EPISTEMIC DIMENSIONS
OF PERSONHOOD

Epistemic Dimensions of Personhood

SIMON J. EVNINE

OXFORD
UNIVERSITY PRESS

OXFORD

UNIVERSITY PRESS

Great Clarendon Street, Oxford OX2 6DP

Oxford University Press is a department of the University of Oxford.
It furthers the University's objective of excellence in research, scholarship,
and education by publishing worldwide in

Oxford New York

Auckland Cape Town Dar es Salaam Hong Kong Karachi
Kuala Lumpur Madrid Melbourne Mexico City Nairobi
New Delhi Shanghai Taipei Toronto

With offices in

Argentina Austria Brazil Chile Czech Republic France Greece
Guatemala Hungary Italy Japan Poland Portugal Singapore
South Korea Switzerland Thailand Turkey Ukraine Vietnam

Oxford is a registered trade mark of Oxford University Press
in the UK and in certain other countries

Published in the United States
by Oxford University Press Inc., New York

© Simon J. Evnine 2008

The moral rights of the author have been asserted
Database right Oxford University Press (maker)

First published 2008

British Library Cataloguing in Publication Data

Data available

Library of Congress Cataloging in Publication Data

Evnine, Simon.
Epistemic dimensions of personhood / Simon J. Evnine.
p. cm.
Includes bibliographical references (p.) and index.
ISBN-13: 978–0–19–923994–8
1. Persons. 2. Philosophical anthropology. 3. Knowledge, Theory of. I. Title.
BD450.E925 2008
126—dc22
2008000194

Typeset by Laserwords Private Limited, Chennai, India
Printed in Great Britain
on acid-free paper by
Biddles Ltd, King's Lynn, Norfolk

ISBN 978–0–19–923994–8

1 3 5 7 9 10 8 6 4 2

To
Rosaly Kruskal Evnine
Giovanna Pompele

Preface

This book is about some of the epistemic features that flow from what it is to be a person. Epistemology and the nature of persons are two very well-trodden areas within philosophy. What I hope is original in this book is that (*a*) I examine the links between epistemology and personhood with a high degree of specificity, linking particular aspects of what it is to be a person with particular epistemic consequences; and (*b*) I bring into confrontation with each other contemporary philosophical debates and bodies of literature that usually exist in isolation from each other.

The book has been long in preparation. Some earlier work of mine—'Believing Conjunctions' (*Synthese*, 118 (1999), 201–27) and 'Learning from One's Mistakes: Epistemic Modesty and the Nature of Belief' (*Pacific Philosophical Quarterly*, 82 (2001), 157–77)—goes over the same ground as parts of Chapters 3, 4, and 6. The later treatment of the issues in the book is generally consistent with the earlier, but all the material has been thought through again, completely rewritten, and (I hope) improved. All these chapters also contain material that has no counterpart in the earlier papers. Two other articles have been largely incorporated into Chapters 2 and 5, though substantial changes have been made in both cases. I thank Oxford University Press for permission to use 'The Universality of Logic: On the Connection between Rationality and Logical Ability' (*Mind*, 110/438 (2001), 335–67) in Chapter 2. 'Personhood and Future Belief: Two Arguments for Something Like Reflection' (*Erkenntnis*, 67/1 (2007), 91–110) is used, in Chapter 5, with kind permission of Springer Science and Business Media.

The writing of this book has been helped by many people, in a variety of ways. The articles mentioned in the previous paragraph contain their own lists of acknowledgements. Here I would like to give special thanks to the following: Jonathan Adler, Oliver Black, Otávio Bueno, Tyler Burge, David Christensen, Risto Hilpinen, Michael Jacovides, Hilary Kornblith, Peter Lewis, Dana Nelkin, Giovanna Pompele, Guy Rohrbaugh, Harvey Siegel, Bill Talbott, Amie Thomasson, and Jennie Uleman. Two referees for the Press made copious and helpful comments. During the summers of 2006 and 2007, work on the book was funded by Max Orovitz Summer Research Awards provided by the University of Miami. I am very grateful for the support. The philosophy department at the University of Miami has proved a very congenial home in which much of this book was written. I thank all my colleagues there, past and present, for making it so.

Simon Evnine
Miami
July 2007

Contents

1. Persons and Other Matters   1

2. Personhood and Logical Ability   23

3. Belief and Conjunction   52

4. Mental Partitioning   83

5. The Epistemic Shape of a Person's Life   108

6. Oneself as Another   138

Conclusion   163

References   166
Index   173

1

Persons and Other Matters

> It began for him almost always with the vision of some person or persons, who hovered before him, soliciting him, as the active or passive figure, interesting him and appealing to him just as they were and by what they were. He . . . then had to find for them the right relations, those that would bring them out.
>
> (Henry James, *The Portrait of a Lady*, 1881)

This book attempts to identify several ways in which being a person necessarily has certain, broadly speaking, epistemic features to it. The idea that there are distinctively epistemic dimensions to being a person is not new. Human beings (among whom are our only uncontroversial examples of persons, although, as I shall argue, the two categories are not the same) obviously stand out from other inhabitants of the world we know in virtue of our intelligence. We think and reason at a far richer and more sophisticated level than any other beings with which we are acquainted. As a result, our culture is hugely more advanced than that of even the most advanced non-humans. And, while this does not necessarily make us morally better or bestow on us greater value, it does put us in touch with morality and value in quite distinct ways. Other animals cannot be moral or immoral and they are, one supposes, severely limited in what they can value and in what forms that valuing can take. Reason, an epistemic feature, thus lies at the foundations of all the things that make us (for better or worse) special. Philosophers fastened on to this fact early and tightly. Aristotle defined us as rational animals, and most subsequent philosophers have concurred, if not with the animal part of the definition, at least with the rational part.

Over the last few hundred years and at an ever-increasing pace, however, this enduring philosophical axiom has been subject to challenge. The 'hermeneutics of suspicion' practiced by Marx, Freud, and

Nietzsche,[1] the post-humanist structuralism of Foucault,[2] a growing wealth of anthropological data from around the world, unflattering studies of human reasoning,[3] postmodernism, and, most recently, the development of neurophilosophy and eliminativism in the philosophy of mind[4] have combined to cast a shadow over reason, and, with it, over the idea that we (whoever exactly *we* are) are, by our very natures, connected with reason.

In many ways, the present book is a rearguard action against these trends. I attempt to delineate a conception of persons that is embedded in what I call our social practices—a nexus of customs, conventions, and institutions within which we 'live, and move, and have our being'. I then argue that anything that falls under this conception must be characterized by a number of distinctive epistemic features that contribute to a fairly traditional portrait of what persons are like. Persons, I claim, necessarily share a core of important logical concepts; have minds that are, to a high degree, unified; have belief systems that improve over time; and are subject to a variety of tensions because they both stand at the origin of a representation of the world and occupy a place within that representation.

In this chapter, I begin by expounding the conception of personhood that will form the basis of the ensuing discussion. The nature of persons is, needless to say, an enormous topic in its own right. I cannot pretend to offer a full treatment of it here but I hope that I can be clear about what exactly the conception is that I will be working with and how my treatment of it relates to the surrounding literature.[5] This being completed, I will preview the rest of the book by explaining three different kinds of connections between personhood and rationality.

Before jumping into the discussion of persons, though, a brief comment on terminology is in order. The word 'person' effectively has two plurals in English—'persons' (its true plural) and 'people'. Of these, the latter is now most common, the former having a literary (see the epigraph to this chapter by Henry James), a legal ('person or

---

[1] The phrase 'hermeneutics of suspicion' and its application to these three figures in particular is from Paul Ricoeur.

[2] See Foucault (1970) and Soper (1986).

[3] Of the kind exemplified by Kahneman and Tversky (1982) and made much of by Stephen Stich (1993).

[4] For example, in Stich (1983) and Churchland (1989).

[5] Authors with whose work I am in sympathy on these issues include Dennett (1976), Wilkes (1988), Brandom (1994), and Rovane (1998).

persons unknown'), or a theological (the persons of the Trinity) ring to it. Perhaps because it is less common, philosophers have tended to use 'persons' in discussing such things as what it is to be a person, personal identity over time, and so on. Judith Jarvis Thomson (1997: 202–4) complains that the singular 'person' has become contaminated by the things philosophers have said using the plural form 'persons'. She therefore favors 'people' as a plural and laments the non-existence of a proper singular form of it. (The singular 'people', of course, means something other than *person*.) I, by contrast with Thomson, am happy to use 'person' and 'persons'. One of the things philosophers have done with the word 'person(s)' is to name a category of beings distinct from (though perhaps, at least in our experience, roughly coextensive with) human beings. As will become evident, I support this distinction. The word 'people', to my ears at least, is too semantically close to 'human being' to make its use in this context comfortable.

1.1 PERSONS

The concept of a person has its home in a network of social, legal, cultural, and moral institutions and practices (social practices, for short). That is to say, the consequences of classifying something as a person lie in these spheres, and hence the importance and significance of the concept are tied to such institutions and practices. If something is a person, that obliges us to treat it with a certain respect and consideration that are not called for, and not appropriate for, things that are not persons. It also entitles us to expect a certain consideration and respect from it that we do not expect from non-persons.[6] These remarks suggest, however sketchily, what follows from something's being a person. They hint at the point of the concept. But in virtue of what, we may ask, is something a person? I distinguish two ways of theorizing about persons. One of these ways, which I call 'realism', takes persons to form a real kind. On this approach, there is no logical or conceptual reason why persons, members of that kind, participate in the social practices they in fact participate in. Rather, the facts (natural facts, if persons are a natural kind) about persons explain and undergird the social dimensions

---

[6] The view that *person* is a forensic concept goes back at least to Locke, in his *Essay Concerning Humane Understanding*. A good modern exposition of this approach can be found in Rovane (1998).

of being a person. The idea that the social practices in which persons are immersed should be explained by (natural) facts about members of the relevant kind characterizes Aristotle's ethical and political project.

The other way of theorizing about persons, which I shall call 'nominalism', is to supply various conditions something must meet if it is to be a person. Since these conditions will be very closely tied to the kinds of things alluded to above about the social and cultural significance of something's being a person, supplying these conditions will not provide a deep *explanation* of those facts in the way that the realist approach might hope to explain them. On the nominalist view, it is a logical, or conceptual, matter that persons engage in the kinds of social practices they do. The point of theorizing in this second way is rather to reveal clearly the lineaments of what must be a social concept. Nominalism, in this sense, is thus an analytical project that seeks explicitness and clarity about an existing concept while realism stands as more of a scientific-anthropological kind of enterprise.

1.1.1 Realism about persons

Perhaps the most obvious way to see persons as constituting a real kind is to identify the kind *person* with the biological kind *homo sapiens* ('human being' in what follows). This approach is Aristotelian in nature and one of its most forceful modern proponents is David Wiggins (1980). It is indeed a notable fact that we know of no paradigmatic actual persons that are not human beings, and this suggests, at the very least, a close connection between the two kinds, if not outright identity. But, even if we accept, as a matter of fact rather than necessity, that all (paradigmatic cases of) persons (with which we are acquainted) are human beings, it may appear problematic for this version of realism that not all human beings are obviously persons. Young children, arguably, are not; nor, arguably, are the severely mentally impaired. That is to say, we do not (and are surely not entitled to) expect from human beings in either of these two groups a high degree of moral sensitivity and we allow ourselves to act towards them in ways that are not appropriate in dealing with paradigmatic persons. (For example, infants are routinely picked up and moved from one location to another.) In fact, such cases are not fatal to identifying the kinds *person* and *human being*, since, although children and the severely mentally impaired are undoubtedly human beings, they are nonetheless lacking with respect to the standards and norms associated with that kind. They are, as the case may be, incomplete, not-yet-fully realized, or functionally impaired human beings. Hence, their failure to be fully persons might be explained precisely by their failure to be fully realized human beings.

A more serious problem for the realist approach, however, is that it rules out *a priori* the possibility of non-human persons. As I noted above, it is true that there are no actual, known cases of non-human persons that are beyond controversy. But it certainly seems as if there might be. The vast literature of science fiction and fantasy is replete with cases of non-human persons. These are beings that, while not belonging to the biological species *homo sapiens* are nonetheless beings to whom one owes and from whom one is entitled to expect the same kinds of moral responsiveness we show to human persons. (There are also cases of beings that seem to fall into the category of persons that belong to no biological species, such as the robot Data from *Star Trek: The Next Generation*.) To deny that such beings really were persons would seem both specious and speciesist. In particular, to deny them the status of persons, when they might have social, cultural, legal, and moral institutions and practices that were commensurable with ours, would be arbitrary and unjust. We would surely be required to treat them in ways that are appropriate to persons and would be quite entitled to expect the same from them. I therefore reject the view that the kind *person* is just the kind *human being*.

Realists might attempt to identify the kind *person* with some other real, but non-biological kind.[7] For example, they may think that Cartesian souls are a real, non-biological kind and that persons, whether humans or not, necessarily are (or have) Cartesian souls. However, lacking any way to identify or investigate the purported real kind in question, I reject this approach.

1.1.2 Nominalism about persons

This brings me to the nominalist option, which I adopt here. On this approach, the concept *person* is associated with a set of conditions that,

---

[7] Jonathan Lowe (1996: 15–21) argues, on grounds stemming from the nature of biological classification, that, if *person* were to be a biological kind, then it could not fail to be the kind *homo sapiens*. And we may note that, if *person* were identified with some other biological kind, objections similar to those offered against the identification of *person* and *homo sapiens* could be raised again. I am not sure what to make of Lowe's own view that persons constitute a real, non-biological psychological kind that nonetheless, unlike Cartesian egos, necessarily has some physical characteristics.

as it were, give the essence of what it is to be a person.[8] Ideally, one should provide necessary and sufficient conditions for something to be a person, but we may usefully proceed even if we fall short of this analytic ideal. (Indeed, the kind may be vague or ill defined and hence not capturable by a consistent set of necessary and sufficient conditions at all.) In fact, I shall confine myself to stating what I take to be some necessary conditions for what it is to be a person. Whether they are together sufficient I shall not attempt to determine. The general kinds of conditions that are associated with the nominalist view are well known and fairly obvious. Daniel Dennett, for example, lists six. Something is a person only if it is rational; it is the subject of psychological, mental, or intentional states; it is treated in a certain (personal) way by others; it reciprocates this attitude; it is capable of verbal communication; it is conscious in some special way (perhaps by being self-conscious).[9]

In the next section, I shall state my own list of necessary conditions on personhood. (My list will be consistent with Dennett's but will differ from it in degree of articulation and in emphasis. Since nominalists claim to be capturing a concept we allegedly have, one ought to be suspicious if different nominalists came up with radically different sets of conditions.) But before we come to that, I will make a few further remarks on realism and nominalism about persons.

The nominalist position has been criticized by David Wiggins (1980) on the grounds that it faces a serious difficulty in providing an adequate and complete analysis of what it is to be a person. And it is indeed true that I do not provide here a complete analysis of the concept, since I limit myself to giving several necessary conditions but make no claim about their joint sufficiency. But, Wiggins argues, if the nominalist is unable to come up with a list of necessary and sufficient conditions, she will either have to 'come down so hard' on some select few necessary conditions as to put 'in jeopardy the personhood of countless human beings' (those, presumably, like the very young or the very impaired, who fail to meet the necessary conditions) or she will have to make constant (and by her own lights illicit) reference back to human beings 'as we know them' to determine the class of persons (1980: 173–4). I have indicated above that I accept the first of these options. It is indeed a consequence of the

---

[8] Of course, the difference between the realist and nominalist approaches would be spurious if necessary and sufficient conditions for membership of the nominal kind were simply membership of a real kind.

[9] Dennett (1976: 177–8). His conditions are endorsed by Kathleen Wilkes (1988: 23).

position I advocate here that not all human beings are persons. (This is the flip side of the coin whose other side is that not all persons must be human beings.) But even realists like Wiggins must agree that those human beings whose personhood the nominalist puts in jeopardy—the very young, the seriously mentally deficient—stand apart in a variety of ways from normal, somewhat developed human beings. The question between Wiggins and the nominalist is only whether these distinctions should be marked by use of the concept *person*, as the nominalist proposes, or by some other conceptual distinction that applies *within* the domain of persons/human beings, as the realist would have it.

Wiggins rightly reminds us of the 'persisting obscurity of the interest of the classification "person" ' (1980: 173). This is reflected in the fact that ordinary linguistic usage does not give us anything like a consistent basis on which to decide difficult cases. Hence the question at the end of the previous paragraph may not have a simple, unequivocal answer and there may be an element of stipulation as to what we say about persons.[10] It is needlessly alarmist, however, to worry that, on the nominalist view, 'we have so much freedom here that we can invent and reinvent at will . . . the *principle of individuation* for persons' (1980: 178 n. 33). The 'interest of the classification "person" ' may be obscure but it is not *that* obscure. The necessary conditions that I offer in the following section will, I hope, pretty clearly capture one important set of interests we have, interests in questions of morality, responsibility, culture, and so on—in short, interests in what I called above social practices. Some persons also pretty clearly have interests in classifying *within* the category determined merely by the necessary conditions. Humans have interests, for example, in whether something that meets those necessary conditions is also human, since this will be necessary if we are to engage in sexual reproduction with it. There might also be interests in classifying based around other biologically based features of human persons. There may be non-human persons, for example, that do not need to eat. There might thus be a whole array of social practices centered around eating and food that are of crucial interest to human persons but might be irrelevant to non-human

---

[10] This is the position of Carol Rovane (1998). Using Strawson's famous distinction, she says that *any* consistent theory of persons must be revisionary rather than descriptive. This seems right to me. See also Ohlin (2005), who argues that the term 'person' serves several different functions in the context of human-rights law (a good example of the kind of context which I claim the concept *person* inhabits.) Ohlin, however, thinks that the concept *person* does little important work in this context.

persons. What I leave open in declining to come down on the question of the sufficiency of my necessary conditions is whether these other interests (sexual reproduction, eating, and so on) should be marked by the use of the concept *person* or by some narrower sub-concept (*human person*, for example). If my conditions are sufficient, then our interest in possibilities of such things as sexual reproduction and eating together should not be marked by application of the concept *person*. Rather, we would simply have interests in classifying not only according to the concept *person* but also within that concept to some more narrowly defined group. If, on other hand, my conditions were not sufficient, one could discuss supplementing them with other conditions that would tie the concept *person* itself to the narrower group. This would be based on interests in classifying that go beyond those that, I contend, are well served by the necessary conditions I give below. But, in that case, we would require some other concept for the wider group, given that we obviously do have interests in classifying based on the most general social, legal, cultural, and moral practices.

Even for the nominalist, however, the *de facto* close connection between the kinds *person* and *human being* is surely worthy of some explanation. The reason for the very high degree of overlap in their extensions is that *our* concept of a person (that is, the concept that features in communities of human persons) has been developed in the context of institutions and practices that are at one and the same time the products of persons and the products of human beings. Their development was enabled by biological facts pertaining to human beings. Thus, the concept has been developed in a way that makes it fit human beings extraordinarily well. Nonetheless, that does not mean that we cannot recognize the possibility of non-human persons. Other concept-developing creatures might develop concepts that reflect their practices and institutions, developed on the basis of natural facts pertaining to their situations. Such concepts might coincide with, or approximate, the concept of a person, or they might not. Human beings may fall under their concepts, or they may not. (They typically will, if their concepts coincide with, or approximate, the concept of a person.) But the fact that the concept of a person is human-centered, in the sense that it has been developed by human beings to fit (most) human beings, does not make it identical with the concept of a human being.

The preceding paragraph suggests that the concept *person* is a historically and culturally situated concept, one which might be developed by some forms of life at some particular historical moments but might fail to be developed by other forms of life (even ones that fall under the extension of the concept), or might, having been developed, fade from use. While I think there is nothing in the nature of concepts to rule out such eventualities, I do not believe that, as a matter of fact, the concept of a person is historically or culturally variable in this way. Of course, since human persons, at any rate, have evolved, there may be questions as to exactly when the concept arose, and whether it was precisely synchronous with the first existence of (human) persons. But the idea that unproblematic cases of persons should lack the concept (or some concept very like it) seems highly implausible. Serious study in history and anthropology would be needed to confirm or disconfirm this view, but I think that the concept of a person is part of what Strawson eloquently describes as a 'massive central core of human thinking which has no history—or none recorded in the histories of thought'. The completion of Strawson's thought, generalized to apply not just to humans but to persons in general, also seems apt: 'there are categories and concepts which, in their most fundamental character, change not at all. Obviously these are not the specialities of the most refined thinking. They are the commonplaces of the least refined thinking; and are yet the indispensable core of the conceptual equipment of the most sophisticated human beings' (1959: 10).

I end this section by pointing out that the ensuing chapters of this book need not be devoid of interest for anyone skeptical of the nominalist view outlined here. According to nominalism about persons, the conditions below, from which certain epistemic consequences will be shown to flow, are analytically necessary for being a person. Thus, if satisfaction of some of these conditions entails possession of a certain epistemic feature E, I will express this by saying such things as 'necessarily, all persons have E', or 'necessarily, nothing that lacks E can be a person'. The necessity here will be logical or conceptual necessity. But a realist about persons, who, for example, equates the kind *person* with the kind *human being*, need not deny that those conditions that I claim are analytically necessary for being a person are, while not analytically necessary, nonetheless deeply important facts about typical, fully developed humans and hence about persons. If those conditions apply to human beings in virtue of the natural facts about humans, there will even be a good sense in which persons (that is, human beings) satisfy those conditions necessarily, though this will be not a logical necessity but a nomological one. Accordingly, the conclusions I come to about the epistemic dimensions of personhood can be re-expressed, for the realist, as 'it is an important fact about typical, fully developed persons that they have E' or even 'as a matter of natural necessity, all typical, fully developed persons have E'. Conclusions of this form are still, I think, significant and interesting.

1.2 NECESSARY CONDITIONS OF PERSONHOOD

Here is my account of some necessary conditions on being a person. These are not alleged to be jointly sufficient, nor are they alleged to exhaust all the necessary conditions. They are those necessary conditions that are relevant to the epistemic dimensions of being a person that I will go on to explore in the following chapters. Since I claim to be giving conditions that are analytically connected with the concept of a person, it will be inappropriate to offer a defense of these conditions. Or, rather, a defense will consist in no more than asking the reader to consider the concept and confirm that the conditions I offer are indeed necessary conditions for the application of that concept. If one does not like the idea that necessary conditions for the application of a concept must, in some sense, be apparent in a mere grasp of the concept, then my defense would take the form of appealing to those social practices that provide the home for the concept of a person and asking the reader to consider whether the kinds of beings involved in such practices could be involved in them without meeting the proposed conditions. And for those reading what follows according to the realist 'translation' scheme offered at the end of the preceding section, my defense would consist in pointing out that these conditions flow from natural facts about human beings and express deep and important features of human life.

1.2.1 Background conditions: Finitude and Belief

I start with two very general background conditions called, respectively, Finitude and Belief. First, persons are spatiotemporally located, causally efficacious particulars. This condition does not, by itself, imply that persons must be material beings. It leaves open the possibility that there may be immaterial, but located and causally efficacious beings.[11] But, taken in conjunction with a background of commonly accepted

---

[11] Of the kind, for example, described by W. D. Hart (1988).

metaphysical views, this condition does imply that persons must be material. I shall assume they are in what follows, though I believe that, if one thinks one can make sense of immaterial persons at all, everything I say will be transposable into that key. In talking of spatiotemporal location, I mean to assert a location within the spatiotemporal universe, and not coextensive with it. Thus, I take the condition to imply that persons are spatiotemporally finite and I take this, in turn, to imply that they are finite in their various capacities, including their epistemic capacities.[12]

A second background condition, Belief, is this. I will be linking the notion of personhood to various views in epistemology that are typically expressed in terms of concepts and beliefs. One or both of the further conditions on personhood I will mention themselves imply that persons necessarily are the subjects of belief.[13] They may also imply that persons must possess concepts. But, partially for the sake of clarity, or as part of a pre-emptive defense of those further conditions, I will require, as an independent condition, that persons necessarily possess concepts and have beliefs. I doubt whether something could have beliefs as its only kind of mental state. In any case, I shall assume that, in having beliefs, a creature must also have those other kinds of mental states, such as desires and intentions, that form part of the same folk-psychological explanatory apparatus as beliefs.

There are two positions from which Belief may be challenged, both of which deny that normal, adult humans have beliefs. Since normal, adult humans are our best and perhaps only examples of persons, if either of these positions were true, Belief would be questionable (though not necessarily false, as I explain in the next paragraph). The first of these is so-called eliminativism in the philosophy of mind.[14] Eliminativists deny that human beings have beliefs or other folk-psychological attitudes. They do this because they think that these notions are part of a scientific theory of human behavior that will be found (or is being found) to be false. The true theory, which will stem from advances in

[12] By imposing Finitude as a necessary condition on personhood, I make the notion of a personal God (at least if the God part of that notion is taken to have its usual monotheistic perfections) incoherent. I do not take this as a reason to reject Finitude as a condition on personhood. It requires a firm appeal to mystery to accept that an infinite, non-located, impassible being could be a person, in the sense at issue.

[13] The condition of Second-Ordinality (that one be capable of having beliefs about beliefs) obviously implies possession of beliefs.

[14] See Stich (1983) for one good example of this approach.

neuropsychology and related disciplines, will come to offer explanations of human behavior that will have no room for things like beliefs and desires, and no room for anything that can plausibly be taken as what people were really trying to get at with their talk of beliefs and desires.

Eliminativists must either deny that Belief is a necessary condition on personhood or deny that (normal, adult) human beings are persons. It may seem as if putting the matter thus is facetious—will they not obviously deny that Belief is a necessary condition on personhood? In truth, though, it is not so obvious which option they should take. It will all depend on how well the eliminativist thinks she can rescue, without the aid of belief or folk psychology generally, those kinds of phenomena by which we anchored the notion of a person: things like morality, sociality, responsibility, culture, and so on. If all these can be recast without belief (or some close surrogate for it), then the eliminativist may coherently deny that Belief is a necessary condition on personhood but continue to hold that the conceptual apparatus of personhood has a role to play in describing important features of typically human life. Since this recasting has not, to my knowledge, even been begun, it is impossible to assess whether the conclusions of this book would be adaptable to the conception of personhood that resulted from it. But, if these anchoring aspects of personhood are supposed themselves to go the same way as belief, then it really does seem as if the eliminativist may be treating the claim that normal, adult humans are persons in the same way as she treats the claim that normal, adult humans have beliefs—namely, as a kind of conceptual confusion to be cleared away by science.[15] In this sense, eliminativism in the philosophy of mind would be of a piece with the more general Structuralist, post-humanist currents that have proclaimed the demise of Man.[16]

---

[15] Hence the eliminativist could still accept that it was part of the concept of a person that persons have beliefs. This would be analogous to the claim that it is part of the concept of a witch that witches summon spirits. In both cases, we would be defining one fiction in terms of another.

[16] I say 'Man' because that is how some famous pronouncements of Foucault (and others) are translated. My own sense is that it is clear that the object of Foucault's criticism was really the concept of a person and not that of a given biological species (still less, the male of the species). Consider the following passage, which I gloss in square brackets with reference to the views and conditions on personhood advocated here and in the next section: 'man for the human sciences is not that living being with a very particular form (a somewhat special physiology and an almost unique autonomy) [a rejection of Realism about Man]; he is that living being who, from within the life to which he entirely belongs [Finitude?] and by which he is traversed in his whole being, constitutes representations [Belief] by means of which he lives [Agency], and on the

A second direction from which Belief could be challenged is by those who advocate the replacement of the notion of belief by a notion of degrees of belief. Ordinary explanations of behavior appear to allow for both types of explanatory framework. We describe people as believing, disbelieving, or being agnostic about propositions, but we also speak of them as believing things strongly, more strongly than other things, and so on. As for what degrees of belief are, there are a number of different views, but by far the most popular is to treat them as subjective probabilities. A person's degrees of belief thereby fall under norms of probabilistic coherence, can be measured by betting behavior, and are generally subject to a large and well-worked-out body of mathematics. A few philosophers, most notably perhaps Richard Jeffrey (1970), have advocated the replacement of belief altogether by probabilistic degrees of belief in our attempts to explain and understand human behavior. Hence Jeffrey is, in his own way, an eliminativist about full belief—not in the name of neuropsychology but in the name of probability and Bayesianism. Most philosophers reject Bayesian eliminativism and continue to treat the notion of full belief as useful and acceptable, but, if one accepts both beliefs and degrees of belief, there are serious and difficult questions about how, and even whether, they can be related.

A proper discussion of all the issues would far exceed the scope of this book but a couple of remarks are necessary.[17] First, I do think that a notion of belief is a significant addition to a notion of degrees of belief. I have no single master argument for this view, but a whole range of quibbles, hunches, and feelings of uneasiness. In any case, I require full belief for personhood. If someone wants to treat that as mere stipulation and argue that a concept very similar to personhood could be characterized that required only degrees of belief and not full belief, so be it. Some of what I say about persons in the following would still go through, some obviously would not, and some I am not sure about. This brings me to a second remark. Two principles discussed in this book are

basis of which he possesses that strange capacity of being able to represent to himself precisely that life [Second-Ordinality].' (Foucault 1970: 352). As the reference to Man as an object of the human sciences at the beginning of this passage makes clear, while Foucault and eliminativists may share a belief in the demise of Man, Foucault puts his origins in the eighteenth century, whereas, if the concept is coeval with the illusion of belief, his origins must surely lie long, long ago.

[17] There is a large literature on this question. For a few recent contributions, see Foley (1993: ch. 4), Kaplan (1996), Christensen (2004) and Weatherson (2005), and the further references therein. I say something more about these issues myself in Section 3.3.

often or even usually discussed within a probabilistic, degrees-of-belief framework. In Chapters 3 and 4, I deal with the claim that it is rational to believe the conjunction of one's beliefs. Challenges to this principle, in the form of the Preface and Lottery paradoxes, are sometimes thought to show something about the relations of belief and degrees of belief. In my treatment of these matters, I make some critical remarks about certain views concerning degrees of belief and their possible relations to full belief that speak, albeit in an incomplete way, to my conviction that belief is an important phenomenon in personhood. In Chapter 5, I deal with the principle of Reflection, which originated in the context of probabilistic epistemologies and says that one should believe something to degree n, conditionally on the hypothesis that one will believe it to degree n at some later time. In this case, I simply move the discussion into a non-probabilistic framework. Although I suggest there that the probabilistic framework within which Reflection is usually discussed obscures some important issues, nothing crucial in what I say depends on taking Reflection to govern full belief rather than degrees of belief.

1.2.2 Further conditions: Agency and Second-Ordinality

On the basis formed by these background conditions, I impose two further necessary conditions on personhood. The first is Agency. This asserts that persons are necessarily agents. Agency includes not only the performance of individual intentional actions but also engaging in relatively long-term plans and projects and deliberating about actions, plans, and projects. No doubt many non-human animals are, in some way, correctly described as performing intentional actions. Unless, however, they also engage in deliberation and have plans and projects, they will not meet the condition Agency. It is sometimes objected that there can be persons who are incapable of action owing to permanent and total paralysis (or, in possible non-human persons, other kinds of immobility). Such conditions do not necessarily imply failure to satisfy Agency. A person who is paralyzed but has the use of her mental faculties will still be able to do things (she will still be able to imagine, think, decide, and so on), to deliberate (about what to think about, for example), and to plan. All this will no doubt be on a limited scale compared to a normally mobile person, but the requirement for being a person is still fully met in such a case. Furthermore, as long as one has some means of communicating one's thoughts, one can intervene in the physical world indirectly. One may induce someone to move one's body into another position or to say something on one's behalf or to fight a war.

A second condition is Second-Ordinality. This is the ability to have beliefs about beliefs, both one's own and other people's. The ability to have beliefs about beliefs is a clear prerequisite for the kinds of social practices within which the concept of a person lives. To give a very simple example, a legal system has to have room for considering not just what people do but what they believe they are doing. Having beliefs about beliefs, in this situation and in other, more quotidian ones, is part of being able to explain persons' actions. So, having second-order beliefs must be accompanied by having second-order desires, intentions, and so on.

Second-Ordinality is one aspect of a more general alleged necessary condition on personhood that would require persons to have the concept of a person, or something along those lines. Such a condition might be called Reciprocity. Versions of Reciprocity are advocated by such thinkers as Strawson (1959), Nagel (1970), Dennett (1976), and Rovane (1998), among others. Since I claim that the conditions I am laying down are analytically connected to the concept of a person, to say that all persons must have that concept means that all persons must classify into a given kind on the basis, at least partially, of satisfaction of the necessary conditions for being of that kind. Since Belief is one of those conditions, Reciprocity would imply that all persons must take persons to have beliefs. In other words, Reciprocity would imply Second-Ordinality. I think Reciprocity is enormously plausible but I shall need only that part of it that is captured by Second-Ordinality. Hence, I do not insist on Reciprocity here.

Second-Ordinality has two important immediate consequences that I will mention here. First, I take it that, if one attributes beliefs to oneself and others, one must have concepts of truth and falsehood to serve as the primary forms of evaluation of beliefs.[18] Secondly, if beliefs are attributed to self and others, there must be principles that

---

[18] Dummett (1991: ch. 7) argues that the origin of our concepts of truth and falsity lies in the linguistic practice of assertion. If so, Second-Ordinality would itself imply that persons must have language. The link between Second-Ordinality and language is also crucial to Davidson, especially (1975). I am sympathetic to this, and I think the possession of language is clearly a necessary condition for personhood, whether or not it is entailed by Second-Ordinality or any of the other conditions I list here. However, the possession of language, as such, plays no role in the following; hence I remain neutral on whether I have framed Second-Ordinality in such a way as to presuppose linguistic ability.

guide the attributions of them in such a way that they can function as explanations of actions. These principles will not necessarily be codifiable and lawlike, but the very point of belief attribution would be moot unless the attribution were tied to at least tacit recognition of the operation of belief-forming capacities and the ways in which they interact with environmental circumstances to generate beliefs. At several points in this work I shall make use of this consequence of Second-Ordinality. In Chapter 3, I shall invoke actual features of our practice of belief-attribution and, in Chapter 5, I shall develop and utilize a fuller conception of the necessary conditions for belief attribution.

These, then, are the conditions that will be operative in what follows: Finitude, Belief, Agency, and Second-Ordinality. What are the relations between these conditions and are they all independent of each other? The question is important. If *person* is a concept determined by a variety of conditions, and those conditions do not, in any intuitive sense, 'hang together', then the suspicion arises that the concept so defined is in some way highly contingent and ephemeral. By contrast, if the various conditions do 'hang together' in some way, the concept so defined will have a kind of stability to it that will indicate that its existence is, relative to the conditions under which it is developed, more than a mere contingency.

In the case at hand, the conditions hang together very well. Besides some obvious overlapping (Second-Ordinality implies Belief), a good case can be made that Agency implies all the remaining conditions. (If so, the present project might merit the epithet pragmatist.) Since Agency includes deliberation, it implies that agents have whatever is necessary for deliberation, and this surely includes beliefs. So Agency implies Belief. Creatures with infinite capacities would not need to deliberate, and creatures with no causal powers could not act. So Agency implies Finitude. The hardest case to make would be that Agency implies Second-Ordinality. Even here, there is a possible connection through Belief. Davidson has argued that one cannot have beliefs unless one has the concept of belief.[19] If so, then Second-Ordinality (which obviously implies Belief) is equivalent to Belief, which itself follows from Agency. This argument, of course, relies on the controversial Davidsonian premise, which I will not attempt to defend here.[20] We

[19] Davidson (1975).
[20] For a different, but very appealing, way of connecting Agency and Second-Ordinality, see Tyler Burge (1998).

might then put, as the most economical expression of the conditions, Agency and Second-Ordinality. Even if neither, strictly speaking, implies the other, they clearly do 'hang together'. For creatures engaged in social practices, who plan and deliberate (and hence have beliefs), it is well-nigh inconceivable that they would not need to take into account, in their plans and deliberations, the beliefs of the other persons with whom they were engaged in such social practices. So Agency would, at least, strongly suggest Second-Ordinality. Conversely, creatures that had beliefs about their own and others' beliefs would, under all plausible circumstances, have to acquire many of those beliefs on the basis of the deliberate actions of others and would themselves have to engage in various actions to gather pertinent information about others' actions (and beliefs).

Despite the possibility of various redundancies among the four conditions, and despite the strong suspicion that all can be derived from Agency, or perhaps Agency plus Second-Ordinality, I posit each of them in its own right. This relieves me of the burden of having to establish that any one follows from another. It also increases perspicacity, since one can see more clearly at various points exactly what is being depended on.

These four conditions are at once quite stringent and quite moderate. They are stringent because we know of only one kind of creature that clearly satisfies them all—namely, normal human beings that have achieved a certain level of development. (I refer to this category as normal, adult humans though it obviously includes children of a certain age, perhaps even quite a young age.) In addition, with the obvious exception of Finitude, I do not think there are any clear cases of anything that satisfies any proper subset of the conditions.[21] (This reinforces the idea that the conditions 'hang together'.) At the same time the conditions are quite moderate. Not only are they satisfied by the only persons we are acquainted with; they are easily and obviously satisfied by them. Furthermore, trying to imagine what a person would be like if, *per impossibile*, it failed to satisfy one or more of them reveals

---

[21] As noted above, many non-human animals might be described as performing intentional actions. They do not, however, clearly meet the condition of Agency unless they also engage in planning, deliberation, etc. Nor is it obvious that animals we would (correctly) describe as acting intentionally, in the absence of the other elements of Agency, have beliefs. Clearly something like belief must be present for intentional action, but it is, I think, quite difficult to say exactly what that is and whether it counts as believing. In any case, nothing substantive hinges on my claim in the text that there are no clear cases of things satisfying a proper subset of the conditions (other than Finitude).

just how central they are to personhood, as that concept functions in the network of cultural, social, moral, and legal contexts within which it is at home. They are not, in any sense, peripheral to the activities and institutions that constitute this network. Without their satisfaction, nothing remotely resembling personal life would be possible. If, then, one is prepared to embrace a nominalist approach to persons in the first place, one will surely have little doubt that the conditions are indeed among the necessary conditions for personhood. And, as I indicated above, even if one is not persuaded by nominalism and identifies the kind *person* with the kind *human being*, one will surely agree that all these conditions are central to the natural history of *homo sapiens*.

1.3 CONNECTIONS BETWEEN PERSONHOOD AND EPISTEMOLOGY

Satisfaction of these four conditions, then, will be my starting point. Satisfaction of these conditions, I shall argue, has a variety of epistemic consequences. The epistemic consequences I will deal with are of three kinds. The first kind I discuss concerns concept possession. In Chapter 2, I argue that various features of personhood are sufficient for the possession of a range of particular logical abilities. (Logical abilities, as I explain, include the possession of logical concepts and the ability to use those concepts in particular ways, most notably in particular kinds of inferences.) Thus, all persons necessarily share a common logical patrimony. Different persons, or kinds of persons, may exhibit variety in how much logic they add to this common core, but the fantasy of other persons with wholly distinct logical abilities, a fantasy that pervades various quarters of epistemology, is just that, a fantasy.[22] According to the view presented here, these fantasies are, like so many of our fantasies, logically incoherent. The logical concepts I shall argue must be had by all persons are conjunction, disjunction, conditionality, negation, and quantification.

The second kind of epistemic consequence that flows from being a person concerns principles that apply to general features of a person's

---

[22] The fantasy is argued for extensively by Christopher Cherniak (1986). It has been echoed as if it were beyond controversy by many others, such as Goldman (1986) and Stroud (1979). Cherniak's work is discussed and criticized in much greater detail in Chapter 2. See also Biro and Ludwig (1994) for critical treatment of it.

beliefs. By saying that these principles 'apply' to general features of a person's beliefs, I mean two things: first, that it is rational for a person's beliefs to conform to these principles; and, secondly, that nothing can be a person if its beliefs do not conform to these principles to at least a sufficient degree. I argue for both these conclusions with respect to two principles:

CP If S believes p and S believes q, then S believes p *and* q;

and

Reflection One should treat one's future beliefs as if they were the beliefs of an expert.[23]

(Reflection means, very roughly, that, if one knew what one's future beliefs would be, one would adopt them as one's current beliefs now.[24]) In Chapter 3, I begin the case for the rationality of CP. This includes disarming a number of objections to it. The most famous of these derive from the Lottery and Preface paradoxes, which purport to show that it is not always rational to believe the conjunction of things that it is rational to believe individually. My defense of the rationality of CP leads me to advance a very permissive theory about what it actually is to believe a conjunction in the first place. According to this theory, to believe a conjunction just is, *under normal circumstances*, to believe its conjuncts. The reference to normal circumstances is to rule out cases in which a person engages in some kind of mental partitioning or compartmentalization. This link between CP and issues of mental partitioning shows that the real thrust of the relation between personhood and the rationality of CP has to do with the irrationality of mental partitioning. In other words, it is rational for persons to have a unified mind, in the sense of 'unified' given by the logical operation of conjunction as applied to beliefs. This is the theme of Chapter 4. At the

---

[23] I call this Reflection because it is a version, or interpretation, of the homonymous principle advocated by Bas van Fraassen which is expressed in the language of probability and degrees-of-belief thus: $P_{a,t}(Q \mid P_{a,t'}(Q) = r) = r$, where $P_{a,t}$ is the probability function (or degree-of-belief function) of a person a at a time t, and t' is later than or equal to t. I take up the relation between my principle and van Fraassen's in more detail in Chapter 5.

[24] Given the notion of conditional beliefs, this can be put by saying that, for every possible hypothesis about one's future beliefs of the form 'I will believe p', one should currently have a conditional belief of the form 'p, given that I will believe p'. I do not assume the apparatus of conditional beliefs in my discussion of Reflection, but I understand treating someone as an expert in terms that are often used to explain what a conditional belief is. See, e.g., Stalnaker (1984: 101–6).

end of that chapter, I also argue that at least a sufficient degree of unity of mind (and hence a sufficient degree of conformity to CP) is necessary for anything to be a person.

In Chapter 5, I argue that Reflection is rational for persons because (a) it is a necessary truth that, in certain respects, the beliefs of persons improve over time and (b) persons must know this. Serious qualifications to (a), however, lead to a deeper understanding of the diachronic character of the epistemic life of a person. As with the treatment of CP, I also go on to argue that nothing can be a person that does not satisfy Reflection to a sufficient extent. Both CP and Reflection have been extensively discussed in recent epistemology. What I add to these discussions here is a sense of the importance of taking into account the nature of persons in any treatment of these principles.[25]

I have mentioned two ways in which principles such as CP and Reflection 'apply' to general features of a person's beliefs. They are rational for persons, and satisfaction of them to a sufficient degree is necessary for persons. I would have liked also to include discussion of a third component in the relation between Reflection and CP, on the one hand, and personhood, on the other. Suppose we have something that satisfies CP and Reflection sufficiently to be a person (and meets any other necessary conditions on personhood). And suppose it is granted that it is rational for this person to satisfy these two principles. This exhausts the ways considered so far in which our principles apply to persons. In addition, though, it seems to me that there is something about what it is to be a person, or, more precisely, something about what it is to lead the life of a person, that makes satisfaction of these principles an ideal.[26] This is in addition to the way in which, since satisfaction of the principles is rational, they form part of the ideal of rationality. Satisfaction of the principles is an ideal for a person's life that is independent of any ideal to be rational; an ideal, perhaps, of narrative coherence, or something along those lines. Nailing down the nature of this further ideal, and getting clear about its relations to personhood, however, proved impossible within the constraints of this work. Since it is logically independent of the other connections between personhood

---

[25] Van Fraassen has tied his defense of Reflection at a number of points to claims about personal identity. I deal with this in Chapter 5, but suffice it to say here that these references to personal identity are not very thoroughly worked out, nor do they by any means exhaust the contribution that a consideration of the nature of persons can make to the discussion of Reflection.

[26] Thanks to Guy Rohrbaugh for helping me get clear about this.

and the satisfaction of CP and Reflection that I do deal with, I defer its exploration to a future occasion.

The first two kinds of connection between personhood and epistemology—concept possession and the applicability (in two senses) of principles governing belief—together constitute a positive epistemic dimension of personhood. They show that persons must have certain logical abilities and that their beliefs must, and will, be rational in certain ways. The third kind of connection that I deal with in this book, in Chapter 6, is of a negative kind. When we form beliefs about the beliefs of persons, or about persons as believers, there are a number of things we might think about them, depending on the state of our evidence. We might think one particular person was an expert, another average in the reliability of her beliefs. We might also have good reason to believe that a person is highly unreliable in her beliefs, or has a very large number of false beliefs. Conclusions of these kinds have further epistemic ramifications. If someone is unreliable, the fact that she believes that p will, other things being equal, not give one a reason oneself to believe that p. On the other hand, if she is an expert on the matter, the fact that she has a given belief may provide one with a reason for adopting that belief oneself. As persons, we can form beliefs about our own beliefs and about ourselves as believers. One aspect of rationality suggests that, in assessing a person's reliability or accuracy, we should be impartial as to who that person is. In forming beliefs about our own beliefs, then, we ought, once again, to be able to follow where the evidence leads and we ought, therefore, to be able to believe of ourselves that we are highly unreliable or have a very large number of false beliefs. And this, in turn, might be thought to have further epistemic ramifications for us. Some judgments about our own beliefs, however, are in various ways inconsistent with the requirements of being a person. For example, there is, I shall argue, something at odds with being a person in believing that most of one's beliefs are false. Being a person, therefore, means being unable to be impartial with respect to our own beliefs. To the extent that such impartiality is itself one aspect of being rational, persons are, necessarily, unable to be completely rational. This, I argue at the end of Chapter 6, is a manifestation of a deep fact about persons: that they stand, in some sense, as the origin of a world, a world that is revealed through their beliefs (one can call this an epistemic world if one wants to avoid sounding overly idealist at this point), and at the same time are a part of, or inside, this very world of which they are the origin. This feature of persons, their standing both at the origin of and inside a world, is the inevitable source of certain epistemic tensions. I call the view that persons are torn between two competing positions within, and outside, the world, aspectual dualism. It is a not unfamiliar Kantian, or Nagelian, strain, but its distinctive application to belief is, I think, something new.

2

Personhood and Logical Ability

Imagine
your mind wandering without its logic
(Jorie Graham, 'Tennessee June',
1980)

In this chapter, I argue that there are certain logical abilities that anything must have to be a person. In other words, satisfying the four conditions on being a person outlined in the previous chapter ensures the possession of a specific set of logical abilities. Even if one were sympathetic to the view that being a person meant having some logical abilities, one might still balk at the idea that one could specify which those logical abilities were. This is, roughly, the view of Christopher Cherniak (1986). He holds that rationality requires the ability to make some (logical) inferences, but not any particular ones.[1] Which logical abilities a creature has, according to Cherniak, depends on natural facts about its psychology. Natural facts about a creature's psychology are contingent; hence, there are no necessary truths about what psychology a rational creature (or person) has, and hence no necessary truths about which logical abilities it has. Cherniak thinks that individuals or species are characterized by feasibility orderings, orderings of inference types in terms of the ease and success with which inferences of those types are typically performed. Different creatures may be characterized by different feasibility orderings. It will be an entirely empirical question which feasibility ordering best describes a given creature.

It is not at all implausible to think that there are differences between groups (and between individuals within a group) as to the extent of

---

[1] Cherniak does not pursue the link between personhood and rationality but I think that, for purposes of comparing his views with mine, nothing is lost by equating his use of the concept of rationality with my use of the concept of personhood.

their logical abilities. Ordinary humans do better than even the best chimps, and there may be creatures that stand to humans as we do to chimps. What is striking about Cherniak's position is that the absence of constraints on the logical abilities of rational creatures would allow that there could be creatures whose feasibility ordering was, say, an inversion of a typical human person's. This would mean there might be rational creatures capable of doing advanced logic who were yet unable to make inferences of the form '*A and B*, therefore *A*', owing to the fact that this type of inference was beyond their logical powers. Against Cherniak's view, I shall argue that, on the basis of satisfaction of the necessary conditions of personhood, there are particular logical concepts that all persons must possess and particular ways in which they must be able to use those concepts. That all persons have these logical abilities is itself a necessary truth.

2.1 METHODOLOGICAL ISSUES

The present section will be devoted to some methodological issues that must be settled before we address substantive claims about which logical abilities are necessary for being a person.

2.1.1 What are logical abilities?

I have so far talked generically about the possession of logical abilities. This rubric covers many diverse kinds of things. We can possess logical concepts, believe logical truths, make or understand logical inferences, use inference rules, 'see' or grasp implications and incompatibilities, and so on. The various phenomena divide naturally into two groups, concept possession and all the others. Broadly speaking, the phenomena in the second group concern conceptual roles, since they depend on logical concepts' featuring in beliefs, inferences, incompatibilities, and so on. Since they will play a large part in the following, I shall for the moment take logical inference rules as representative of conceptual roles. We may then inquire into the generic notion of logical abilities by asking the question: what is the relation between possession of logical concepts and the use of, or ability to use, logical inference rules? The answer to this question raises a number of complex issues.

To say of a creature that it makes, or accepts, or is prepared to make inferences of a given form seems to presuppose that that creature possesses the logical concepts that feature in inferences of that form. For example, to say that a creature accepts inferences of *A* from *A and B* presupposes that it possesses the concept of conjunction. It could not even entertain propositions of the form *A and B* without possessing that concept.[2] This suggests that an attempt to argue for the claim that persons must have certain logical abilities should take the form of first trying to show that any person must possess certain logical concepts (that is, meets a necessary condition for being able to make certain inferences) and then arguing that that condition is also sufficient for being able to make those inferences. In order to do that, one would need some account of the individuation of logical concepts, an account that specified the conditions that were necessary and sufficient for possession of a given logical concept. And here we may appear quickly to be brought round in a circle. For it has seemed to many that the individuation of certain logical concepts is to be explained in terms of inference forms (or other conceptual roles). At the very least, which inferences a creature is prepared to make, and perhaps which inferences it finds obvious, are seen as contributing to the individuation of its logical concepts. We thus have a problem: if we attempt to discuss the acceptability of inference rules, we are thrown back on concept possession, while if we attempt to discuss concept possession, we are directed to inference rules. We thus need some way of dealing with concept possession and conceptual role in one go.

2.1.2 A strategy

Here is a schematic, and idealized, description of the three-stage strategy I shall use in the arguments that follow.[3] The strategy relies on a notion of what I call canonical inference rules.[4] Before proceeding with

---

[2] I should note that throughout I mean by 'possessing a concept' merely the ability to have thoughts of which the given concept is a component. It should not be taken to imply a discursive ability such as being able to give an account of the nature of the concept. In the case at hand, therefore, I mean only to say that having thoughts of the form *A and B* is sufficient for possessing the concept of conjunction. This is consistent with allowing that, for *some* concepts (of which, pretty clearly, basic logical concepts are *not* examples), it is a necessary condition for having thoughts of which those concepts are components that one be able to give a discursive account of them.

[3] My strategy is heavily indebted to Peacocke (1987).

[4] As always in this section, it must be remembered that inference rules are only one example of a range of conceptual roles that may be relevant. We will need to countenance such things as canonical incompatibilities as well, as will become clear below.

a description of the strategy, therefore, I shall attempt to clarify this notion. Roughly, the idea is that, among the various types of inference in which a logical concept features, there are some that are associated with that concept in a particularly immediate way. (It is not a requirement on a rule's being canonical for a concept that a possessor of the concept have any concept of canonicity, or even of validity. The canonical status of the rule for the concept, however it is to be explained, may be manifested in inferential behavior, or dispositions thereto, that do not suffice to give the possessor of the concept an explicit grasp of the nature of rules, validity, or canonicity.) There are two key questions raised by my claim that there are canonical inference rules associated with logical concepts. First, why should one think that there are canonical rules at all? Among the various inferential (or other) roles that a given logical concept can feature in, is it actually true that some are to be distinguished as being more central to their associated concepts than others? Secondly, supposing there are such things, what exactly is it for an inference rule to be canonical? What is the nature of the relationship between concept and rule that makes a rule canonical?

The case for the existence of canonical rules is intimately bound up with another issue: whether there can be distinct but logically equivalent concepts. The possibility of distinct, logically equivalent concepts is a necessary condition, and possibly a sufficient one, for the existence of canonical rules. Even if it fails to be sufficient, however, it nonetheless strongly recommends the thesis that there are canonical rules. The reason the two issues are connected is as follows. Associated with each logical concept is a set of all inference types that are valid for it. Suppose, then, that we have two logical concepts, C and D, about whose identity or distinctness we assume nothing but that are both associated with exactly the same set S of valid inference types. C and D are, therefore, logically equivalent. If there are canonical inference rules, then there is no reason why C could not be associated canonically with one subset of S, while D was associated canonically with a distinct subset of S. In such a case, C and D would be different concepts, even though they were logically equivalent. This shows that the existence of canonical rules is sufficient for the possibility of distinct, logically equivalent concepts (and, hence, that the latter is necessary for the former). Conversely, suppose there can be logically equivalent but distinct concepts. Let C and D be two such concepts. Since they are logically equivalent, the set of valid inferences associated with C will be the same as the set of valid inferences associated with D. If, therefore, they are distinct concepts nonetheless, something other than which inferences are valid for them must be appealed to in explaining that distinctness. One obvious way to understand the distinctness is offered by the notion of canonicity. To give an example: ... *or* ... and *if not* ... *then* ... are logically equivalent (in classical logic). One can infer from *p* both *p or q* and *if not-p then q*. If one were to hold that they were different logical concepts, nonetheless, this might be accounted for by the fact that being inferable from *p* was associated with *p or q* in a particular way, a way that does not characterize the inference from *p* to *if not-p then q*.[5]

That canonicity provides an obvious way of explaining the distinctness of logically equivalent concepts, however, does not mean that it is the only way. There may be other ways to do that. Hence I do not think it is correct that the possibility of distinct, logically equivalent concepts is sufficient for the existence of canonical rules. But to the extent that logical concepts are exhausted by their logical roles, it seems *prima facie* unlikely that other ways can be found that will not themselves, ultimately, come down to a matter of canonical inferences. For example, one might think that a logical concept is a mode of presentation of the underlying set of valid inferences. Logically equivalent but distinct concepts are different modes of presentation of the same set of inferences in just the same way that the concepts expressed by 'Mark Twain' and 'Samuel Clemens' are different modes of presentation of the same man, on Frege's theory of sense. While this approach does not appear to make use of the notion of canonicity, it might well turn out that one could understand what a mode of presentation of a set of inferences was only in ways that amounted to a theory of canonical inferences. I am not here claiming that this must be so. But I think that the notion of canonical inferences will end up being very congenial to anyone who thinks that there can be distinct but logically equivalent concepts.

Cherniak, not surprisingly, holds that there cannot be distinct, logically equivalent concepts, and this leads him, in effect, to deny the existence of canonical inferences.[6] However, I think he is mistaken on this point. The argument for the existence of distinct, logically equivalent concepts is simply a version of Frege's test for sameness of

---

[5] Nothing hangs on this particular example, though of course something does hang on the existence of some such examples.

[6] In fact, what he explicitly denies is the stronger thesis, that there are canonical rules that determine the meanings of logical constants (which I discuss below). His objections to this thesis, however, would clearly carry over to the weaker claim that there are canonical inferences at all.

sense or concept. One could, for example, think that a sentence of the form *p and q* was true and yet doubt the truth of *not-(not-p or not-q)*. One would, in such a case, be making a logical error, but the error does not seem to be ruled out merely in virtue of possession of the concepts. (If one finds this example implausible, consider the logical equivalence of *p and q* and some very, very long transformation of it.) As a particularly striking case of this test consider the equivalence (again, in classical logic) of *p* and *not-not-p*. There is clearly a conceptual difference involved in these two propositions, despite their equivalence. Someone could think that *p* and yet doubt that *not-not-p*. If one were to object to this claim by saying that one could not think *p* and yet doubt that *not-not-p* if one had a full grasp of the concept *not*, then it might be replied that fully grasping negation is not necessary for having a thought of the form *p* at all. That is what makes the case striking. There is an equivalence between a substantive logical concept and something like the absence of a logical concept (or, if one prefers, the presence of the null logical concept).

Supposing, then, that we recognize that there are canonical inferences associated with logical concepts, what is it for some inference to be canonical for a concept? Here, unfortunately, I have no comprehensive story. Let me review a couple of possible answers. Christopher Peacocke, whose work I am drawing on heavily here, talks about how certain inferences are primitively obvious: 'the impression of obviousness is primitive in the sense that it is not consequential upon [one's] acceptance of some more primitive principle; nor upon iterated applications of any single principle; nor upon any other belief not already presupposed in grasp' of the propositions featured in the inference (1987: 154–5). But this cannot help in the context of the given project, for I am attempting to draw conclusions about logical abilities of persons in advance of any empirical psychological questions. Yet it is empirical psychology that would be needed to establish whether an inferential principle was primitively obvious in Peacocke's sense.

A more promising way to understand canonical inference rules is in terms of rules that give the meaning of the logical constant that features in them, or (to speak in the material mode) that individuate the relevant concept. Gentzen (1964), for example, held that the introduction rules for logical constants in his natural deduction system determined the meaning of those constants. A number of other philosophers were drawn to this position, or variants thereof (Popper 1946/7, 1947; Kneale 1956). This view of the meaning of logical constants was subject to a serious attack by Arthur Prior (1960). Prior described an alleged logical constant, 'tonk', defined by the introduction rule 'from *A* infer *A tonk B*' and the elimination rule 'from *A tonk B* infer *B*'. If deducibility is transitive, these rules have the consequence that an arbitrary *B* is inferable from an arbitrary *A*. Conversely, if it is not the case that anything can be inferred from anything, then deducibility must not be transitive. Either of these options is hard to accept. The challenge to the holders of the Gentzen view was that they would have no way of denying the validity of the offensive tonk-inferences, since, if 'tonk' were defined by the inference rules, those inferences would be valid for 'tonk' by definition. I shall not follow further the course of the debate.[7] If the Gentzen view can be successfully defended, then it will provide the needed account of the nature of canonicity (and, furthermore, establish conclusively the existence of canonical inferences). If it cannot, then I will have to settle for something weaker, according to which certain inference rules, while not determining the associated logical concepts, are in some way more reflective of the essence of those concepts than other equally valid inference rules.

The first stage of the three-stage strategy I will follow in the arguments below will be to identify canonical inferences (or other conceptual roles) for a range of logical concepts under discussion. In all cases, the roles identified at this stage as canonical for a given concept will be valid for it. Suppose, then, that we have a given logical concept, *CON*, with an associated canonical role, *R*.[8] I shall next attempt to show that any creature meeting one of the necessary conditions of personhood must have a concept, *X*, for which *R* is canonical. It is this second stage of the argument that carries the real philosophical weight, for it is here that the attempt to forge a connection between personhood and a given logical ability is made.

A third, and crucial, stage is still required. For even if we have so far succeeded in showing that any creature satisfying a given condition (and therefore, any person) must have a concept *X* for which *R* is canonical, it may be objected that we have not yet shown that that concept is *CON*. There is not even any guarantee that *X* is a concept for which *R* is valid. Perhaps, it will be alleged, there are creatures who

---

[7] Belnap (1962) gives a classic defense of the Gentzen view.

[8] There may be more than one inference associated canonically with a given concept. In my description here of the strategy I will pursue, I simplify by assuming just one such conceptual role.

are sufficiently confused that they have a concept of disjunction and yet take the inference from *p or q* to *p* to be valid, or even canonical, for that concept. (Perhaps they treat disjunction as if it were conjunction.) Such an objection makes dubious sense, in my opinion, but we must be clear that, and how, we are ruling it out. We shall rule it out by an application of a version of the Principle of Charity. The version of the Principle tells us that, wherever possible, we should take someone's logical concepts to be such that the inferences she takes to be canonical (or non-discursively treats as canonical) for those concepts are indeed valid for them.[9] Thus, if *CON* is a concept for which *R* is the associated canonical (valid) inference rule, and a creature has a concept *X* for which *R* is canonical (these are the results of the first two stages of the argument), then the third stage tells that, if there is a concept for which *R* is valid (as we know there is, since we have already established that *R* is canonical and valid for *CON*), then *X* is a concept for which *R* is valid. Since *X* is then a concept for which *R* is both valid and canonical, there seems absolutely no basis on which to deny that *X* is *CON*.

Notice that this third stage of the argument would be trivial if we took the Gentzen view about the relation of canonical inferences to the concepts to which they apply. If the canonicity of an inference rule were determinate for the identity of the concept featuring in it, then the fact that a creature had a concept, *X*, for which a rule *R* was canonical, would ensure that *X* was *CON*, if *R* was canonical for *CON*.[10] Thus, if the Gentzen approach could be successfully defended against Prior's objections, it would provide a particularly smooth way of establishing the third stage of the argument. The appeal to the Principle of Charity would, in effect, be *pro forma* only. On the other hand, if we show that a creature has a concept *X* with which it makes and accepts inferences of the form *R*, but cannot show that *R* is canonical for *X*, then the appeal to the Principle of Charity risks proving too much; for it will make it difficult (though not necessarily impossible) to show that a creature could ever misuse logical concepts.[11] So the success of the

---

[9] Although I shall not dwell on this in the following, I think we should add to this statement of the Principle of Charity the methodological scruple that, if there is more than one such concept, we should take that person to be using the weakest of them.

[10] The method does not run the risk of attributing to a creature a concept like Prior's 'tonk', since we are running arguments of the kind described only for canonical roles associated with concepts that we have, and recognize as legitimate.

[11] This, of course, is a version of the familiar objection to the Principle of Charity, that it makes it hard to explain error and irrationality.

strategy depends on showing that whatever conditions on personhood we appeal to imply that a creature not only has a concept with which it makes inferences of the kind *R*, but that those inferences are genuinely canonical for that concept.

This last point is particularly important because it is just here that the description of the arguments I will be giving is idealized. I do not know how, in general, to show that, for an arbitrary concept of a given creature, a concept the exact identity of which is still unknown, certain of the inferences made using that concept are indeed canonical for it. The best approximation I can make to showing that given inference rules are canonical for some arbitrary concept of a given creature is this. The arguments I shall give will show that any person must have a concept with which it makes inferences of a certain kind, *R*. If the context provided by the argument in which the agent must make inferences of kind *R* is sufficiently unspecialized, basic, or fundamental (I leave all these notions undefined), then it will be plausible to treat the relevant inferences as canonical for the concept involved. To do otherwise would be to assume that the person might, in these very basic contexts, rely on a concept for which the needed inferences were *not* canonical, but secondary or derived. While it is not impossible that a person should, in some very basic and fundamental contexts, use a concept for which the inferences needed in that context were secondary or derived, this would certainly be odd.[12]

Above, I mentioned that Cherniak rejects the existence of canonical inferences and individuates logical concepts broadly, so that there cannot be, on his view, distinct but logically equivalent concepts. I offered an argument against the broad view of the individuation of logical concepts and showed why the view that there can be distinct, logically equivalent concepts naturally supports the existence of canonical inferences. However, even if I am wrong about all of that, one should note that the arguments I am about to give would still be effective against Cherniak's view that there are no logical abilities that any rational creature, or person, must have, so long as one accepted a slightly stronger version of

---

[12] The impression of oddity would be even stronger for creatures subject to evolutionary pressure, since one might expect evolution to favor the development and acquisition of concepts for which needed inferences were canonical in order to minimize the chances of logical error in important situations. But, needless to say, relying on evolutionary claims would be contrary to the *a prioristic* spirit of my project. Or, to put the point another way, nothing in the account of persons that I am relying on requires that persons be the product of a process of natural selection.

the Principle of Charity than the one I gave above. The stronger version of the principle would hold that, if possible, we take rational creatures not to be making invalid inferences with their logical concepts not just in cases where those inferences are canonical for the concepts involved (as the weaker of the version of the principle states) but in a wide range of basic, unspecialized, or fundamental cases generally, whether the inferences are canonical for the concepts involved or not. Each of the arguments I give in the following will show that any person must have some logical concept with which she makes certain inferences. Given the stronger version of the Principle of Charity, that is enough, by Cherniak's lights, to identify the logical concepts she is using, and to establish that she must be able to use those concepts in certain ways. In other words, not relying on the notion of canonical inferences (and taking the broad view of the individuation of logical concepts) makes the task of showing that there are particular logical concepts and particular ways of using them that must be shared by all persons (slightly) harder, by requiring the use of the stronger version of the Principle of Charity. But, once that stronger version is adopted, what remains to be shown is much easier, since one can identity a creature's logical concepts from the inferences it makes with them without worrying about whether those inferences are canonical for the concepts concerned.

Having given this detailed and idealized description of the arguments to come, I shall not be overly concerned to squeeze them into the described schema. It will be obvious enough how what I say below meets the requirements of the first two stages of the strategy. Since the third stage, the final application of the Principle of Charity, is invariant across all the different arguments, I shall not include it in the various arguments.

2.2 CONJUNCTION

I come now to the arguments that possession of certain logical abilities is indeed necessary for anything to be a person. In the present section, I shall deal with conjunction. In many respects, conjunction is the simplest of the logical concepts to deal with. There will surely be no argument with the claim that the usual introduction and elimination rules for conjunction are canonical for it. We must therefore show that any person must have a concept, *Conj*, for which the following inference rules are canonical:

(1) Infer *p* from *Conj(p,q)*;
(2) Infer *q* from *Conj(p,q)*;
(3) Infer *Conj(p,q)* from *p* and *q*.[13]

Which condition, among the various conditions discussed in the previous chapter, will ensure that any person must have such a concept? Agency. The basic point is that agency requires the integration of information that, owing to Finitude, is gained at different times and places. Action, especially in the form of long-term plans and projects, would be impossible unless this disparately gathered information could be put together or synthesized. One can think of this synthesis either more narrowly or more broadly. Narrowly speaking, a given action will often depend on a number of pieces of information the acquisition of which must happen at different times and places. In order to know at what time to leave for a destination I must put together information about what time I must arrive by with information about how long the journey will take. These will have to be put together because, owing to Finitude, they will generally be acquired in different contexts, at different times and places. Information necessarily comes to finite creatures piecemeal. More broadly speaking, we need to take account of the way in which any action will rely, if only implicitly, on a whole host of background beliefs that need to be integrated in some way to provide us with any guidance. These background beliefs will include such things as that a material object cannot be in two places at once, what given words of a language mean, what one's name is, how long various types of things typically continue to exist, and so on without definite limit. They operate in all cases of action in different respects and there is no knowing which of them will be relevant on which occasions. We are thus required to maintain, as it were, a running account of the world. This account need not contain all the information we are in possession of, but it must contain a vast amount of it.

Either the narrower kinds of synthesis, in which particular relevant bits of information are put together in the context of a given action, or the broader kind, in which we assemble a background theory that, in its various parts, is ready to inform all manner of actions, must be logically equivalent to the conjunction of the elements that are synthesized. That is to say, the synthesis must logically imply all and only the beliefs

---

[13] These conditions, of course, do not fully characterize the English word 'and', which serves other functions besides expressing the concept of logical conjunction.

it synthesizes. If it were weaker, then not all the individual bits of information that went into the synthesis would be derivable from it. The synthesis would fail to preserve all of the information of which it was a synthesis. If, on the other hand, the synthesis were stronger than the conjunction of the individual elements that it comprised, it would run ahead of whatever basis we had for the individual elements themselves. It would thus contain information unwarranted by whatever justification attached to the individual elements.

It is important not to misconstrue these remarks about the relation of the synthesis to the elements it synthesizes as saying anything about the relation of the synthesis to the historical vicissitudes of a person's evolving beliefs. For example, the requirement that the synthesis not be stronger than its elements does not imply that persons cannot forget individual bits of information. Only, as individual bits of information are forgotten, so the synthesis derived from them itself must become correspondingly weaker. Nor does it imply that we cannot, for example, draw inductive conclusions from a number of individual observations. There is no requirement here that the individual elements of the synthesis must be observational. If an inductive conclusion is derived from a number of observations, it itself is an element in the overall synthesis and hence the synthesis must imply it, and not just the individual observations. Nor are issues of justification at all relevant here. When one has drawn a generalization from a number of observations, that generalization is itself an element in the overall synthesis. It may continue to be part of the synthesis even if the observational beliefs on which it was based are forgotten (or dropped for some other reason). Whether one is *justified* in believing the generalization when one has forgotten the evidence is a wholly separate issue on which opinions differ.

To say that the synthesis must by logically equivalent to the conjunction of the elements synthesized does not settle the question of whether it requires a concept for which (1) to (3) are *canonical*, however. It merely shows that it requires a concept for which they are valid. As I mentioned in Section 2.1.2, this is the point at which the strategy I am pursuing becomes problematic, since I do not know exactly what would be required to show that someone must have a concept for which given rules are canonical. How is one to show that, of the many truth-functionally equivalent concepts that would form a synthesis out of individual bits of information in the way described above, it is, precisely, conjunction that a creature has, and not some other equivalent concept?[14] The best answer I can give is this. The point of the synthesis is to keep an up-to-date integration of the information that a creature has. The way in which the synthesis is kept up to date is that, from the synthesis at any moment, and the acquisition of a new piece of information, a new synthesis is formed immediately on the basis of nothing other than those two elements. Thus, it is of the essence of how this synthesis is maintained that it be revisable according to (3). This would be strange unless the concept that united the elements of the synthesis were one for which (3) was canonical. Moreover, since the background synthesis contains much more information than is needed for any particular action, the information contained in it must be readily detachable. Hence, (1) and (2) ought to be canonical for the concept as well.[15]

The foregoing should not be confused with a general theory of belief revision of the kind given by Peter Gärdenfors (1988). The process described in connection with (3) corresponds more or less to what Gärdenfors calls 'expansion' of a set of beliefs. But the thrust of his work is to spell out what happens when an added belief is inconsistent with something already believed. In this case, it is not rational simply to move to the expansion of the original belief set. Beliefs must also be removed to avoid inconsistency. None of what I say is meant to be inconsistent with this. If a new piece of information is added that is inconsistent with something already believed, then it may not simply be conjoined with the existing synthesis. But it will be conjoined with some subset of the existing synthesis. So the basic point about the synthesis maintaining its up-to-date status through conjunction will still obtain.

The claim about extraction of information via (1) and (2) also requires some clarification. Not all information contained, in some sense of containment, in the synthesis need be extractable by inferences of these forms. For example, if I believe p and *if p then q*, I will not (unless I also believe q) be able to extract q from the synthesis by one of these inferences even though q is somehow contained in the totality.

[14] If one thinks there cannot be distinct, truth-functionally equivalent concepts in the first place, then, given the strengthened Principle of Charity discussed above, no further work is needed to show that any person must have a concept of conjunction with which it can make inferences of the forms (1) to (3). See the last paragraphs of Section 2.1.2 for elaboration of this point.

[15] One point of detail. The argument just given concerns a logical operator of variable polyadicity, whereas (1) to (3) are stated in terms of a dyadic operator. There is, I believe, nothing essentially dyadic about conjunction. Hence, ideally, (1) to (3) should be restated in terms of an operator of indeterminate polyadicity.

One might wonder, then, whether in synthesizing, the logical form of the information is altered in such a way that none of it might be extractable by such inferences. For example, if I learn that p, this might be registered in the synthesis in the form $pv\perp$ (where $\perp$ represents some logically false proposition). p is itself not extractable from this by a simple application of (1) or (2). Might it be possible that synthesizing information always involves alterations of logical form in this way? Again, reflection on the point of the synthesis suggests not. Such an alteration makes any information that comes in as a unit harder to extract. It thus, pointlessly, increases the possibility that the synthesis will fail to fulfill its function, which is to guide action successfully in the light of information possessed. The point of having the synthesis would be undermined if the information held were harder to get out than to get in.

I should add that the remarks made here about the synthesis should be taken together with the discussion, in Section 3.4, of what it is to believe a conjunction. It will turn out there, to anticipate, that to believe a conjunction simply is, under normal circumstances, to believe the conjuncts. This means that all reference here to the synthesis of information is actually not to be taken in an overly psychologically realistic way.

Before proceeding with further arguments to identify additional logical abilities that any person must possess, let us use the argument of this section to clarify my response to Cherniak in less abstract terms than the ones I had to use earlier. Cherniak claims that a sophisticated rational creature with various logical abilities might yet fail to have a concept of conjunction, or, having it, might fail to be able to infer p from p *and* q. Although he does not use the apparatus of persons, nothing in his view requires that a rational creature unable to reason with conjunction must lack any of the features I hold are necessary for being a person. We may therefore say that Cherniak thinks that there can be persons that lack a concept of conjunction or, having one, still cannot infer p from p *and* q. The argument of this section purports to show that this is false. Persons are necessarily agents, and agency requires the ability to synthesize information gathered bit by bit into something with the logical strength of the conjunction of those individually gathered pieces of information. It also requires being able to recover those pieces of information from the synthesis. The synthesis, therefore, must relate the pieces of information in such a way that it is inferable from them (collectively) and they are inferable from it. If those inferences do not involve misuse of the logical concept involved (as there is no reason to think they do), then, according to Cherniak's broad theory of the individuation of logical concepts, that is sufficient to show that any agent, and hence any person, must have a concept of conjunction with which it can make inferences of the types (1) to (3). For one such as myself, who takes it to be possible that there are distinct, logically equivalent concepts, something more needs to be shown to establish that it is a concept of *conjunction* that a person must have, and not just any concept from a class of concepts equivalent to conjunction. That 'something more' is that inferences of the types (1) to (3) are not only valid for the concept used but canonical for it. Although I have not firmly established that (1) to (3) must be canonical for the concept that performs the function of synthesizing the separately gathered pieces of information, I have suggested why it is plausible to suppose they are.

2.3 CONDITIONALITY

No other cases fall into place as easily and unqualifiedly as does conjunction. I turn next to conditionality. I take the canonical fact about conditionality to be the inference rule *modus ponens*—infer *q* from *if p then q* and *p*. Thus, we must consider whether conditions on personhood require that all persons have a concept, *Cond*, with which they can make inferences of the form:

(4) Infer *q* from *Cond(p,q)* and *p*.

Conditionality, however, is not analogous to conjunction in at least one important way. In the case of conjunction, the requirement that the concept make valid (1)–(3) narrowed down the range of possible candidates for the concept to those truth-functionally equivalent to conjunction. Conjunction was then picked out from this equivalence class by the further requirement that (1)–(3) be canonical for the concept. But if, as I maintain, the only canonical fact about conditionality is given in (4), then we do not have an initial determination of a truth-functional equivalence class of concepts. This is so for two reasons. First, taken from a purely syntactic point of view, (4) leaves it open that *Cond* may be, for example, conjunction. Since conjunction is monotonic, *q* can be inferred from *p and q* together with *p* as well as it can be inferred from *p and q* alone. To avoid interpreting *Cond* as conjunction, further conditions would have to be laid down, either in the form of some introduction rule for the concept or at least in some specification that both premises in (4) are necessary for the derivation of q.[16] Since I do not think that any introduction rule is canonical for conditionality as such (as opposed to one or another particular variety of conditionality), I shall assume that some fix of the latter type can be provided to deal with this issue.

The second reason, however, why (4) fails to pick out a truth-functional equivalence class of logical concepts is that there are many conditionals for which (4) is valid, both truth functional and non-truth functional. In fact, the lack of specificity about the canonical logical facts of conditionality is a good thing. Classical logic has the material conditional, but it would, I think, be a mistake to argue that any person must have a concept of *material* conditionality.[17] Both psychological research and the anecdotal experience of logic teachers show that many humans have great difficulty with material conditionality. One obvious interpretation of this difficulty is that such people do not have, and in many cases cannot acquire, that concept. On the other hand, a creature that had a concept of material conditionality but of no other kind would nonetheless have a concept with which it could make inferences of the kind specified in (4). What we should strive to show, then, is that any person must have *some* concept from a family of concepts for any of which (4) would be canonical.[18]

Let us say that a creature meets the condition Inference if it is able to make some inferences which are either logically or materially valid.[19] The argument of the previous section shows, in effect, that Inference is a derived condition on personhood. Some of the arguments below will also support that claim. It is satisfaction of Inference that implies possession of a concept with which inferences of the form (4)

[16] Though this would have to be amended to deal with cases where, for example, q was a necessary truth.

[17] It might be thought that, since I argue that all persons must have concepts of conjunction and negation, all persons should be able to have thoughts of the form *not-(p and not-q)*, which is equivalent to the material conditional *if p then q*. However, as I argued in Section 2.1.2, the logical equivalence of the material *if ... then ...* and *not-(... and not ...)* does not entail that they are the same concept. Furthermore, the possession of the concepts of negation and conjunction does not guarantee the ability to combine those concepts into arbitrarily complex combinations.

[18] We thus have a case where the Gentzen approach, even if it could be defended against Prior's objections, could not work for present purposes.

[19] A materially valid inference is one whose premises guarantee its conclusion in virtue of the non-logical concepts involved. An example Brandom (1994: 98) gives is the inference from 'A is to the west of B' to 'B is to the east of A'.

can be made. To be able to make or understand an inference, one must understand that the conclusion is reached owing both to the supposition of the premises and to the existence of a relation between the premises and the conclusion. Where the conjunction of the premises is abbreviated as p and the conclusion as q, this means that, to make or understand an inference, one must have a concept, *Cond*, such that one can infer q from p and $Cond(p,q)$. To put it simply, to make or understand an inference, one must see that the conclusion is in some sense conditional on the premises.

This simple argument requires a number of comments and clarifications. First, I noted above that, given the argument of the previous section that any creature meeting Agency must be able to make and understand inferences of the forms (1)–(3), any creature satisfying Agency will automatically satisfy Inference. In fact, we now see that the connection between the concept of conjunction and a concept of conditionality is more substantial. In the previous paragraph, I talked of a relation of conditionality between the conjunction of the premises of an argument and its conclusion. There are, of course, single-premise arguments, and the argument of this section will show that any creature that can make or understand even single-premise arguments must have a concept of conditionality that behaves according to (4), and this independently of whether the arguments about conjunction in the previous section are good.[20] But, if a creature is able to make and understand many-premise arguments, then we have another way of showing that such a creature must also have a concept of conjunction. This alternative argument would be a kind of theoretical counterpart to the practical argument already given.

A second point is this. The relation between conditionality, which is a propositional operator, and things like validity and entailment, which are features of arguments, is a controversial topic.[21] Some philosophers caution us to keep them well apart, while others see a very close connection between them. Obviously, my argument here puts me in the latter camp. But I have not confused the two sets of concepts. I pointed out that one concept for which (4) would be valid is the material conditional. But the validity of an argument must consist in more than

---

[20] 0-premise inferences—inferences whose conclusions are logically valid—are, I think, a logician's extension of the ordinary concept of an inference in much the same way that the empty set or singletons are a logician's extension of the ordinary notion of a set.

[21] See Sanford (1989: 121–41) for discussion of this issue.

the truth of the material conditional consisting of the conjunction of the premises as antecedent and the conclusion as consequent. What this means is that, although I have argued that all persons must have some concept of conditionality on the basis of an ability to make and understand inferences, this does not guarantee that all concepts of conditionality that might satisfy this requirement are sufficiently strong to provide a concept of logical validity. In other words, a creature meeting Inference must have some concept of conditionality on that basis, but may not have any concept of logical validity as such. As with the failure of the argument to establish that all persons must share the concept of material conditionality, the failure to guarantee that all persons must have a concept of logical validity is an advantage. For it is by no means obvious that all humans, let alone all possible beings meeting Inference, *do* have such a concept.

A final observation I wish to make is this. The essence of the argument for conditionality that I made was that, to make any inference at all, a creature must have a concept of conditionality, since in any inference the conclusion is conditional on its premises. But my argument should not be confused with the view that all arguments are enthymematic and depend for their validity or their persuasiveness on a premise that is a conditional the antecedent of which is the conjunction of the other premises and the consequent of which is the conclusion. This is the view that Lewis Carroll (1895) criticized effectively. I have made no claim that the ability of an argument to convince one of its conclusion, let alone its validity, depends on the acceptance of such a conditional. Obviously the argument '*p and q*, therefore *p*' is valid, and a creature with a concept of conjunction is rational in accepting it, without the provision of the further premise *if p and q, then p*. My argument was only that one cannot understand what an argument is, and hence make or accept arguments at all, without having a concept of conditionality.

2.4 DISJUNCTION

So far, the kinds of inference rules that have been taken as instances of canonical facts about logical operators closely mirror the typical introduction and elimination rules of natural deduction systems. With disjunction, things are different. The introduction rule for disjunction in natural deduction systems is usually this:

(5) From *p* infer *p or q*.

Though this is simple and straightforward, it will not do as a canonical fact about disjunction. The reason is that research shows that many humans, even after being coached in inclusive truth-functional disjunction, fail to accept inferences of this form.[22] We cannot try to show that any person must have a concept with which it makes inferences of the form (5) when the only examples of persons with which we are acquainted typically fail to have any such concept. The usual elimination rule,

(6) If *r* is derivable from *p* and a set of assumptions S, and *r* is derivable from *q* and S, then infer *r* from *p or q* and S,

is implausibly complex to characterize a logical ability necessary for personhood.

A more likely candidate for a canonical rule for disjunction is *modus tollendo ponens*:

(7) From *p or q* and *not-p*, infer *q*.

However, from our present point of view, (7) is problematic. The problem is that, in order to show that a creature had the relevant conception of disjunction, we would need an independent way of establishing that it had a concept of negation. There is no problem in principle with doing this, and indeed, in the next section, I shall give an argument for the possession of a concept of negation based on the same condition that I will use in this section to establish the necessity for persons of possessing a concept of disjunction. This same approach, however, provides a way of showing the necessity of having a concept of disjunction in a way that is independent of negation, and I take this to be preferable.

In fact, the tactic I will use with respect to disjunction is adapted from an idea proposed by Gilbert Harman, and taken up by Christopher Peacocke, in dealing with the conceptual role of negation.[23] So far, the only conceptual roles for logical operators that we have been considering are their roles in inferences. In treating negation, Harman suggests that we consider, besides inference rules, incompatibility or exclusion rules. This allows one, for example, to characterize negation as a concept *Neg*

---

[22] See Braine *et al*. (1984: 346–6, 354) and Osherson (1975).
[23] See Harman (1986) and also Peacocke (1987). Brandom (1994) also emphasizes the coordinate statuses of inference and incompatibility in understanding logical vocabulary.

such that p and $Neg(p)$ are incompatible, or mutually exclusive. This gets at the essence of negation much better than the somewhat complex introduction and elimination rules provided for it in natural deduction systems. (I shall follow this up in the next section.)

What is the appropriate exclusion rule concerning disjunction? If we try and adapt (7) we get:

(8) p *or* q and *not-p* exclude *not-q*.

This, of course, doubles our problem with (7), since we now have negation occurring on both sides of the rule. By contrast, the following is much simpler:

(9) p *or* q and p exclude q.

(9), though, unlike (7) and (8), is valid only for exclusive disjunction (appropriately enough, since it is an exclusion rule). Nonetheless, it does seem to me as if (9) is really canonical for exclusive disjunction. I shall therefore argue that any person must have a concept, *Disj*, that is governed by the rules:

(10) $Disj(p,q)$ and p exclude q;
(11) $Disj(p,q)$ and q exclude p.[24]

Once again, the relevant condition on personhood that is needed here is Agency, in particular that part of Agency that requires of persons that they be able to deliberate about what to do. The objects of deliberation are one's takings of various courses of action. That is, one deliberates about whether one shall do y or z. Taking a course of action, or doing y, is an event. But since, by the condition Belief, all creatures within the scope of this discussion have beliefs (and other propositional attitudes), there is no harm in taking the objects of deliberation as the propositions corresponding to one's taking various actions. Corresponding to the course of action of my doing y is the proposition that I do y.

Now the argument that any creature that satisfies Agency must have a concept governed by (10) and (11) is this. Deliberation is a process of choosing, or trying to choose, among incompatible alternatives. If the

---

[24] These rules do not completely determine a concept of exclusive disjunction. As a referee pointed out, $Disj(p,q)$ might be interpreted as something like '*(p and x is black) or (q and x is white)*', where the 'or' could be inclusive. Here would be a case in which the methodological scruple mentioned in n. 9 would be necessary. The deviant interpretation of *Disj* is stronger than is necessary to see a person using a concept characterized by (10) and (11) as making valid exclusions with it.

alternatives in deliberation were not incompatible, it would be unclear what was involved in deliberating over which to take.[25] One who deliberates, therefore, must be able to relate two (or more) alternatives in such a way that the realization of one excludes the realization of the other(s).[26] If, as suggested, we take these alternatives as propositions, that means that one who deliberates must be able to relate two or more propositions in such a way that the obtaining of one excludes the obtaining of the others. This requires a concept behaving as *Disj* does in (10) and (11).

This argument for the possession of a concept of exclusive disjunction by all creatures capable of deliberating is silent on whether such a concept must be truth functional or not. As with the conditional, this silence seems to me appropriate. As mentioned above, inferences that are valid for a purely truth-functional (inclusive) disjunction are routinely rejected by people, and this suggests they lack such a concept. If so, our argument would have proved too much by requiring all deliberators to have a concept of truth-functional disjunction. Nonetheless, a purely truth-functional concept of disjunction would be adequate for deliberation, so long as it was exclusive.

There is a long-running argument over whether disjunctive terms in natural languages, such as the English 'or', represent inclusive or exclusive disjunction. In arguing, as I have, that any creature capable of deliberation must have a concept of exclusive disjunction, I do not mean to imply that the English 'or' does, in fact, primarily represent exclusive disjunction. For, even if all speakers of English, as creatures meeting Agency, must have a concept of exclusive disjunction, this is quite consistent with there being no term of English given over to representing only that concept. It would, however, be odd if natural languages had no way of expressing exclusive disjunction. Hence I am inclined to accept

[25] One may, of course, deliberate over whether to eat cake, ice cream, or both, and this, it may be suggested, shows that the alternatives of eating cake and eating ice cream are not incompatible. But, if eating both is a genuine alternative in the deliberation, then the options of eating cake and eating ice cream must be understood as eating cake only and eating ice cream only.

[26] As with conjunction, (10) and (11) describe a two-placed operator, whereas the argument in the text implies the possession of an operator with variable polyadicity. Again, (10) and (11) should be rephrased in terms of an indefinite number of propositional schematic letters. Or perhaps, in this case, one might reformulate the argument to show that there is a special, fundamental type of deliberation between two alternatives, the options of doing or not doing a given action. Hence the condition on the basis of which all persons must have a concept of disjunction is tied in a special way to a dyadic version of disjunction.

that some uses of such terms as 'or' do express exclusive disjunction and hence that exclusivity is sometimes a genuinely semantic and not always merely a pragmatic feature of the use of sentences containing that word.

2.5 NEGATION

Negation is difficult to deal with because all the standard logical principles governing it, Excluded Middle, Non-Contradiction, Double Negation, *Ex Falso Quodlibet*, and so on, have been challenged by proponents of different forms of negation. There is, therefore, little one can appeal to about negation without becoming embroiled in debates over relevant logic, intuitionism, and so on. Compare the situation with the conditional, another logical concept over which debates have raged. Proponents of all different varieties of conditionals agree that *modus ponens* is a valid rule for a conditional.[27] But a more basic problem with negation is that it introduces a polarity that seems to resist capture by anything other than itself. As Richard Sylvan puts it:

Negation is indefinable in positive terms . . . By virtue of negation itself there are positives and negatives, elements of a multiple pole story. Now positive functors, in terms of which negation (and its circle) might pragmatically be defined, do not move outside the orbit of their respective aspects (positive or negative). Negation however changes polarity, whence its indefinability. Negation is, to repeat, so to vaguely say, *sui generis*. (1999: 305)

This has the consequence that any conditions on the basis of which a concept of negation might be shown to be possessed by all persons are liable to seem as if they simply beg the question, as if they are already being described in terms of negation, or concepts very close to it. Yet the existence of this polarity is incontrovertible. The difficulty of supplying any grounds for its presence in thought that avoids question-begging is simply the reverse side of its utter basicness to all thought and reasoning.[28]

[27] There have been a few ready to question the validity of *modus ponens* for some conditionals, but they are a small minority. See, e.g., Lycan (1995).

[28] Any Parmenidean attempt to deny its existence is bound to lead to paradox. See the closing lines of Sally Potter's verse film whose title, *Yes*, might have served Parmenides himself: 'There's no such thing as nothing, not at all. | It may be really very, very small | But it's still there. In fact I think I'd guess | That "no" does not exist. There's only "yes" ' (2005: 73).

As noted in the previous section, and following Harman, I shall take the canonical fact about negation to be given by an exclusion rule, rather than an inference rule. The usual introduction and elimination rules for negation in natural deduction systems are rather complex, making them unlikely to capture features of the concept necessary to personhood. Some of them also require that negation be mentioned in the conditions of application for the rules. This would make it impossible to show that a creature had a concept for which those rules were canonical (or even merely valid), without our first being able to show that it had a concept of negation. Consequently, I shall take the canonical fact about negation to be that a proposition and its negation are mutually exclusive, or incompatible with each other. If we do not say too much about the nature of this exclusion, we seem to have something here that all parties to the debate over the nature of negation can agree to.[29] This approach seems to capture the essence of negation, as Sylvan's remarks on polarity suggest.[30] We are therefore looking to show that any creature meeting certain conditions must have a concept, *Neg*, such that

(12) *p* and *Neg(p)* are mutually exclusive

and such that (12) is a canonical fact about that concept.

There are a number of different avenues to showing that a concept of negation is necessary for personhood, none of them, however, without some serious problems. I shall look at two here. As Sylvan goes on to point out, after the long quote above, there are various cases of exclusive pairs of positives, such as in/out, up/down, danger/all clear, living/dead, etc. If we introduce a condition on personhood that a person must have, for example, spatial concepts, not an implausible condition for intelligent creatures meeting the condition of Finitude, then there will certainly be mutually exclusive pairs of beliefs of which such creatures are capable of having either, and such that it will follow from a grasp of the concepts involved (for example, *up* and *down*) that the beliefs in the pairs are treated as mutually exclusive.

The trouble is that we have nothing here that deserves to be called a concept of negation, for negation is an all-purpose propositional function, not tied in its application to any particular range of concepts

---

[29] 'Opposition, manifested in contradiction, contrariety or other conflict or contrast, is at the core of negation' (Sylvan 1999: 305). See also Priest (1999: 103).

[30] Of course, this approach does not alleviate the difficulty discussed in the previous paragraph, since exclusion itself depends on just the kind of polarity that negation is supposed to make possible.

such as spatial concepts. We do, however, have an all-purpose opposition in the concepts of truth and falsity. Just like the pairs up/down, in/out, and so on, truth and falsity are, by their nature, exclusive of each other.[31] And, in fact, the condition of Second-Ordinality (which requires of persons that they be able to have beliefs about their own and others' beliefs) implied, as we saw in Chapter 1, that any person must have concepts of truth and falsity. Second-Ordinality, then, provides the basis for an argument that any person must have a concept for which (12) is canonical, for falsity itself can be taken as the value of *Neg*.

There are at least two problems with this approach. It may be true by virtue of the nature of the concepts that anyone who has the concepts of truth and falsity must understand that they are exclusive in their application. It will, therefore, be canonical for the concept of falsity that 'it is true that p' and 'it is false that p' are mutually exclusive. But *Neg*, as it features in (12), is not a semantic concept. *Neg(p)* is exclusive not of the claim that it is true that p, but simply of p. Now this may be partially overcome if we also hold, as seems reasonable, that a grasp of the concept of truth ensures that one will accept a disquotational schema such as:

(13) It is true that p if and only if p.[32]

We will thereby obtain the result that any creature that has concepts of truth and falsity must, in virtue of those concepts, recognize, for any proposition p, that (i) p if and only if it is true that p, and that (ii) 'it is true that p' and 'it is false that p' are mutually exclusive. Yet there is still some logical work involved in putting these two claims together to yield the result that (iii) p and 'it is false that p' are mutually exclusive. So it remains open for someone to argue that, even with possession of the concepts of truth and falsity, and even with a grasp of (i) and (ii), a creature might still not have a concept for which (12) is canonical.

---

[31] This is exactly what dialetheists, such as Graham Priest, deny. So here is one point where I cannot help becoming embroiled in substantive debates over the nature of negation. However, I shall exempt myself from having to defend here the principle that no proposition is both true and false. See Priest (1999: 108–9).

[32] If it is true that anyone who has a concept of truth must grasp (13), then it will also follow from satisfaction of Second-Ordinality that a creature must have a concept of biconditionality (and hence of conditionality and of conjunction), thus providing further grounds for the necessity of those concepts for personhood. This seems like a lot of logic to build into the possession of a concept of truth, so perhaps we have a reason to be wary of asserting that a grasp of (13) must come with possession of the concept of truth.

A second problem with this avenue for establishing that all persons must have a concept of negation is that falsity and negation are so obviously related that to argue that any creature with a concept of falsity must have a concept of negation has a serious air of begging the question. In a certain sense, this need not be a problem. After all, if the argument presupposes its conclusion, it is at least guaranteed to be valid. The real question will then become, how plausible is it to make Second-Ordinality a condition on personhood? If we can argue that it is plausible, and if there is no real gap between falsity and negation, then in effect, we will have argued directly that a grasp of negation is a condition on personhood.

I turn now to a second avenue for establishing that possession of a concept of negation is necessary for personhood. This springs from our earlier discussion of disjunction. I said that deliberation involves incompatible alternatives. The nature of this incompatibility, as Peter van Inwagen (1983) notes, may stem from nothing more than an agent's decision not to take both of them. Thus, if I deliberate about whether to have ice cream or cake for dessert, that implies that I am not going to have both. But this may be only because I have decided that it would be greedy to have both. In other cases, the incompatibility may be physical. If I deliberate about whether to be in New York or Miami to see in the New Year, it is because I physically cannot be in both places at the same time.

In one prominent kind of deliberation, the incompatibility of the alternatives is of a logical variety. This is deliberation over whether or not to perform some action. If we continue to treat the alternatives in deliberation as propositions, such deliberation requires that one have a concept that modifies any given proposition that provides a suitable object of deliberation to produce another alternative that stands in a relation of mutual, logical exclusion to the original alternative. In other words, it requires a concept that is governed by (12). All we need, therefore, to get the conclusion that any creature meeting Agency must have a concept of negation is the further premise that any creature capable of deliberation is capable of deliberation about whether or not to perform an action.

As with the attempt to establish the universality of negation on the basis of the concepts of truth and falsity, so here too there is a sense of assuming what needs to be proved. If the relevant conditions include that a creature must be able to deliberate about whether or not to perform an action, it may seem as if we need a premise that a creature has a concept of negation in order to show that it must have a concept of negation. As indicated above, however, I think that this cannot be avoided. Another potential weakness with this means of establishing the necessity of possessing a concept of negation to be a person is that, although it seems highly plausible that any creature capable of deliberation must be capable of deliberating over whether or not to perform some action, and not just between options the incompatibility of which is not a logical matter, I do not see any way to prove this.

Despite the unresolved problems with these two arguments for showing that any person must have a concept of negation, my conviction that any person must have such a concept is so strong, and the arguments given in this section come so close to proving it, that I shall suppose this conclusion established. If one bears in mind also that the arguments concerning the other logical concepts we have looked at so far do not seem open to such objections, and it can therefore be taken as proven that persons must have concepts of conjunction, disjunction, and conditionality, the thought that a person might not have a concept of negation is, frankly, unbelievable.

2.6 QUANTIFICATION

When it comes to quantification, much of the work needed to show that all persons must possess concepts expressed by 'some' and 'all' and be able to use them in certain ways has been done by Jaakko Hintikka (1973: especially chs. 3 and 5). Hintikka argues that the meanings of these quantificational expressions is to be found in their connection with what he calls the games of searching and finding. An existentially quantified claim is to be understood as a claim that instances of a certain kind of thing can be found, a universally quantified claim as a claim that nothing can be found that is not of a given kind. The notions of searching for something of a given kind and finding it are treated elastically to include producing (as in 'there are transuranium elements') and scanning (as in 'there is a tree in front of me'). If anyone is worried about anti-realist implications of Hintikka's view, that it seems to preclude quantification over things that cannot be searched for or found in *any* sense, we may note that such worries can be summarily dispatched in our present context. What is important to us here will be the sufficiency of the activities of searching and finding for quantificational thought and not their necessity. As long as we can show that any creature that can engage in activities of searching and finding must have quantificational concepts that it can use in certain ways, we may leave it entirely open whether these concepts can also apply to cases in which possibilities of searching and finding do not apply at all, or apply only in a highly attenuated sense. Despite my own realist sympathies, I do not have a firm intuition that any person must have a conceptual grasp of a realm of objects that transcend its abilities to search and find.

It will be impossible to carry over the techniques we have developed in Sections 2.2–2.5 to apply to the case of quantification. This is because we relied on the condition Belief to guarantee that creatures in the scope of our discussion could grasp propositional contents and we could then go on to isolate the extra content added by the various logical operators we were looking at and ask what conditions would guarantee that a creature could have that extra content. In the case of quantification, however, we are dealing with logical operations that affect not complete propositions but propositional functions. But, if we simply stipulate, to correspond to the use of Belief in the previous arguments, that it is a necessary condition on personhood that a person can entertain propositional functions as contents, we effectively beg the question, since what it is to grasp a propositional function cannot be given independently of a grasp of some form of quantification. For this reason, I shall conduct the following discussion in a less precise fashion than previously adopted and simply try to indicate the underlying point without a full-dress application of the strategy employed in the other arguments of this chapter.

Hintikka develops his insights into the relations between quantification and the activities of searching and finding into a game-theoretic analysis of quantification. The essentials of the game that Hintikka associates with quantificational language are these. (I skip over various details in his account, especially those concerned with how other logical vocabulary besides the quantifiers is dealt with in his game-theoretic framework.) A person is thought to be playing against nature. One starts with a given quantified sentence. When the left-most quantifier is existential, it is the turn of the person, who advances by eliminating the quantifier and replacing all free occurrences of its variable with the name of some object in the domain of the game. When the left-most quantifier is universal, it is the turn of nature, which advances in exactly the same way—by eliminating the quantifier and replacing the free occurrences of the variable with the name of some object in the domain. When all the quantifiers have been eliminated in this way, the person wins if the resulting sentence is true and loses if it is false. This game provides the basis for a semantics for quantification since an arbitrary sentence of first-order logic is true if and only if there exists a winning strategy in this game.

The game described is somewhat too elaborate and theoretically involved for us simply to say that anyone capable of searching and finding must be capable of playing it, and hence logically competent with respect to quantification. But we can extract from it a more basic structure that will serve the same purpose. The existential quantifier is associated with a description, expressed by the propositional function obtained by removing the quantifier from the sentence. The person in the game is in the position of someone who is looking for something. She has a general description of the kind of thing she is looking for. She attempts to identify an individual to which that description applies. Success is finding something of the right kind. The ability to search and find is thus the ability to start with a general description that I do not know to apply to anything in particular and to identify a particular that fits the description. Thus, the ability to search and find is sufficient for the possession of the concept of an existential quantifier and sufficient for the ability to use that quantifier in inferences that have the form of existential instantiation.[33]

The universal quantifier is also represented, in the game, by a move from a quantified sentence to one in which the quantifier is removed and the variable replaced with the name of an object in the domain. Structurally, it acts identically to the existential quantifier. What connects that structural pattern to the universal quantifier is that the move is made by nature, not the person, and nature wins if the final sentence is false. Hence, to anthropomorphize, nature has an incentive to replace the variable with the name of an object that does *not* satisfy the description expressed by the propositional function, rather than one that does. But what is it, in the *person* rather than in the some anthropomorphized opponent, that reveals a grasp of the universal quantifier? Nature, in the game, is given the role of looking out for counter-examples. Thus, for a person to grasp the universal quantifier is for that person to be sensitive herself to the possibility of counter-examples to some claim. If a universally quantified proposition

---

[33] Hintikka (1973) is very good on the relation of the rules of the game described to the logical rules of existential and universal instantiation, to which they bear an obvious relation but with which they are not identical. See especially pp. 104–14.

is adopted tentatively, if someone, as it were, asks herself whether all Fs are G, then the paradigm manifestation of this is another search, a search for something that meets the description 'an F that is not G'. This brings out the equivalence of a sentence of the form $\forall x(... \; x \; ...)$ to one of the form $not\text{-}\exists x\text{-}not(... \; x \; ...)$. Where a universally quantified proposition is accepted, this is manifested in the tendency to select, without checking, an F if one is after something that is G. Its acceptance is freedom from the expectation that a given F may fail to be G.

We are thus in a position to say that any creature that is in a position to search for and find something that meets a given description must grasp the existential quantifier. And any creature that can search for and find something that does not meet a given description must grasp the universal quantifier. These two abilities are surely inseparable from each other. Hence, anything that can grasp one of the quantifiers can grasp the other. So we can say, with Hintikka (though without having to introduce the particular apparatus of the game he associates with quantification) that any creature capable of searching and finding must have a grasp of quantification.

But must any *person* be capable of searching and finding? Such capability was not explicitly enumerated among our conditions of personhood. Persons are necessarily finite agents. Agency involves identifying particular things. Finitude means that the particular things required by agents will not always be already given to them. Together, these facts imply that persons must be capable of searching for and finding what they need to act. The kinds of things that action requires will range from the most mundane and basic physical objects to abstract objects of various kinds: a twig of the right shape, a branch dry enough to light a fire, a telephone that works, another person to be friends with, a place to shelter in from the rain, a number by which to distribute certain goods equitably, a plan for further action, or a means to accomplish a goal. (It should be recalled that searching and finding can be interpreted very widely in this context. Hintikka talks of both producing and scanning as involving them, but there may be even more abstract modes of searching and finding.) Thus, I conclude, any person must indeed be capable of searching and finding. So all persons must have a grasp of quantification.

3

Belief and Conjunction

Everything only connected by 'and' and 'and'.
(Elizabeth Bishop, 'Over 2,000 Illustrations
and a Complete Concordance', 1955)

In the previous chapter, we looked at how conditions on personhood put requirements on concept-possession. The remainder of the book will be about some of the ways in which personhood has implications for belief. In this chapter and the next, I shall be concerned with a principle that requires closure of belief under conjunction; it requires, in other words, that a person believe the conjunction of her beliefs:

CP If S believes p and believes q, then S believes p *and* q.

I shall argue that this principle has two important features. First, satisfaction of it is rational. Secondly, satisfaction of it, to a sufficient extent, is a necessary condition for something's being a person. After explaining these two claims in more detail, the remainder of this chapter will be concerned with the case for CP's rationality. That will continue in the next chapter; the end of the next chapter will deal with whether satisfaction of CP, to a sufficient extent, is a necessary condition for persons.

It may initially be thought that the question of whether and why a person believes the conjunction of her beliefs is a rather uninteresting one. Nothing could be further from the truth. In fact, conjunction gives a precise way of dealing with the unity of the mind at a given time. The unity of the mind is a grand theme in philosophy and has meant many different things at different times and in different philosophical contexts, but the notion of conjunction gives a relatively simple way to get a handle on the problem. Conjunction is itself an operation of unification—it makes one thing out of two. What it unites, in the first instance, is propositions. But when these contents are the objects of belief, we can capture one sense of the unity of mind by means of the logical operation of conjunction. In believing the conjunction of two things one believes, one gathers into a system elements that might otherwise have nothing to do with each other. If a person believes the conjunction of all her beliefs, then her beliefs are, in this way, unified into a single whole, a body of beliefs rather than a mere heap of them. Believing the conjunction of all one's beliefs is one important way of having a unified mind. Failure to believe the conjunction of all one's beliefs is a failure of unity. We will also see in this chapter and the next, however, an even deeper sense in which conjunction is linked to the unity of the mind. To anticipate briefly, I shall argue that, in normal circumstances, what it is to believe a conjunction simply is to believe the conjuncts. Abnormal circumstances, in which this does not hold, are when the conjuncts belong to different mental partitions in a person's mind. Thus, satisfying CP implies that one is not subject to mental partitioning. This is the deeper sense in which conjunction is connected to the unity of the mind.

3.1 CLARIFICATION OF THE THESIS

3.1.1 What does it mean to say that satisfaction of CP is rational?

Satisfying CP means believing the conjunction of one's beliefs. What does it mean to say that it is rational to satisfy CP? Or, to put it another way, to say that CP is rational? In fact, this can mean more than one thing. I will defend two precisifications of the original claim. The first is:

> CPR1 If S believes *p* rationally and S believes *q* rationally, then, if S believes *p and q*, S believes it rationally.

Here, the point is that conjunction is a conduit for the transmission of rationality from the conjuncts to their conjunction. One need say nothing directly about what it is to believe something rationally in the first place. Whatever your favored account is, CPR1 would have it that belief in the conjunction is rational if the beliefs in the conjuncts are. In Section 3.2, I shall defend CPR1 against a number of objections.

The second claim I will defend that might be expressed by saying that CP is rational is:

> CPR2 If S is rational, then, if S believes *p* and believes *q*, S believes *p and q*.

CPR2 might be seen in terms that are either pragmatic or epistemic. Seen in a more pragmatic light, the idea behind CPR2 is that it is rational for a person to conjoin her beliefs. In more epistemic-sounding language, one could rephrase CPR2 as holding that the belief that *p and q* is rational relative to the beliefs that *p* and that *q*. However one sees it, however, the point of CPR2 is that, whatever the status of a person's beliefs is—whether they are themselves rational or not—there is something good to be said for bringing those beliefs together via the operation of conjunction. Indeed, there is more than something good to be said for it. It is what a person should do. To illustrate the difference between CPR1 and CPR2, suppose that someone believes *p* irrationally and *q* (either rationally or irrationally). If that person also believed *p and q*, CPR1 would not deem that conjunctive belief rational. The irrationality of the belief that *p* would infect it. CPR2, though, still recommends believing *p and q* in the circumstances described. Even if the belief itself is not rational, it may be rational to have it, given that one believes *p* and believes *q*. In Section 3.3, I shall defend CPR2 against a line of criticism stemming from naturalized epistemology. Then, in Section 3.4, I shall argue for the view that

BC Under normal circumstances, what it is to believe a conjunction simply is to believe its conjuncts.

Hence, under normal circumstances, a person does bring her beliefs together. Non-normal circumstances, in which a person believes two things but not their conjunction, are those involving mental partitioning. This leads to a further argument for CPR2, pursued in Chapter 4, that a person ought not to partition her beliefs.

I take both CPR1 and CPR2 to be highly intuitive and plausible. The main work in supporting these claims is to show why certain objections made to them do not in fact succeed.

3.1.2 The necessity of satisfying CP

My other claim is that satisfaction of CP to a sufficient degree is a necessary condition of something's being a person. The point of discussing this here, rather than in Chapter 1, where a number of other necessary conditions on personhood were offered, is that we here move from fairly generic necessary conditions on personhood (which are either non- or only weakly epistemic) to a specifically and strongly epistemic condition, which, I shall argue, derives from the generic conditions. A further, but related, difference between the necessary condition here, satisfaction of CP, and the necessary conditions in Chapter 1, is that here satisfaction of the principle comes in degrees. Whereas something is either finite or not, an agent or not, a possessor of beliefs or not, and so on, one can satisfy CP to a greater or lesser degree. That is, one can believe many, or few, of the conjunctions of one's beliefs. My claim here is that it is a necessary condition on personhood that one satisfy CP to a sufficient extent. This is, of course, vague, but the vagueness is, I think, ineliminable for two reasons. First, I doubt there is a good way of counting beliefs (is a belief that *p and p and p* distinct from a belief that *p and p?*) and it is also quite plausible that persons have an infinite number of beliefs. It would, therefore, be hard to formulate a meaningful precisification of our claim. But, even if such a precisification could be meaningfully formulated, it would surely be arbitrary to suppose that belief in at least some precise number of conjunctions was necessary for personhood. There will be clear cases where something does believe enough of the conjunctions of its beliefs to be a person. And there will be, at least notionally, clear cases in which something does not.[1] But there will also be, at least notionally, cases in which we simply do not know what to say. This vagueness in the concept of a person seems to me right and just what we should expect.

I take it to be of some significance that satisfaction of CP is both rational and necessary for personhood. These two features are independent. There may be things that are rational and yet such that something can fail in them and still, unequivocally, be a person. More controversially, there might be beliefs or constraints on belief that are necessary for personhood and yet not rational (or are even irrational). For example, Kant argues, quite plausibly in my opinion, that it is necessary for a person to see herself as acting under the idea of freedom. One could put this by saying that it is a necessary condition on persons that they believe they are free. Yet, arguably, there is no good reason to believe that one is free. The standard criticism against transcendental arguments for some conclusion, that such arguments may succeed in showing why we must believe the conclusion but give us no reason to think it is true, is well taken. Happily, in the case of satisfaction of CP (and similarly for the

---

[1] I say 'at least notionally' because I suspect that having beliefs itself will ultimately turn out to be sufficient for being a person (i.e. it will imply the other necessary conditions mentioned in Chapter 1). In that case, if the claim I am making here is correct, nothing could have beliefs and yet fail to believe enough of the beliefs' conjunctions to count as a person.

principle of Reflection discussed in Chapter 5), the transcendental and the rational coincide. (However, we shall explore in Chapter 6 an area where they threaten to come apart.)

3.2 OBJECTIONS TO CPR1: A BUDGET OF PARADOXES

Suppose I rationally believe that today is Wednesday and I also rationally believe that dodos are extinct. If I believe the conjunction of these two propositions, if I believe that today is Wednesday and that dodos are extinct, would that belief also be rational? It would. Given that it is rational for me to believe each of the conjuncts, where could the irrationality of believing their conjunction come from? After all, in a certain sense, to be capitalized on when I come to say, in Section 3.4, what it is to believe a conjunction at all, a conjunction is nothing over and above its conjuncts. If each of the conjuncts is rational, there is nothing else left in the conjunction that could be irrational. One might even say that the canonical way to show that belief in a conjunction is rational is to show that belief in its conjuncts is rational. What superior method could there be? One might show that belief in a conjunction was rational because, for example, it followed from some other proposition one believed rationally, but such a method would fail to address the rationality of the components of the conjunction. It would, therefore, be inferior to showing that the conjuncts themselves were rational.

Better to understand this characterization of CPR1, we should take care not to be misled by the following scenario. One might believe two things independently that, when one puts them together, one sees cannot both be true. If one is committed to the view that contradictions cannot be true (or rationally believed), one will take this fact as a reason for suspending belief in one or both of the propositions involved. One might further specify this scenario in either of two ways. According to one of those ways, one comes to see that, whatever one's initial impressions were, belief in one or both of the propositions was, after all, not rational. According to the second way, one was rational in believing the conjuncts previously, but ceases to be so when one sees that they cannot both be true. Such a scenario, taken in either of these ways, is not a counter-example to CPR1. CPR1 applies in cases in which belief in the conjuncts actually *is* rational. So the first way of taking the scenario fails to be one in which the antecedent of CPR1 is true. The second way of taking the scenario is, effectively, calling for a relativization of the notion of rationality to either a time, a body of evidence, what one has already thought, or something like that. Belief in the conjuncts is rational relative to one time, or to one body of evidence, or to what one has thought up to a given point; belief in the conjunction is not rational relative to another time, another body of evidence, or to what one has thought up to a later point. Relativization of the notion of rationality in this way is not something I object to on principle (though I shall not pursue it here). But, if one were to take that step, CPR1 as stated would be incomplete. The version of CPR1 I would seek to defend would be the one in which the rationality invoked in the antecedent and the rationality invoked in the consequent were relativized to the same index. The scenario as taken in the second way we are considering, though, appears to present a counter-example to CPR1 only because it relativizes the rationality in the antecedent and the consequent to different indices. So it fails to address CPR1 as actually formulated and would not be a counter-example to the appropriately relativized version of CPR1.

Notwithstanding CPR1's high initial plausibility, it has garnered a large amount of criticism. Henry Kyburg (1970) even takes support of it to be a philosophical pathology—'conjunctivitis'.[2] Arguments against CPR1 typically (though, as we shall see, not invariably) involve two propositions that one believes rationally but that contradict each other. This seems to enable an easy route to showing that belief in their conjunction is not rational, since it will be a contradiction and it is alleged by the proponents of such cases that belief in a contradiction is *ipso facto* not rational. That cases against CPR1 take this form is indicative of just how strong the intuitive case for it really is. Absent contradictoriness, what grounds could there be for holding that belief in the conjunction was not rational? Contradiction plays the role of a kind of *deus ex machina*, showing that belief in the conjunction is irrational regardless of the fact that belief in each of the conjuncts is (alleged to be) rational.

3.2.1 The Lottery Paradox

One argument against CPR1 is the Lottery Paradox, developed by Kyburg (1961, 1970). Here is a statement of the paradox. There is a

---

[2] Kyburg's formulation of the principle is in terms of 'bodies of reasonably accepted statements' rather than a person's rational beliefs, but I don't think anything substantive hangs on the distinction here.

lottery with 1,000 tickets. Exactly one will be randomly selected as the winning ticket. You rationally believe this. For any ticket, the odds that it will be selected are one in a 1,000. Hence the probability that it will not be selected is 0.999. You therefore rationally believe, of each ticket, that it will not win. The conjunction of these thousand beliefs is equivalent to the proposition that no ticket will win.[3] According to CPR1, belief in this conjunction is rational, since belief in each of its conjuncts is. The conjunction of this rational belief with the rational belief that one ticket will win yields, according to another application of CPR1, the rational belief that one ticket will win and no ticket will win. But this belief is a contradiction, so it cannot be rational. Since Kyburg finds all the assumptions involved in this argument more compelling than CPR1, he concludes that CPR1 is false.

The basic mistake with this argument is the move from the fact that each ticket has a 0.999 probability of losing to the claim that it is therefore rational for someone to believe, of each ticket, that it will lose. The mistake is not that 0.999 is not a high enough probability to license this move. After all, we can increase the number of tickets in the example to make the probability of any ticket's losing arbitrarily close to one. The point is rather that whether it is rational for you to believe something does not depend simply on how probable it is. True, the probability of a given ticket's losing may be much higher than the probability of many things you do have good reason to believe—for example, that your bicycle has not been stolen. But it is precisely knowledge of the circumstances of the lottery that make the belief that a given ticket will lose irrational, even though the probability of its losing is very high.

A number of authors agree that statistical or probabilistic evidence is not sufficient for knowledge and/or rational belief. Dana Nelkin (2000), for example, suggests an externalist condition for knowledge that would imply that a person does not, in the lottery situation, know that a given ticket will lose. The condition is that there be a causal or explanatory relation between a belief and the fact that makes it true. Where a person's belief is based on mere probabilities, as it is in the lottery case, such a relation is lacking. My subject in this chapter, however, is rational belief and not knowledge. Even if, owing to the

---

[3] The conjunction of the beliefs, of each ticket, that it will not win is not, strictly speaking, equivalent to the belief that no ticket will win. I take up this issue in my discussion of the Preface Paradox below. I ignore it here because I believe there are other problems with the Lottery Paradox.

absence of the right kind of causal or explanatory relation between the belief and the fact that makes it true, a person does not know a given ticket will lose, that does not imply that her belief that it will lose is not rational. And, while many philosophers agree that some externalist conditions are appropriate for knowledge, rationality of belief seems a much more internal matter. Nelkin, however, extends her treatment of the knowledge case to cover rational belief as well in an intriguing way that parallels an important part of my argument in Chapter 5 in support of the rationality of Reflection. She calls it an 'internalized version of the "connection" requirement' (2000: 396). The idea is that, although, for a belief to be rational, it is not required that there actually is a causal or explanatory relation between the belief and the fact that makes it true (and, of course, a belief may be rational even if there is no fact that makes it true), it is a requirement that 'one be able to posit the existence of an explanatory connection between one's belief and the object of one's belief' (2000: 398). As Nelkin stresses, one need not be able to tell a detailed story about the causal or explanatory relations between one's belief and its object, but one must have some idea of how one's belief is explained by what makes it true (or would be explained by what would make it true). In the lottery case, where the belief that a given ticket will lose is based solely on knowledge of probabilities, one cannot point to any way in which one's belief would be explained or caused by the fact (if it is a fact) that that ticket will lose.

Returning to CPR1, it should be easy to see, with a little reflection, that the problem in the Lottery cannot stem from CPR1. To see this, simply give up CPR1. Now, how is the epistemic situation of a person in the Lottery any better? Such a person (according to the propounder of the argument) still rationally believes, of each ticket, that it will lose and rationally believes that one ticket will win. Nothing in the statement (or in Kyburg's resolution) of the paradox depends on the person's not knowing that she has these beliefs and realizing that they are inconsistent. We may, therefore, suppose that she does know all this. In other words, even though without CPR1 we are unable formally to derive the result that the person rationally believes a contradiction (that is, has a single rational belief of the form *p and not-p*), we are still in a situation in which all the elements of the contradiction are present, accepted as rational, and, typically, may well be realized to be present and rational by the subject. It is hard to see wherein the subject's epistemic situation is any better than if CPR1 were accepted.

To suppose that the Lottery is an argument against CPR1 is to rely on a distinction between having contradictory beliefs (for example, believing *p* and believing *not-p*) and believing a contradiction (believing *p and not-p*). CPR1 is alleged to lead us to the rationality of belief in a contradiction. If that is worse than rationally having contradictory beliefs, then indeed there may be some argument against CPR1 in the offing. But, although in the abstract we may be able to conceive a difference between having contradictory beliefs and believing a contradiction, in many actual cases it is hard to see how the former is any better than the latter. Imagine that I profess to believing *p* and, a moment later, to believing *not-p*. You remind me that I have just expressed belief in *p*, but I calmly say that I remember perfectly well, and that indeed I still believe *p*. Exasperatedly, you say: 'But how can you?!' I answer complacently: 'Well, I don't believe *p and not-p*; I just believe each of them.' Hardly a defense at all.

It may be objected that, in the circumstances described, I do, I must, believe the conjunction, whatever I say about it. I am inclined to agree. But in that case, the same goes for the Lottery. The point of distinguishing having contradictory beliefs from believing an outright contradiction lies in the fact that psychological realization of the distinction is likely to involve situations of repression, forgetfulness, compartmentalization, lack of self-knowledge, or, at the very least, lack of awareness. None of these psychological phenomena has any essential connection to the Lottery situation. A lottery is apt to be a situation in which it is crystal clear what all my various beliefs are, what their logical relations are, and so on. (I shall return to this issue below extensively.) So I conclude that, whatever the problems are that are generated by the Lottery Paradox, they do not specifically concern CPR1 or conjunction in general.

3.2.2 The Paradox of Compounding Doubt

The Preface Paradox, first formulated by David Makinson (1965), raises related, though somewhat different, issues. The following is an informal presentation of the paradox (a slightly more formal version will be given below). An author completes a book, rationally convinced of every claim she makes in it. In the preface to the book, she writes, quite rationally: 'Although I have been as careful as possible, I am sure that there are some mistakes still remaining in the book. I urge critics to point them out to me as they have done for my previous books.' She thus rationally believes each claim made in the book, and also rationally believes that at least one claim made is false. By CPR1, she should be rational in believing the conjunction of all these propositions. But together they constitute a contradiction and she cannot be rational in believing a contradiction. Hence, CPR1 is false.

Douven and Uffink (2003) point out that the paradox as just described is different from another paradox with which it is often run together in the telling.[4] This other paradox is far closer to the Lottery than the one just described, since it depends, as does the Lottery, on assumptions about the relation between probability and belief. I shall call it, to distinguish it from the Preface as described above, the Paradox of Compounding Doubt. I shall discuss this paradox before returning to the Preface Paradox.

The Paradox of Compounding Doubt rests on some version of what Richard Foley has called the Lockean Thesis, which is a principle about the relation between beliefs and degrees of belief or degrees of confidence. Foley's way of putting the Lockean Thesis is this: 'It is rational for you to believe a proposition just in case it is rational for you to have sufficiently high degree of confidence in it, sufficiently high to make your attitude toward it one of belief' (1993: 140). Although Foley rejects a probabilistic understanding of degrees of confidence, his treatment of the paradox we are about to look at suggests that he takes degrees of confidence to behave as if they were probabilities in the relevant respect.[5] Hence, I shall feel free to recast the Lockean Thesis in terms of degrees of belief understood as subjective probabilities.[6] Thus recast, the Lockean Thesis can be seen as comprising two claims, one analytic and the other normative. The analytic claim is that what it is to believe a proposition is to accord it a sufficiently high probability. In the light of the Lottery, I shall charitably weaken this to the position that according a proposition a sufficiently high probability is a necessary

[4] Having made the distinction, they use the name 'Preface Paradox' for the paradox from which I withhold it. The distinction between these two kinds of arguments, although in a more general context than that of the Preface, is previously noted by Olin (1989).

[5] The relevant respect is that the degree of confidence in a conjunction of logically independent claims believed with less than certainty will be lower than the degree of confidence in any one of them. Foley (1993: 144) implies commitment to this in his treatment of what he calls the Preface Paradox and I am calling the Paradox of Compounding Doubt.

[6] This is how other supporters and critics of the Lockean Thesis usually take it. Other supporters of the view include Daniel Hunter (1996) and James Hawthorne and Luc Bovens (1999). Mark Kaplan (1996) argues against it. So does Brian Weatherson (2005).

condition for belief in it. By sufficiently high, I shall mean a value above some threshold r, $0.5 \leq r < 1$.[7] The second, normative, claim is that according a probability of greater than r to a proposition makes it rational to believe it.[8]

Suppose, then, we accept the Lockean Thesis and CPR1. The Paradox of Compounding Doubt goes as follows. An author expresses in her book a number of claims, all probabilistically independent of each other, each of which she rationally believes. By the Lockean Thesis, that means that she accords to each of them a subjective probability greater than r (but less than one). By the probability calculus, the probability of their conjunction is their product. Let us suppose that the numbers are such that the probability of the conjunction of these propositions falls at or below the threshold r. Hence, again by the Lockean Thesis, it is not rational to believe their conjunction. But, by CPR1, if the author rationally believes each of the claims, then she is rational in believing their conjunction. So, their conjunction both is and is not rational.

This paradox, of course, is only an argument against CPR1 on condition one accepts the Lockean Thesis. Without the Lockean Thesis, all that we have is a reminder that, under common conditions, the probability of a conjunction is less than the probability of its conjuncts and that, with a large number of conjuncts, the probability of the conjunction may be quite low even though that of each conjunct may be quite high. Thus, like the Lottery, the argument against CPR1 here depends on a view about the relation between belief and probability or degree of belief. Yet the Lockean Thesis itself is surely much more dubious than CPR1. To see this, take the simplest possible version

---

[7] Note that this rules out the case that $r = 1$. For $r = 1$, alleged problems about belief via the Paradox of Compounding Doubt cannot be generated by means of CPR1 since, for any two beliefs, their conjunction will also have a probability of one. For this, and other reasons, some have sought to integrate the logic of belief and the logic of degrees of belief by taking belief to be degree of belief of probability one. I do not consider this position in what follows since it seems obviously wrong. If one takes a betting approach to the assignment of probabilities, to assign a proposition a probability of one is to be prepared to bet any amount of money on its truth for arbitrarily small winnings. I doubt I would be prepared to do that for any of the things I believe; certainly not for many of them. More simply: I believe many things of which I am not certain.

[8] It is important not to confuse the Lockean Thesis with eliminativist Bayesianism of the kind espoused by Richard Jeffrey (1970). The latter does away with full belief in favor of degrees of belief. The former, by contrast, analyzes full belief in terms of degrees of belief. My argument here is against the Lockean Thesis, with which I am in agreement so far as the existence of full belief goes, not with the eliminativist Bayesian, whose views I discuss somewhat in Section 1.2.1.

of the paradox just rehearsed. Let the author's book contain only the following two propositions: (*p*) Lima is the capital of Peru; and (*q*) dodos are extinct. I assume that *p* and *q* are probabilistically independent of each other and that neither has any special psychological significance for the author. Suppose the probabilities she assigns to each are above the threshold for (rational) belief, but their product is below that threshold. (If the threshold is 0.9, she might believe each to a degree of 0.92. The probability of their conjunction is around 0.85.) Now the analytic part of the Lockean Thesis implies that, in such a case, since it is a necessary condition for belief that one have a subjective probability greater than 0.9, the author simply does not believe the conjunction *p and q*. But this is clearly absurd. She has just finished her book. Both claims are clearly present to her mind. On what grounds could we possibly suppose that, in these circumstances, she does believe *p* and she does believe *q*, but does not believe *p and q*? As in the discussion of the Lottery above, it seems that the author *must* believe the conjunction here. Hence the analytic part of the Lockean Thesis cannot be sustained.

The normative part of the Lockean Thesis, which of course may be detached from the analytic part, is almost as absurd. We could hardly say to the author that, although we agree she is rational in believing each of *p* and *q*, she is nonetheless irrational in believing their conjunction. What remedial action might she take? There is, we agree, no rational need for her to withdraw her belief in either of them. She cannot very well say that she will believe each of them, but not believe their conjunction, since, as we saw above, in the circumstances, she cannot but believe their conjunction, and can defend herself by pointing to the rationality of each of the conjuncts. When we deal with a situation in which the number of propositions is sufficiently high, as in an ordinary book, it may seem as if there is some plausibility to the idea of believing the conjuncts but not their conjunction. Hence, the charge of irrationality leveled at believing the conjunction may seem more reasonable. But, if we accept the Lockean Thesis, it must apply even in such a simple case as the one described. Hence, I reject the Lockean Thesis, and, with it, the argument against CPR1 stemming from the Paradox of Compounding Doubt.[9]

[9] I do not pursue here a different objection to the Lockean Thesis—namely, that the threshold for belief is bound to be arbitrary. See Weatherson (2005: 420–1) for a developed account of this objection.

One might be tempted to see Sorites-like issues at work here. In fact, there are two possible dimensions along which they might be thought to arise. First, perhaps the problems noted with the Lockean Thesis arise from attempting to find a precise threshold. If one saw the threshold as vague, the kind of argument just given against the Lockean Thesis might no longer apply, and, in that case, the argument against CPR1 on the basis of the Paradox of Compounding Doubt might still be in business. But, in fact, I do not believe this invocation of vagueness would undermine the argument against the Lockean Thesis, for an amended version of it could still run as follows: let the two propositions that comprise the simple book have probabilities that make them determinately rational and determinately believed and let their conjunction have a probability that makes it not determinately rational or determinately believed. Such cases will always be available on the vague threshold view, but they are (nearly) as objectionable as the original case on which their conjunction comes out as determinately not believed and not rational.[10]

The second way in which one might think that Sorites factors were at work is in the number of applications of CPR1 that are acceptable. In a classic Sorites, a single grain added to a non-heap always produces a non-heap. But it does not follow that any number of grains added to a non-heap results in non-heap. In the current case, one might agree that, for any two rational beliefs, their conjunction is rationally believed, but deny that, for any number of rational beliefs, their conjunction is rationally believed. But, first of all, this is simply inconsistent with the Lockean Thesis, which characterizes whether a given degree of belief in a proposition is enough to meet the necessary condition for belief and enough to make belief rational in terms simply of whether the degree of belief is high enough. In other words, the Lockean Thesis has no genetic component that concerns how one gets to a given degree of belief. Secondly, it is unclear why one should seek to shore up an argument against CPR1 by assimilating it to another paradox. The whole point of the Sorites, after all, is that, while it seems to be obviously true that one does not turn a non-heap into a heap by adding one grain to it, and it seems to be obviously true that one can turn a non-heap into a heap by adding a lot of grains, these turn out to be inconsistent (given some other plausible assumptions). To say that one is rational in believing

---

[10] Weatherson (2005: 420–1) also argues that vagueness-based defenses of the Lockean Thesis against the objection that the threshold must be arbitrary do not succeed.

the conjunction of two rational beliefs but not, say, in believing the conjunction of fifty rational beliefs is to court the same inconsistency as in the Sorites. Conjoining fifty beliefs can be decomposed into forty-nine conjunctions of two beliefs. Advocating CPR1 unrestrictedly would be like holding that no addition of any number of grains ever turns a non-heap into a heap. But, while that is demonstrably false in the case of heaps, it is merely controversial in the case of conjunction. My advocacy of CPR1 does mean that I am committed to the view that it can be rational to believe something that has a low probability. But it begs the question against CPR1 to suppose that, when that improbable proposition is a conjunction whose low probability comes merely from the number of (let us stipulate) highly probable conjuncts, it cannot be rational to believe it despite its low probability. The advocate of CPR1 should not allow herself to be led from the plausible view that it can be rational to believe something with a low probability (that is, a large conjunction of highly probable conjuncts) to the implausible view that low probability is never an objection to rational belief. Whether, and how, low probability is an objection to rational belief all depends on the circumstances of the case. This is the flip side of what we saw in the Lottery Paradox case—that high probability is not sufficient for full belief.

3.2.3 The Preface Paradox

I now take up the Preface Paradox proper. What lies at the heart of the Preface is the problem of how to acknowledge one's own fallibility. As can be seen at a glance, this does not require any notion of degree of belief at all, and hence does not rely on the Lockean Thesis or any other dubious principle linking belief and probability. One might see the replacement of an epistemology of belief by an epistemology of degrees of belief (without any reference to belief, and so without anything like the Lockean Thesis) as part of a *solution* to the Preface Paradox, but the problem is stated purely in terms of belief. Anyone committed to accepting belief cannot respond simply by advocating a belief-free epistemology and describing the situation solely in terms of degrees of belief. In fact, there are two distinct problems for CPR1 that are raised by the Preface Paradox and it will be important to deal with them separately.[11] The first problem takes the following form. An

---

[11] My own discernment of the existence of two *distinct* problems is due to Christensen (2004).

author rationally believes the various things she asserts in the body of her book. She also rationally believes the disclaimer she enters in the preface to the book, to the effect that some of what is expressed in the book is false. Following Christensen (2004), I call this disclaimer the Modest Preface Proposition (MPP). But, it is held, if we accept CPR1, we will be forced to say that the author rationally accepts the conjunction of MPP and all the claims in the book, that this is a contradiction, and that no contradiction can be rationally accepted. Therefore CPR1 must be false.

There are two problems with this argument against CPR1 that I want to focus on. The first is this. What form is the contradiction, rational belief in which is allegedly foisted on one by CPR1, supposed to take? If each of the propositions $p_1 \ldots p_n$ expressed in the book is rationally believed, CPR1 commits one to the rationality of their conjunction p_1 *and* $\ldots p_n$. Call this conjunction BOOK. MPP, as expressed in the preface, is 'something in this book is false' or something like that. A further application of CPR1 implies the rationality of the conjunction of MPP and BOOK. But this is not a contradiction and there need be nothing at all irrational in believing it.[12] To yield a contradiction we have to get either a second-order correlate of BOOK, such as 'everything in this book is true', or a first-order correlate of MPP, of the form *not-*(p_1 *and* $\ldots p_n$). In either case, certain other beliefs must be present that have the effect of bridging the first-order/second-order divide. For example, if a person believes '$p_1 \ldots p_n$ are all the propositions expressed in this book', one could, with a little more machinery, go from MPP to a first-order correlate or from BOOK to a second-order correlate.

The question that then needs to be asked is this. How is the case for the rationality of MPP affected by the supposition that the person accepts some bridging belief between the first- and second-order levels? In other words, will it be rational for a person to accept MPP if she also accepts a bridging belief? Imagine a very simple case. In the last minute I have acquired two beliefs, p and q. I believe that p and q are the only two beliefs I have acquired in the last minute. (This is the bridging belief in the case.) I am now given very good reason to believe that something I have come to believe in the last minute is false. Surely, in this case, I suspend belief in both p and q. It will be objected that the

---

[12] Of course, the conjunction of MPP and BOOK is necessarily false. My point is that this is not evident merely from its form. Further information is required to see that it is necessarily false.

small number of beliefs accounts for this. But take a case with a greater number. I go through a deck of cards and look at each card and judge that it is unmarked. Again I accept a bridging belief, here to the effect that I have a belief for each card in the deck that it is unmarked. Now I am given excellent evidence to believe that there is exactly one marked card in the deck. Again, it seems, the rational thing to do is to suspend the fifty-two judgments about each card's being unmarked.

The point of these cases is that, if I do rationally believe each proposition in a given set, and I am aware that they are exactly the propositions in that set, then it will not obviously be rational for me to accept 'some proposition in that set is false'.[13] To the extent that it is rational for me to believe 'some proposition in that set is false', and rational to believe each member of the set, it follows that I had better not have any clear idea of exactly what the propositions in that set are. If an author writes in her preface 'there are errors in this book', then she will write this rationally only if she either does not believe everything in her book or does not know exactly what the propositions are among which she is asserting the existence of some error. If she believes everything in the book, and knows exactly what is in the book, she will not rationally believe that there are errors in it. When one moves the Preface Paradox onto the larger canvas of a person's beliefs in general, the modest belief that one has some false beliefs is likely to be rational precisely because we do not have a very good idea of exactly what we believe.

Perhaps not everyone will agree with this. The second objection to the first argument against CPR1 stemming from the Preface is, however, decisive. Suppose CPR1 relinquished. How does this help our author? She still, according to the proponent of the paradox, rationally believes each of the claims she makes, and still rationally believes some of them are false. Although, without CPR1, we cannot derive the conclusion that her belief in the conjunction of MPP and BOOK (itself leading to a contradiction given a bridging belief) is rational, we have all the elements present, and all, we may suppose, fully present to the author's mind. Unless the Preface Paradox is thought to turn essentially on the author's not being able to have in mind (whatever exactly that means) all the relevant beliefs at once, relinquishing CPR1 will simply not ameliorate the epistemic situation of the unfortunate author. The situation of one who is forced by reason to accept *p*, *q*, and *not-(p and q)*

---

[13] I switch into direct, rather than indirect, discourse to make clear that 'some proposition in that set' is to be taken *de dicto*, not *de re*.

is no better than that of one who is forced by reason to accept *p and q and not-(p and q)*, unless, in the former case, there is some lack of awareness involved. But the Preface Paradox does not depend upon such a lack of awareness. And, if it did, then the first response would be even more apt, since we could not then be dealing with a case in which there was a bridging belief present. The presence of a bridging belief would guarantee the kind of awareness that erases the difference between having inconsistent (or contradictory) beliefs and believing an inconsistency (or a contradiction). (I return in greater detail below to the distinction between believing a contradiction and having contradictory beliefs.)

In fact, a careful look at David Makinson's original presentation of the Preface reveals that, at least in its pristine form, it was not, unlike the Lottery, intended to be about conjunction. Makinson says that the paradox seems to show that someone can be rational 'even though he believes each of a certain collection of statements, which *he knows* are logically incompatible' (1965: 205; emphasis in the original). There is a paradox if he believes each of them, regardless of whether he believes their conjunction. Makinson's solution is that we distinguish between the attribution of rationality to each of a set of beliefs from its attribution to the set as a whole. The Preface shows that one cannot reduce the rationality of the set to the rationality of its members. If one considers a given set of propositions, then it is true that, if the set as a whole is not rational, nor is the conjunction of the members of the set. So it is true that, on Makinson's account, the Preface is supposed to show the irrationality of believing a given conjunction. But that cannot be the point of the paradox, since the author is still saddled with belief in a set of inconsistent propositions, each of which is itself rational, even if he does not believe their conjunction. He is still in a situation of believing 'each of a certain collection of statements, which he knows are logically incompatible'. Hence, giving up CPR1 cannot be said to be part of Makinson's solution to the paradox.[14]

There is, however, a further and distinct problem for CPR1 that is supposed to stem from the Preface Paradox. The problem is this. It is alleged that CPR1 commits the author to what Christensen calls an Immodest Preface Proposition (IPP) such as 'this book is 100 percent error free'. (Of course, this is just an in-your-face version of 'all the

[14] So I disagree with Douven and Uffink's claim (2003: 413, n. 7) that Makinson is among those whose solution to the paradox is to abandon CPR1.

beliefs expressed in this book are true'.) The argument against CPR1 is that it would be irrational for anyone to accept IPP. Notice that this argument is quite different from the preceding one. There, we were concerned to avoid a formal problem, having to pronounce belief in a contradiction rational. CPR1 would make rational the putting-together of beliefs that should not be put together. Here, the problem is that CPR1 seems to lead to the conclusion that a belief whose content is itself alleged to be preposterous will nonetheless be pronounced rational. This is regardless of whether one is also committed to MPP, and whether there is any contradiction in the offing. Here, then, we have the exception to the general rule that objections to CPR1 are based on contradictions.

Like the previous problem, however, we are also here dealing with a transition between first- and second-order beliefs. What CPR1 commits one to is only the conjunction of the beliefs in the book—namely, BOOK. That is not equivalent to IPP. One can derive IPP from BOOK only if one adds the premise that the conjuncts of BOOK are all the propositions expressed in one's book. If one believes BOOK but does not believe this further premise, CPR1 will not commit one to the rationality of IPP. Such a person can believe the conjunction of the beliefs in her book and remain agnostic as to whether her book is indeed 100 per cent error free. Still, it will be objected that there is no reason why someone should not believe of $p_1 \ldots p_n$ that they are all the propositions expressed in her book. Will we not have to say of such a person, if we accept CPR1, that she would be rational in believing IPP? Yes. But I question whether there is anything irrational in believing IPP for a person in that situation. It is precisely when we have no clear idea of the extension of the expression 'all the propositions expressed in my book' that it is immodest—and irrational—to believe that the book is entirely error free. For someone who really believes a given set of propositions and knows exactly which propositions she is talking about, to say that her beliefs in those propositions are error free (that is to say, that her beliefs in those propositions are true) is not at all irrational or preposterous.

Hence I conclude that, while the Preface Paradox may show some-thing, it is not the source of effective arguments against CPR1. What it may show is, first, that one can be rational in having inconsistent beliefs; and, secondly, that we must take care to separate the first-order issues, where CPR1 does play an important role, from the second-order issues, where CPR1 may still be important, but does not operate alone in producing phenomena that some have found troubling, though mistakenly so.

3.3 CPR2 AND NATURALIZED EPISTEMOLOGY

In the discussion of the Lottery and Preface above, I alluded to a distinction between believing a contradiction and having contradictory beliefs. Although I argued that this distinction could not help in the Lottery and Preface situations, it might be thought, nonetheless, to be a valid distinction. In the next section, we shall examine head on the conceptual question of what it is to believe a conjunction. But, for now, let us continue to focus on questions of rationality, and consider a possible objection to CPR2:

> CPR2 If S is rational, then, if S believes p and believes q, S believes p *and* q.

This principle, it will be remembered, focuses on the rationality of conjoining beliefs, rather than on the rationality of the (content of the) conjunctive belief, which is what CPR1 deals with.

Almost everyone agrees that it is a rational desideratum that one not believe a contradiction or something that implies a contradiction. This is expressed in the following weak consistency requirement:

> W-Con If S is rational, then no belief of S's is such that it implies everything.

For those who stress the distinction between believing a contradiction and having contradictory beliefs, this is to be distinguished from a stronger consistency requirement:

> S-Con If S is rational, then no finite subset of S's beliefs is such that it implies everything.

Someone whose beliefs include either of the following belief sets is in violation of S-Con but not W-Con: $\{p, not\text{-}p\}$, $\{p, p \supset q, not\text{-}q\}$.

W-Con together with CPR2 implies S-Con. For the above sets, if one adds to them the conjunctions of their elements, one will obtain, in the first case, p *and* $not\text{-}p$ and in the second p *and* $p \supset q$ *and* $not\text{-}q$. The first is, and the second implies, a contradiction. Thus, for anyone who accepts W-Con, an argument against S-Con is an argument against CPR2. And there is, indeed, an important objection to S-Con by philosophers who accept W-Con, an objection that derives from the perspective of naturalized epistemology, and, more specifically, from work in Computability Theory. In this branch of mathematics, a distinction is made, among tasks that can be performed by the application of an algorithm, between those in which the performance time increases as an exponential function of an input parameter and those in which performance time increases as a polynomial function of that parameter. Since, for any exponential function and any polynomial function, there will come an argument past which the value of the exponential function will exceed that of the polynomial function, algorithms the execution time of which increases exponentially are considered inherently inefficient.[15] Checking each belief to see whether it is inconsistent is a task for which the execution time increases polynomially as a function of the number of beliefs being checked. But checking for consistency *between* different beliefs is a task for which the execution time increases exponentially as a function of the number of beliefs being checked. To give some idea of the scale of the problem, it is worth quoting one impressive statistic. Christopher Cherniak considers the question of how large a body of beliefs a computer could check for consistency by the truth-table method.

Suppose that each line of the truth table for the conjunction of all these beliefs could be checked in the time a light ray takes to traverse the diameter of a proton, an appropriate 'supercycle' time, and suppose that the computer was permitted to run for twenty billion years, the estimated time from the 'big-bang' dawn of the universe to the present. A belief system containing only 138 logically independent propositions would overwhelm the time resources of this supermachine. (Cherniak 1986: 93)

Since a normal person will certainly have more than 138 logically independent beliefs, these numbers suggest an in principle unfeasibility about satisfying the demands of S-Con, but not W-Con. The objection to CPR2 then goes like this. The claim that S-Con is a rational principle for belief is taken to mean that it is not rational to believe two (or any finite number of) things that, if conjoined, would be or imply a contradiction. That means, in turn, one ought not to believe such things. But one cannot be required to do or abstain from doing things that one cannot, feasibly, do or abstain from doing. 'Ought' implies 'can'. As we have just seen, it is in principle unfeasible to check one's beliefs to

---

[15] See Lewis and Papadimitriou (1978) for a good introduction to these issues.

ensure that, if conjoined, they would not be or imply a contradiction. It therefore cannot be required of us that we do so. S-Con is therefore not a requirement on rational belief. W-Con, however, is. Since W-Con and CPR2 are together equivalent to S-Con, CPR2 must be rejected.[16] One might put the objection more informally like this. Every time you add a new belief to your belief corpus, you are able to check it to make sure it is not self-contradictory. Hence you can be required not to have any beliefs that are themselves contradictions. But you cannot check indefinitely many new beliefs along with each and every existing belief to make sure that no two contradict each other. Hence you cannot be required not to have any beliefs that contradict each other. CPR2 (given W-Con) makes just this unfeasible demand, since it requires you, every time you add a belief to your corpus, also to add all the conjunctions of it and each of the existing beliefs (which would then have to be checked to make sure they were not contradictions).

Naturalized epistemologists are certainly right that it would be an absurd waste of time to police our beliefs tirelessly to make sure that each was consistent with the others. It would be a waste of time not only because we could never hope to complete the task but also because there are simply better uses of our time. But no one who suggests CPR2 or S-Con as rational principles has such a scenario in mind. If one accepts W-Con, recognizing a belief of one's own that is a contradiction is a cause for alarm. Someone who finds one within herself should be perplexed by it, and perhaps give it up immediately. But one cannot give it up by simply ceasing to believe the self-contradiction but continuing to believe its contradictory conjuncts. This would represent no epistemic progress whatsoever. So one cannot naively embrace W-Con and ignore the issues raised by S-Con. Conversely, recognizing within oneself two beliefs that contradict each other, even if they are not so recognized as part of a thorough policing of one's beliefs, should produce exactly the same sense of discomfort as the recognition of a self-contradiction. From the point of view of the rational undesirability of what they seek to rule out, I cannot see any difference between S-Con and W-Con.

---

[16] The basic move behind this argument ('ought' implies 'can' in the sphere of rationality) is the theme of the whole of Cherniak (1986). It is approached, without being explicitly stated, in Kornblith (1989). After quoting an earlier version of the Cherniak passage as part of an argument that beliefs cannot be arrived at by processes that in fact check for coherence (including consistency), Kornblith draws the moral that 'all versions of the coherence theory propose an ideal which is very far out of our reach' (1989: 211).

In particular, the fact that checking each belief to see whether it is a contradiction is a task whose performance time increases polynomially with respect to the number of beliefs, while checking for consistency among beliefs increases exponentially, seems neither here nor there.

Nor should S-Con (or CPR2 with W-Con) be seen as violating the maxim that 'ought' implies 'can.' There are two reasons for this. First, if one thinks that the existence of a 'can' requires some method a person can employ to ensure compliance with the principle, there are, surely, fairly easy things one can do to satisfy S-Con, short of checking all of one's beliefs to make sure no finite subset of them is inconsistent. For example, when one realizes that one has contradictory beliefs, one can drop one or both of them. More ambitiously, one might spend limited amounts of time checking for inconsistencies in cases where one thinks there is a special likelihood of finding them. Secondly, the 'ought' of S-Con is that none of our beliefs taken together should form an inconsistent set. Considerations of the computational complexity of *checking* whether that is the case say nothing about whether it is impossible for it to *be* the case. And there is nothing to suggest that such consistency is impossible, even for creatures such as us.[17] I do not doubt that it is a hard goal to live up to, and perhaps one that in practice is rarely, or never, lived up to. But there is nothing impossible about it, even if there is something impossible about checking up on it. So I do not see any reason for rejecting CPR2 that derives from the naturalized epistemological considerations examined here.

3.4 WHAT IS IT TO BELIEVE A CONJUNCTION?

An important question that has arisen several times in this chapter is under what circumstances somebody *does* believe the conjunction of two propositions that she believes individually. In various places, I have said one cannot get round the various problems generated by the arguments against the rationality of CP at which we have looked simply by giving up believing a conjunction and yet continuing to believe each of its

---

[17] Recall, from the discussion of the Preface Paradox above, that, even if one thinks that rationality requires one to accept that some of one's beliefs are false (a claim I disputed), that would still not entail that one had contradictory beliefs but only beliefs that could not be all true. This need be no more irrational or contradictory than believing that water is not H_2O.

conjuncts. This suggests that there are circumstances in which, if one believes each of two propositions, then, necessarily, one believes their conjunction. How extensive are these circumstances? And, in general, what is it to believe a conjunction, and how is that related to believing the conjuncts? In this section I shall defend the view that

> BC under normal circumstances, what it is to believe a conjunction simply is to believe its conjuncts.

(What normal circumstances are will be examined in the next chapter.)

I take it as uncontroversial that believing a conjunction is analytically sufficient for believing each of its conjuncts. Hence, believing the conjuncts is necessary for believing their conjunction. What other conditions, if any, are necessary and/or sufficient for believing a conjunction? There are a number of conditions that are clearly sufficient for believing a conjunction—sincerely asserting it, for example, or inferring *r* on becoming convinced of the conditional *if p and q, then r*. Given some of the discussion in Sections 3.2 and 3.3 above, perhaps special mention should also be made of being aware of *p* and *q* at the same time. Any other alleged necessary conditions must therefore be entailed by conditions such as these. In fact, there are several suggestions that have been made for necessary conditions on believing a conjunction that exceed the minimal necessary condition of believing each of the conjuncts. I shall make my case for the claim that believing a conjunction simply is, under normal circumstances, believing the conjuncts and then go on to examine these suggestions.

Before giving my argument for BC, though, I want to consider a preliminary objection that purports to show that it *cannot* be right. It could be objected that to believe something is to bear a certain relation to a proposition that gives the content of the belief. The proposition *p and q* is distinct from the proposition *p* and the proposition *q*; there are three distinct propositions here in question. Whether one bears a given relation to one of these propositions is therefore independent of whether one bears it to any of the others. Hence, believing that *p*, believing that *q*, and believing that *p and q* must be three distinct states. But then it cannot be true that, in normal circumstances, to believe that *p and q* just is to believe that *p* and believe that *q*. This objection is, I think, mistaken. First, the argument seems to prove too much. For it seems to suggest that one could believe that *p and q* without believing that *p* or believing that *q*. But there surely is a conceptual link between believing a conjunction and believing its conjuncts in one direction at least.[18] A deeper reason, though, for questioning the objection to BC is that we should not presuppose that what it is to believe a logically complex proposition is the same kind of thing as what it is to believe a logically simple one. The wisdom of (at least considering) keeping these things apart is revealed by the vigorous debate over whether there is a phenomenon of conditional belief and whether, and if so how, this relates to belief in a conditional. The issues here are highly complex, and there is, besides, some latitude in terminology (that is, concerning the word 'belief'), but one way of putting one view in this debate might be that what it is to believe a conditional is to be in a state of conditional belief that is of a different kind from that associated with belief *simpliciter*.[19] Obviously the issues surrounding conjunction are quite different from those surrounding conditionals, but I raise the topic of the latter only to show that what it is to believe a conjunction *might* be of quite a different kind from what it is to believe its (propositionally simple) conjuncts.

My argument for BC is provided by our interpretative practice. According to that practice, if someone is taken to believe *p* and to believe *q*, then, absent special circumstances, she is taken to believe *p and q*. Generally speaking, when we have reason to describe someone as believing *p* and believing *q*, we do not require any further justification for describing her as believing *p and q*. Moreover, in general, someone can repudiate the attribution to someone (herself or another) of a conjunctive belief only by repudiating belief in one of the conjuncts or by invoking non-normal circumstances. (Note that if, as this suggestion has it, under normal circumstances, the only necessary condition of believing a conjunction is believing its conjuncts, this is indeed entailed, indeed trivially so, by those sufficient conditions

---

[18] As I said above, I assume this is true. Not everyone, however, agrees. Although he is not explicit with regard to belief, Graham Priest (2005: 66) argues that it is not in general true for intentional operators that, if they apply to a conjunction, they apply to its conjuncts. He analyzes 'I am trying to find a hotel' as 'I am trying to bring it about that something is a hotel and I find it'. To the potential objection that the *analysans* implies, as the *analysandum* does not, that I am trying to bring it about that something is a hotel, he rejoins that, since intentional states are not closed under entailment, the *analysans* does *not* imply 'I am trying to bring it about that something is a hotel'. His semantics for intentional operators would imply the same about belief unless one supplied some special axiom to deal with that state in particular. There are, however, many independent reasons for doubting his semantics.

[19] I think this is Mellor's view (1993) with respect to *some* conditionals.

we posited above. If someone sincerely asserts *p and q*, for example, then, since that is sufficient for believing that *p and q*, and that in turn is analytically sufficient for believing *p* and believing *q*, it follows that someone who sincerely asserts *p and q* does believe *p* and believe *q*.)

Here are three comments on the argument just given. First, in tying claims about belief to claims about the attribution of belief I am staking a position (albeit one I do not defend or even fully articulate here) on what I have called elsewhere (Evnine 1991: 155–60) the idealist wing of debates about the nature of belief. Looking at attributive practices reveals more than merely our contingent views about the circumstances under which people have various beliefs. These practices are to some extent constitutively tied to the phenomena they concern. Secondly, it may be objected that, although it is our practice to attribute, with no further justification, conjunctive beliefs where we attribute belief in the conjuncts in a given context, this practice does not generalize across contexts. If I attribute to someone the belief that dodos are extinct on one day, when we are discussing natural history, and a belief that there is no largest prime on another day, when we are discussing mathematics, it will not be in line with our practice of belief attribution, according to this objection, to attribute, without further justification, a belief that dodos are extinct and there is no largest prime. But the problem here is simply one of conceiving of contexts in which we might be interested in whether someone believes the conjunction of these two things. If we had some idea of such a context, I think we would, absent special reasons to think otherwise, attribute a belief in the conjunction under such circumstances. We should also not be misled by reflecting on cases where the attribution of a conjunctive belief seems wrong because the person simply no longer believes one of the conjuncts. I may now recall, for example, that, forty years ago, someone believed there was an ant colony in her garden. If I now justifiably attribute to her the belief that dodos are extinct, it could easily fail to be the case that she believed that there was an ant colony in her garden and dodos are extinct. But this could be because, without ever having changed her mind, she no longer believes that there was an ant colony in her garden. The example shows something about the decay of belief and not the falsity of BC. Thirdly, I wish to detach my support for BC from any claim about the closure of belief generally under logical entailment. The argument I have just given for BC does not support the wider claim. BC reflects the special nature of conjunction: one might say that a conjunction simply is its conjuncts.[20] If something like this is true, of course, it holds without any proviso. The same cannot be said for conjunctive beliefs, though, where there is a restriction to normal circumstances.

It is possible to agree with my claims about interpretative practice, and even to accept that our practice is a good guide to the truth, and yet not accept the claim that belief in a conjunction simply is, in normal circumstances, belief in the conjuncts. The practice might, for example, rest on the fact that persons often enough satisfy whatever further conditions there are on believing the conjunction of things they believe. Let us now turn to examine these alleged further necessary conditions.

The most obvious candidate for an additional necessary condition, advocated by David Armstrong, is that believing a conjunction requires some mental act of bringing together the two beliefs in the conjuncts, what Armstrong calls a 'movement of thought' (1973: 106–8).[21] But this condition surely cannot be necessary, and equally, not entailed by the other sufficient conditions mooted above, such as sincerely asserting a conjunction. One reason why it cannot be necessary is that one may come to believe a conjunction at the same time as its conjuncts. One might infer it from *r*, if one comes to accept *if r, then p and q*. But a more profound reason why Armstrong's proposed condition cannot be necessary is that, if we take a person who, by stipulation, has not performed the requisite mental movement, but believes *p* and believes *q*, and ask that person what they think about *p and q*, they may well sincerely assert the conjunction, thereby fulfilling a sufficient condition for the conjunctive belief. It is no doubt open to Armstrong to insist that the exchange itself prompts the required mental movement. But, if the mental movement is some real happening, this is an empirical claim, whereas, under the given circumstances, it seems a conceptual truth that the person has the conjunctive belief in question (or, at least, that she has the conjunctive belief unless she ceases to believe one of the conjuncts). Armstrong might try and meet this demand for conceptuality by holding that the exchange in question constitutes,

[20] I mean here by 'is' either identity or whatever other relation exists between something and its mereological components. In other words, I remain neutral here on the 'composition as identity' question.

[21] Davidson also speaks of cases in which someone does not believe the conjunction of two things she believes individually as cases in which 'the thinker fails to put two and two (or one and one) together' (1985: 198). I think, however, that Davidson's view will turn out to be much closer to the one I advocate below than it might seem at this stage. This will become apparent in the discussion of Davidson in the next chapter.

rather than prompts, the required mental movement. But that would deprive us of the ability to *explain* the person's assertion in terms of her belief, since the assertion would now constitute part of the acquisition of the belief.

Setting aside these objections, would Armstrong's position allow us to explain our interpretative practice? Might it be the case that people do perform some mental act of putting their beliefs together sufficiently frequently that we are justified in assuming, absent special circumstances, that, if someone believes *p* and believes *q*, she believes *p and q*? This seems unlikely. We saw above that the time for checking for consistency among beliefs multiplies exponentially as a function of the number of beliefs. This makes the task of checking a large body of beliefs for consistency unfeasible. If we require for conjunctive belief an act of putting together, the same argument could apply here to show that it would be unfeasible to perform that act sufficiently many times to justify, for any reasonably large body of beliefs, our interpretative practice. So, if our practice is to attribute, as a default mode, belief in a conjunction when we have belief in the conjuncts, and if this practice is taken to be reliable, it cannot, practically speaking, be the result of our performing sufficiently often a mental act of putting together our various beliefs into conjunctions.

Another necessary condition suggested for believing a conjunction is that the believer must have the concept of conjunction.[22] In other words, someone might believe that *p* and believe that *q*, and yet, allegedly, fail to believe that *p and q*, owing to the fact that she did not possess the concept of conjunction (Barnes 1969: 303–4). I agree that, in order to have a conjunctive belief, one must possess a concept of conjunction. The only real issue is whether someone could satisfy what I consider to be the conditions for believing a conjunction—namely, believing each of the conjuncts—and yet fail to have a concept of conjunction. On this question, I refer the reader to Section 2.2 of the present work, in which I argue that all persons must have a concept of conjunction. To elaborate just a little in the present context, consider that, if lacking the concept of conjunction is taken as a reason for holding that it is not always true that a creature that believes *p* and believes *q* also believes

---

[22] I speak of *the* concept of conjunction, though of course there may be more than one such concept. The assumption of singularity is warranted if we restrict ourselves to truth-functional concepts. Additionally, it should be remembered, from Chapter 2, that by possessing a concept here I mean merely the ability to have conjunctive thoughts.

their conjunction, then it would hold, for such a creature, that it never believed a conjunction. This, in turn, would seem to undermine any attempt to explain its behavior in terms of the attribution to it of conjunctive beliefs. For example, if we assume that a primitive creature can want to chase a rabbit, and can believe that the rabbit hole is ahead of it, and believe that the rabbit is down the hole, we cannot explain its running towards the hole by saying of it that it believes that the rabbit is down the hole and that the hole is just ahead of it. But now it begins to seem as if all intentional explanations of behavior will be ruled out, since surely all require, for their cogency, complex interrelated sets of beliefs. An explanation that has as *explanans* that a creature performs some action φ because it believes *p* and believes *q*, but where this does not imply that it believes *p and q*, is not an intentional explanation in anything like the ordinary sense.

It may be replied that the very fact that a creature, say, runs towards the rabbit hole, given that it believes the rabbit is there and that it believes the hole is just ahead, shows that it does have a concept of conjunction. Perhaps so; but then it is hard to see how a creature could have beliefs at all and not have the concept of conjunction, since the attribution of beliefs to something makes sense only when those beliefs can enter into explanations of its behavior. The idea that a creature could genuinely have beliefs and yet not have the concept of conjunction seems incoherent.

It is important to keep separate the having of a concept from the recognition of one's having it. As Routley and Routley (1975: 210–15) stress, the fact that a creature may disavow an attribution to it of a given belief, perhaps owing to its failure to understand the attribution, cannot be decisive in assessing the truth of that attribution. For example, if someone believes that A gave a book to B, we might describe her as believing that B was given a book by A. This might be a fair description of her belief, even if, for some odd reason, she disavowed the passive-voice attribution. Suppose someone did this routinely, although the grounds for attributing to her the corresponding beliefs in the active voice were firmly in place, it would be wrong to argue that such a creature had no conception of passivity, say (that is, no ability to have passive-voiced beliefs). The explanation for this state of affairs would, presumably, say something about the person's linguistic competence or ability. But the attribution of belief cannot be so sensitive to language that we should give up the principle that S believes that A gives something to B if and only if S believes that B is given something by A.

Finally, another necessary condition for believing a conjunction, suggested by Foley (1979: 249, n. 7), is that the conjunction be psychologically considerable by its believer. The idea is that, although someone may believe p and believe q, the conjunction p *and* q may be too long, or complex, for a person to be able to bring before her mind. While the considerability condition may seem to have little application if we take any two of our ordinary beliefs, we must remember that, on my account of what it is to have a conjunctive belief, it will fall out that, under normal circumstances, a person believes the conjunction of all her beliefs. And this would certainly make a very long conjunction of precisely the kind Foley wishes to save us from having to believe. The considerability condition assumes, however, exactly what is under dispute here—namely, that we cannot exhaust what it is to believe a conjunction in terms of belief of its conjuncts. To put this in terms of psychological considerability, we might say that one way to be able psychologically to consider a conjunction is by being able psychologically to consider its conjuncts. Foley bases his condition on the more general principle that 'a person non-occurrently believes some p only if he is *able* to consider p' (1979: 249). But to assume that this applies to conjunctive propositions in just the same way as to simple propositions begs the question.

Besides these alleged additional necessary conditions on believing a conjunction, there is one further source of opposition to my claim that what it is to believe a conjunction is, under normal circumstances, to believe the conjuncts. It is held by a number of philosophers that, while it is possible to have contradictory beliefs, it is impossible to believe a contradiction (at least of the simple form p *and not-p*). Thus, Henry Kyburg writes: 'I probably cannot believe a contradiction, or act on one. But I can certainly believe, and even act on, each of a set of statements which, taken conjointly, is inconsistent' (1970: 60). Others have been less cautious than Kyburg in their assessment. For example, Davidson says: 'We cannot, I think, ever make sense of someone's accepting a plain and obvious contradiction . . . someone can believe p and at the same time believe not-p; he cannot believe (p and not-p)' (1985: 198). Likewise, Jonathan Barnes (1969) argues that it is logically impossible for someone to believe a contradiction. While Davidson leaves his assertion unsupported, Barnes holds that, with the help of a few plausible principles, one can derive from the statement that someone has a belief of the form p *and not-p* the absurd conclusion that she both does and does not believe p (and likewise for *not-p*). If these philosophers are right, then one cannot hold, as an analytical claim, that belief in a conjunction simply consists in belief in its conjuncts.[23]

But these philosophers are not right. I suggest that it is clearly possible for people to believe contradictions, even explicit and obvious ones of the form of *p and not-p*. I am convinced of this because many people, people of whom we have no reason to suppose that they are confused in their conceptual grasp of the notions of belief, of conjunction, and of negation, people including philosophers and logicians, say they do. It is, of course, possible that in all such cases there is some underlying confusion, or perhaps equivocation over the meaning of the logical constants or the concept of belief, but the onus must surely be on someone who denies the possibility of what seems to be actual to give us a good enough reason to look for such confusion. As for the kinds of argument proposed by Barnes and others, Routley and Routley (1975: 218–19) do a good job of showing that they are dialectically ineffective, since among the principles on which they rely must be found one that is plausible only if one accepts the conclusion of the argument. In the case of Barnes, the premise is that, if one disbelieves *p*, then it is not the case that one believes *p*. To disbelieve something is surely to believe its negation. Hence, the premise asserts that, if one believes *not-p*, then one does not believe *p*. But this is exactly the question at issue and so cannot be appealed to in an argument for the conclusion that one cannot believe a contradiction.

Ruth Marcus (1981: 505) suggests another reason for supposing that one can believe two contradictory propositions but cannot believe their conjunction. She takes it to be a condition on belief that one cannot believe what is impossible. Thus, one can believe each of *p* and *not-p* (assuming that neither is itself an impossible proposition), but cannot believe their conjunction, since it does not represent a possible state of affairs and hence cannot be the object of belief.[24]

---

[23] Actually, since my claim is that, under normal circumstances, belief in a conjunction just is belief in its conjuncts, it is open to me to respond by saying that, when a person has contradictory beliefs, circumstances are not normal. Hence my claim about what it is to believe a conjunction might be made consistent with the various views quoted in this paragraph. As will emerge in the next chapter, however, I do not think that having contradictory beliefs is enough to plead 'abnormal circumstances'. Hence, I prefer to take on these views directly, as I do here.

[24] As the philosophical Lady Davenant remarks in Maria Edgeworth's *Helen* (1834): 'we cannot believe what is impossible, you know, only because it is impossible' (1987: 118). (Though the impossibility in question is merely that someone should be glad not to have met Sir Walter Scott!)

Marcus's claim—that, if one can believe that p, then it is possible that p—however, is quite implausible. She bravely points out, and accepts, a number of consequences of the principle. Someone, for example, who assented to the sentence 'water is XYZ', where XYZ is some chemical formula other than H_2O, could not have believed that water is XYZ, even if the matter was, at the time, open to speculation. That is because it is, according to Marcus, a necessary truth that water is H_2O. Her response is that, on learning that water is H_2O, our assenter would hold, not that she had mistakenly believed that water is XYZ, but that she was mistaken in having claimed to believe that water is XYZ. But this is surely to let a philosophical theory drive out all common sense. Other examples abound in which people appear to believe something that is, in fact, impossible (one need think only of logic and mathematics). To deny that in all such cases people believed what they took themselves to believe is untenable. I conclude that we can believe what is impossible, and hence there is here no argument against believing a contradiction.

Kyburg also suggests that one cannot *act* on a contradiction and hence cannot believe it for that reason. This is a somewhat difficult claim to assess in the absence of a clarification of what it is to act on a belief. If one believes that p *and* q and acts on the belief that p, is one also acting on the belief that p *and* q? Presumably Kyburg must say no, but I have no clear intuition as to why this should be the right answer. But, in any case, here are some ways in which one might, I suppose quite uncontroversially, act on a contradiction: one might try to prove it true, one might write a book about it, one might assert it, and so on.[25] I conclude that the alleged impossibilities of believing a contradiction or acting on one do not constitute the thin end of a wedge against the view that if one believes p and believes q, under normal circumstances, one also believes p *and* q.

The question of what circumstances are normal can no longer be deferred. But, to paraphrase Hilaire Belloc: 'I'm getting tired and so are you. | Let's cut the chapter into two.'

---

[25] Some of these ways are suggested by Graham Priest (1985/6), himself one of the most vigorous agents of contradiction.

4

Mental Partitioning

One cannot agree to disagree with oneself.
(Robert Stalnaker, *Inquiry*, 1984)

I have said that our interpretative practice takes belief in two propositions to be sufficient for belief in their conjunction, under normal circumstances, and I treated this as an argument that

BC under normal circumstances, what it is to believe a conjunction simply is to believe its conjuncts.

Under what circumstances would we moderate or suspend our practice? I shall suggest that the 'abnormal' circumstances associated with not automatically attributing belief in a conjunction when we attribute beliefs in its conjuncts are those in which mental partitioning is an issue. This will lead me to embrace a variant of BC according to which

BC' if a person is not engaged in mental partitioning, what it is for her to believe a conjunction just is for her to believe its conjuncts.

In order to make good on the equivalence of BC and BC', it is necessary not only that we should suspend our usual practice concerning attribution of conjunctive beliefs under conditions of mental partitioning but that these should be the only such circumstances under which we do so. I know of no way of establishing this, but I am not aware of any other such circumstances. The only possible candidate is circumstances of insanity. In such cases, one might be tempted to say, it may be true that there is no mental partitioning, but nonetheless our interpretative practices are held sufficiently in abeyance that we would not routinely ascribe to someone in those circumstances a belief in a conjunction just because we ascribed belief in its conjuncts. I am doubtful of the plausibility of this potential counter-example to BC', however. Where the circumstances of insanity are extreme enough to suspend our practice concerning conjunctive beliefs, I contend that they are enough to undermine the attribution of beliefs to the subject altogether.[1]

In this chapter, then, I turn to the notion of mental partitioning. In the first instance, this will result in support for the claim CPR2 of the previous chapter, the claim that it is rational for a person who believes *p* and believes *q* to believe *p and q*. This, it will be recalled, was one of the senses given to the thesis that satisfaction of CP (if S believes *p* and believes *q*, then S believes *p and q*) is rational. The other thesis of Chapter 3 was that satisfaction of CP to a sufficient extent is a necessary condition of being a person. Through the links between, on the one hand, mental partitioning and conjunction, and, on the other hand, mental partitioning and personhood, I will argue for this at the end of the present chapter.

4.1 MENTAL PARTITIONS

Mental partitioning is an often-invoked but little-clarified concept in philosophy. It has, of course, a lengthy history, going back at least to Plato. The nature of mental partitions has often been cast in terms of better and worse parts, reason and appetite or passion, moral and immoral, and so on.[2] One of Freud's topographies of the mind depends on the modality of mental states—namely, whether they are conscious or unconscious. The notion of mental part I wish to invoke is much simpler and less morally loaded than any of these. I will take a mental part to be a subset of a person's beliefs that meets certain further conditions. Some of these further conditions will be of a logical, or at least quasi-logical, nature. Others will be more substantive and, correspondingly, less easy to state formally or precisely.

Appeals to mental partitioning in existing literature are motivated by one of two concerns. First, there is a link between mental partitioning and mental conflict—a link that extends to treatments of irrational

---

[1] This is, of course, a large and controversial claim and I cannot defend it here. See Evnine (1989) for a discussion and defense of the claim.

[2] I do not mean to suggest that in this tradition there can be, or have always been thought to be, only two parts to a mind. Plato and Freud offer famous, and not dissimilar, tripartite accounts. See Anthony Kenny (1973) for a good discussion of the similarities between their accounts.

thought and action but also to issues in the logic of belief and the formal modeling of belief. Secondly, the notion of partitioning has been approached out of interest in the 'architecture' of mind, and in particular in the question of whether the human mind is, or should be, modular. My treatment of the issue will be conducted under the first of these rubrics. I shall address the second approach to mental partitioning somewhat obliquely in Section 4.2.

4.1.1 The logic of mental partitioning

I start by proposing some axioms that capture some, but, as we shall see, not nearly all, of the notion of mental partitions.

P1 If a belief p is in one partition and a belief q is in another, it does not follow that a belief p *and* q is in any partition.

A stronger version of this would hold that, if p is in one partition and q in another, then p *and* q is not in any partition. For reasons that will become clearer below, this stronger version is untenable. Briefly, a single belief may occur within two partitions. In that case, it may be true that two beliefs exist in different partitions but also true that they exist in the same partition. And, if they exist in the same partition, then it is at least not impossible that their conjunction should also exist in that partition. However, this qualification of the stronger version still holds:

P2 If a belief p is in one partition only, and a belief q is in another partition only, then p *and* q is in no partition.

P2 is basically equivalent to the very plausible principle that, if a conjunction is in a given partition, then so are each of its conjuncts. This is so plausible because one way for a belief to be in a partition is for a conjunction of which it is a conjunct to be in that partition. Just as, in the previous chapter, I assumed that believing a conjunction is analytically sufficient for believing its conjuncts, so, here, P2 represents the same view relativized to partitions.

Finally, I propose

P3 If a belief p and a belief q are in the same partition, then so is the belief p *and* q.

The motivation for P3 is this. We were led to partitioning precisely in order to account for the circumstances under which someone may believe each of two things without believing their conjunction. P1 and

P2 are the formal expression of the separateness of partitions. The idea that the separateness of partitions is captured by P1 and P2 makes sense, however, only against the background view that, absent partitioning, people do believe the conjunctions of their beliefs. To put this another way, if someone rejects the idea that, absent partitioning, people always believe the conjunctions of their beliefs, she will not find in P1 and P2 a central and defining feature of the notion of partitions. For if, even within a partition, someone may fail to believe the conjunction of beliefs in that partition, then failure of conjunctivity will not be a special feature of beliefs occurring only in different partitions. This fact is represented by P3, which has the effect of making failure of conjunction to apply to two beliefs sufficient for assigning them to separate partitions.

However, although P1–P3 may give the formal defining characteristic of partitions, if this is all we can say about them, we cannot hope illuminatingly to *explain* failure to believe a conjunction of one's beliefs by adverting to partitioning.[3] Something more needs to be said about the phenomenon if we are not merely to utter a tautology in saying that persons believe the conjunctions of their beliefs except where those beliefs belong (exclusively) to different partitions. Given only P1–P3, this amounts to no more than that persons believe the conjunctions of their beliefs except when they do not.

4.1.2 Partitions and conflict

In fact, the main motivation for invoking partitions is their connection with conflict and inconsistency. P1–P3 say nothing about this crucial aspect of partitioning. How far can we formalize the connection between partitioning and conflict? Not very far, I will argue. One might think to begin by supplementing P1–P3 with the further principle:

P4 If a person believes *p* and believes *not-p*, then these beliefs belong to different partitions.

Many theorists of the logic of partitioning do accept P4 and, in addition, treat partitions as if they were fully characterized by P1–P4.[4] Such

---

[3] This echoes David Pears's criticism (1984: 84) of what he calls functional theories of systems (of which the theory under development would be an example).

[4] This is true of Rescher and Brandom (1980), Lewis (1982), and Stalnaker (1984). My description of their view is slightly inaccurate, since they accept something stronger than P3—namely, that partitions are closed under logical consequence generally and not just under conjunction, as P3 requires.

theorists are motivated by three principles that are inconsistent with each other. (1) Belief is closed under entailment: a person believes the logical consequences of any finite subset of her beliefs. (2) The appropriate logic to determine what is entailed by what is classical logic, in which a contradiction entails everything. (3) People can have contradictory beliefs without believing everything. The inconsistency of these three principles is easy to see. Suppose a person has contradictory beliefs. By (1), that person believes their conjunction, which is a contradiction. By (1) and (2), it follows that that person believes everything; but that contradicts (3). Partitioning helps by denying the unruly letter of (1) while keeping its peaceful spirit. As long as contradictory beliefs are consigned to different partitions, we can keep (2) and (3) and a version of (1) limited to partitions.

All this is given by P1–P4. P1 and P2 ensure the separateness of partitions; P3 gives the closure of partitions (under conjunction — but one could adopt a stronger version to guarantee closure generally); P4 ensures that contradictory beliefs are assigned to different partitions. However, although P4 may seem highly plausible, I shall argue below that it should not be accepted. Before coming to that, though, I want to argue that, even if P4 were to be accepted, a notion of partitioning that is based exclusively on P1–P4 is inadequate.

In order to see this, we will need to distinguish between two uses the notion of partitioning is used to serve that are not always clearly separated. One is the use of the account of partitioning in the context of a logic of belief. The other is its use in the context of a theory of reasoning. Starting with the logic of belief, we have seen that the following inconsistent set of principles has recommended itself to those trying to develop a logic of belief. (1) Belief is closed under entailment: a person believes the logical consequences of any finite subset of her beliefs. (2) The appropriate logic to determine what is entailed by what is classical logic, in which a contradiction entails everything. (3) People can have contradictory beliefs without believing everything. The solution to the inconsistency of (1)-(3) offered by a number of advocates of partitioning is to weaken (1). By seeing a belief corpus as falling into fragments, they are free to insist that each fragment exhibits closure as long as inconsistent beliefs always occur in different fragments. Hence the importance of P4.

Seen in this light, the resort to fragmentation is a logical solution to a logical problem. The difficulty with it is, however, that beliefs, to which a logic of belief is supposed to apply, are not, as the propositions to which regular logic applies are, purely logical entities. Thus, if a person's beliefs are to be described as falling into distinct partitions, this cannot be seen as a purely logical fact about propositions in a belief corpus. It must be matched by some empirical story about partitions in a person's belief system. David Lewis, a philosopher whose views are close to those outlined in the preceding few paragraphs, clearly recognizes this, since he says, of a fragmented corpus of belief, that 'something about the way it is stored, or something about the way it is used, keeps it from appearing all at once. It appears now as one consistent corpus, now as another' (1982: 104). These claims about storage, use, and appearance are empirical claims about belief as an empirical phenomenon. But now one must ask how, and why, do the facts about storage or appearance mirror (if they do) the logical relations among beliefs in just the right way to allow us to avoid inferring, from a logic of belief, that someone who has contradictory beliefs believes everything? Take storage, for example. It would make perfect sense to conjecture that our beliefs about, say, how to speak our first language are stored in some quite different way from that in which our beliefs about medieval history are. The two types of belief are acquired and manifested in such different ways it would be remarkable if there were no differences in their neural underpinnings. Thus a theory of partitioning that posited that these two sets of belief constituted different partitions would have the right kind of empirical credentials. But it would not seem to serve any logical purpose, since there is unlikely to be any conflict between the beliefs in these sets.

Now consider the example in which Lewis invokes partitioning:

I used to think that Nassau Street ran roughly east–west; that the railroad nearby ran roughly north–south; and that the two were roughly parallel . . . Now, what about the blatantly inconsistent conjunction of the three sentences? I say that it was not true according to my beliefs. My system of beliefs was broken into (overlapping) fragments . . . The first and second sentences in the inconsistent triple belonged to . . . different fragments; the third belonged to both. (1982: 103)

The beliefs that need to be kept separate here are of entirely the same order. What ensures that the facts about storage or appearance keep them apart? What one must avoid here, on pain of incoherence, is tacit reliance on the following model: a person 'recognizes' the inconsistency involved and imposes the separation deliberately. If such a hypothesis made sense, it would provide an answer to the question just posed. But the problems with such a view are well known from discussions of self-deception and are sufficiently evident that I will not rehearse them here.[5] Nor will it help to start talking as though the inconsistency is 'unconsciously recognized'. Perhaps some story that avoided this recognition of inconsistency could be concocted, but, keeping in mind that it must be an empirical conjecture, it seems fairly unlikely that it would meet the test of plausibility.

The notion of fragmentation associated exclusively with P1–P4 does, however, work much better in the context of the second of the two issues that I warned against confusing: the issue of how to reason from one's beliefs. It is clear that this role for a theory of partitioning was evident to Lewis in the work of his that we have been considering, since he cites, among authors who have worked out the details of a theory of fragmentation, a piece by Schotch and Jennings (1980).[6] These authors write:

On the classical view, reasoning from a set of premises ceases upon its detonation [by inconsistency]. But consider how imperfectly this approach reflects the way we actually reason. Our normal data set is the set of sentences that we believe to be true, and few of us imagine that among our beliefs are lurking no inconsistent pairs . . . Nor are such pairs always hidden from us. Our response is sometimes to reject one thesis but on other occasions we have *no* basis on which to decide what must be discarded. In these cases we decide to live with the embarrassment . . . In the meantime the data remains and if our decisions are to be rational we must reason with what we have. (Schotch and Jennings 1980: 329)

What is being suggested is that, if one recognizes that one has inconsistent beliefs but needs to reason from one's beliefs anyway (and does not want to give up classical logic as the organon of such reasoning), one simply reasons from some consistent subset of them. Here, the explanation of what is going on with the fragmentation is clear and explicit and does involve the recognition by a person of her own inconsistent beliefs. Fragmentation is deliberately performed by the agent in response to a

[5] A classic warning against this way of thinking is to be found in Sartre (1958: 47–54).

[6] Lewis also cites Rescher and Brandom (1980), and Jaśkowski (1969), and says 'these authors' intended applications of fragmentation differ to some extent from mine' (1982: 103). If Lewis is thereby intending to distance his own use of fragmentation from the use I am now considering in the text, his disclaimer strikes me as rather understated. And there is much else, in all these authors' use of the notion of fragmentation, that Lewis might have in mind with his disclaimer. But it is, of course, possible that that is what he intends.

specific problem. The reason this is not problematic here, as it was in the case where we were looking at a logic of belief, is that we are not trying to avoid the conscious awareness of inconsistency, which, indeed, is central to fragmentation in *this* story. And the reason we are not trying to avoid the conscious awareness of inconsistency is because we are not dealing with a logic of belief at all, in the sense in which I have been using this expression. We are not looking at a theory that says what a person does believe (given various facts about what else she believes). Nor are we even dealing with a normative version of this, which would say what a person ought to believe (given various facts about what she does believe). We are dealing, as I indicated, with a theory about how to reason, how to infer some beliefs from others.

But for this very reason, it is not clear that the notion of fragmentation employed by Schotch and Jennings (and so perhaps by Lewis) must rule out a belief in the conjunction of the inconsistent beliefs. If, in order to reason non-explosively from a belief that *p*, along with related beliefs, one can simply set aside one's simultaneous belief that *not-p*, there is no reason why one cannot also set aside one's belief that *p and not-p*. One might believe the contradiction and simply always set it aside when reasoning. And, in favor of attributing belief in the conjunction to such a person is the fact that, if she did not believe the conjunction, she would be in the position of saying of herself that she believed *p* and believed *not-p* but did not believe *p and not-p*. If one were to press her on why she did not believe the conjunction, she could have nothing to say, since she would acknowledge believing the conjuncts and (let us suppose) accept that a conjunction follows from its conjuncts.

In fact, there is a deeper problem with this second use of the account of partitioning. Some of the work behind such proposals as this has come from dealing with inconsistent databases in computer programming and in AI more generally. The language that Schotch and Jennings use reflects this. They speak of a data-set. Although this is connected with belief ('our normal data set is the set of sentences that we believe to be true'), it is so, in some sense, only incidentally. If we have to employ some database that has inconsistent information in it, we may, somewhat arbitrarily, decide to use one of the inconsistent propositions and not the other(s) to avoid explosion. But, when we are dealing directly with *belief*, this policy would seem somewhat stranger. We are to suppose that someone who believes *p* and believes *not-p* will set aside her belief, say, that *not-p* and reason only with her belief that *p*. But, if she genuinely *believes not-p*, why should she set it aside from her reasoning? What is meant by saying, in such a case, that she does genuinely believe *not-p* if she simply ignores it in the course of reasoning to which it is evidently relevant?[7] A person who realizes that she believes *p* and believes *not-p* and wants to reason about something that these beliefs are relevant to has one of two options (on both of which we may also attribute to such a person a belief in the conjunction *p and not-p*). She might retain classical logic and infer any arbitrary proposition. This is a hard way, but it is surely the right way for someone who knows that she believes *p* and believes *not-p* and thinks that classical logic really does say what follows from what. A much better option, however, would be to adopt some other logic according to which a contradiction does not entail everything.[8] In either case, the question of which logic a subject uses to reason with should be kept distinct from the question of which logic a theoretician uses in a logic of belief that is supposed either to describe what a person does believe or spell out what she should believe.

I thus conclude that, even if we accept P4 along with P1–P3, we fail both to give an adequate account of fragmentation in the context of a logic of belief (since no plausible story seems at hand as to how and why the fragments necessary from a logical point of view to prevent the attribution to the subject of belief in everything should dovetail with any empirical story about mental partitions) and to give an adequate account of fragmentation in the context of reasoning from one's beliefs.

Even if all this is accepted, however, we have not yet tackled head-on whether one should accept P4. For one might accept P4 even if one thinks that P1–P4 do not give an adequate account of mental partitioning. Support for P4 goes back to perhaps the earliest discussion of the topic, in Plato's *Republic* IV. Plato's own treatment of the question is less than conclusive. It will be remembered that he argues, invoking what is often cited as an early statement of the law of non-contradiction, that 'it's plain that the same thing won't be willing at the same time to do or suffer opposites with respect to the same part and in relation to the same thing' (436b5; the translation is Allan Bloom's). Accepting

---

[7] The point being made by this rhetorical question will be true by definition if one accepts Robert Brandom's view that 'thinking that things are thus-and-so is undertaking a distinctive kind of *inferentially* articulated commitment: putting it forward as a fit premise for further inferences' (2000: 11). But, even if one does not accept this, one still might wonder exactly what it means to attribute the belief in this case in which a person, investigating consequences to which it would be relevant, deliberately leaves it out of account.

[8] It is precisely to avoid such recourse to a non-classical logic that Lewis appeals— confusingly, as I hope I have shown—to the idea of partitioning.

and refusing, embracing something and thrusting it away, and other such pairs are agreed to be opposites. Then, from the fact that a single person can accept and refuse something, or embrace it and thrust it away, it is concluded that there must be parts to the person, such that one part is affected by one of the pair of opposites, and another by the other. The chief problem in Plato's argument is his notion of opposition. Accepting and refusing are not logical contradictories, no more than are believing that p and believing that $not-p$. If 'opposites' in the sentence quoted means contradictories, it is a plausible principle, but Plato's argument will suffer from equivocation, since the examples he gives to show that a person's mind must have several parts are not in fact examples of contradictories. If, on the other hand, 'opposites' in the principle includes such pairs as accepting and refusing, or believing that p and believing that $not-p$, then the principle is no more obvious than the conclusion of the argument, that a person who accepts and refuses something must have two parts to her mind, one doing the accepting and the other the refusing. Plato's mistake, in effect, is the same as that attributed to Barnes and others in the previous chapter who argued that it was impossible to believe a contradiction, of assuming that, if someone disbelieves p, then she does not believe p. And, as I have observed already, whether or not they should, many people do believe obvious contradictions. It thus seems to me that P4 should be rejected. The fact that two beliefs contradict each other is not sufficient to assign them to different mental partitions.

What about the converse of P4? If being contradictory is not sufficient for assigning two beliefs to separate partitions, it is at least necessary? Should we accept

P5 If two beliefs are assigned to different partitions, then they are inconsistent with each other?

In other words, even if conflict does not automatically entail partitioning, is it true that, wherever one has partitions, there is conflict between them? Davidson, in his discussion of partitioning, says firmly he wants a view of partitions as 'overlapping territories' (1982: 181), and this view has, I think, been accepted by many of those working with the idea of partitioning, whether to employ or to criticize it.[9] This implies

---

[9] Pears (1984), for example, takes it for granted in the course of a sympathetic discussion of Davidson; as do Mele (1987) and Heil (1989) in the course of critical ones. Lewis (1982), as we have just seen, also wants overlapping partitions.

that the letter of P5 will be false. For any two beliefs that are part of the overlap between partitions S1 and S2, it will be true that one is in S1 and the other in S2, and yet, both being in S1 and both being in S2, there is good reason why they should be consistent with each other. However, Davidson also holds that 'a part of the mind must show a larger degree of consistency or rationality than is attributed to the whole' (1982: 181). This seems to imply that, even though it is not necessary for two beliefs to be assigned to different parts that they be inconsistent, nonetheless, if there are two parts, there must be some beliefs in one that are inconsistent with some beliefs in the other. Without that condition, it would not be true that a part of the mind must show greater consistency than the whole. Thus Davidson is committed to a weaker version of P5, namely:

P6 If S1 and S2 are distinct parts of a mind, then there is a belief p in S1 and a belief q in S2 such that p and q are inconsistent.

Needless to say, the beliefs to whose existence P6 commits one will not be in the overlapping parts of S1 and S2. P6 preserves a clear link between partitioning and conflict while not taking the implausibly strong stances of P4 and P5. However, as will become clear in the following section, while P6 is often true, it is not a necessary truth about partitioning. Briefly, my reason for not accepting P6 outright is that the host of questions that arose in connection with P4, about how the empirical facts about partitions would manage to track the logical facts about inconsistency without some deliberate efforts on the part of the agent, would arise again.

4.1.3 The Japanese astronomer

I would like to suggest that what is crucial for partitioning is not the actuality of conflict but the perceived threat of conflict. Partitioning is a deliberate choice made by agents to avoid inner conflict. Although there may be many reasons for wanting to avoid dealing with a conflict in our beliefs, such as laziness, confusion, and others, the root cause is surely the reluctance to give up cherished beliefs that threaten to be challenged by other beliefs. It is attachment to our beliefs, and the sense that they may be under threat, that leads to mental partitioning. The phenomenon has nothing to do with the explosion that arises if classical logic is applied to inconsistent beliefs. The difficulty with attempts to link partitioning to conflict in the form of principle like P4 and P6 is that, as emerged in my discussion of P4, we are faced with a kind of confusion between the logical or conceptual, on the one hand, and the empirical, on the other. We cannot suppose that empirical conditions for partitioning just happen to be met whenever, but only when, we are dealing with inconsistent beliefs. But we cannot, without the threat of incoherence, suppose that partitioning is imposed, even unconsciously, by the person herself when she is cognizant of the inconsistency. If we tie partitioning to the perceived threat of inconsistency, though, we avoid the potential incoherence. A person may impose partitioning on her beliefs without actually being cognizant of any actual inconsistency. Partitioning is a precautionary measure undertaken to avoid conflict. Needless to say, it often happens that, when one senses the possibility of conflict, there really are inconsistent beliefs present. That is why P6 will very often be true. But we sometimes fall into defensive measures even when there is no actual inconsistency. Hence, P6 should not be taken as axiomatic for mental partitions.

With this in mind, let us look at a description of a case of mental partitioning. Peter Geach gives us the elements of a good example:

> I once heard the story of a Japanese astronomer who seemed to succeed very well in treating the sun alternately as an inanimate natural body whose properties can be investigated by the techniques of mathematical physics, and as a divinity, the ancestress of the Japanese imperial dynasty; when challenged about the matter by a European colleague, he said 'Here in Europe I know it's all nonsense, but in Japan I believe it'. (1976: 9)

When the astronomer makes his final admission, he is, I contest, well past the point of successful partitioning. (He might be suggesting merely that his beliefs change as his location changes. This would not require any appeal to partitioning, though it would raise problems of a kind explored at length in Chapter 5.) Let us, then, imagine the astronomer at a period prior to his admission. He simply goes to conferences, where he discusses the sun in terms of mathematical physics, and then goes back home, where he worships the sun in traditional ways. But he never reflects explicitly on the apparent inconsistency his behavior manifests. This is an excellent example of mental partitioning, because it makes clear how the partitions match the fault lines in a person's life. Although (we may suppose) it turns out that the astronomer does have inconsistent beliefs, that is not essential to his predicament. Rather we see a cultural division (tradition versus modernity), a geographical division (Japan versus Europe), and a division of subject matters (religion and science) coming together to constitute separate areas of his doxastic life. It is over just such divisions as these that we all sense the possibility of conflict. Aspects of our lives come under threat; the old ways may come to seem outdated and childish; the new, outlandish and iconoclastic. Here, I think, we find the link between partitioning and conflict. Partitions arise to ward off potential conflict between different sides of our lives.

If this is so, then I fear that we cannot capture the connection between partitioning and conflict axiomatically. Partitions will be subsets of a person's beliefs that meet conditions P1–P3. They will often, though not necessarily, satisfy P6. Beyond that, we can say that partitions will embody distinctive, psychologically significant parts of a person's doxastic life across which there threaten to be inconsistencies. This last claim is, I recognize, vague. But, if we take it as the root of the notion of partitioning, then it does explain why partitions should be characterized by P1 and P2. (As we saw above, the roots of P3 lie elsewhere.) The fact that partitions are imposed precisely to avoid potential conflict helps to *explain* why we do not take people to believe the conjunction of things that exist uniquely in different partitions.

I might add at this point that I have expressed what I take to be the root of the phenomenon of partitioning in terms of conflict rather than inconsistency. Inconsistency is a logical notion; conflict is a psychological one. It is true that many of us do see conflict in inconsistency. Those who do will be moved to engage in partitioning if they take there to be a threat of inconsistency in different areas of their doxastic lives. But, of course, one may find conflict in many other things than inconsistency and so may be led to partitioning even when there is no threat of inconsistency. Furthermore, some, such as dialetheists, do not see conflict in inconsistency. Such people, therefore, are not likely to resort to partitioning where they feel a threat of inconsistency. This is part of the reason for rejecting P4, which would have the effect of tying partitioning too closely to inconsistency, ignoring conflict's further dimensions and not allowing for those who do not find inconsistent beliefs to be in conflict.

Despite the difference in motivation between the conception of partitioning I advocate and that found in the work of writers on irrationality, such as Donald Davidson (1982, 1985) and David Pears (1984), the conception I have outlined is not, I believe, all that different from theirs. Davidson takes partitions to be what I will call well rounded. By this I mean that they contain a large number of beliefs that hang together in a network of relations of implication and support. This is similar to the view I have just advocated, according to which partitions embody psychologically significant areas of a person's doxastic life. Davidson's reason for holding that partitions must be well rounded, however, is not, as mine is, that this is the only way we can understand partitions if they are to play an explanatory role in the contexts envisaged. Davidson has a distinctive reason for requiring partitions to be well rounded—holism. The content of a belief, for Davidson, is determined (at least in part) by other beliefs with which it has logical relations.[10] Hence, each partition must contain within itself a sufficient number of beliefs to give content to those beliefs in the way that holism demands. This virtually guarantees the picture of overlapping territories, since so many beliefs will be required to make sense of, and give content to, conflicting beliefs that belong to different partitions. This reason for well-rounded partitions that largely overlap will be irrelevant to any who do not share Davidson's holism about content.

A second reason for thinking of partitions as well rounded also derives from their role in explaining irrationality. It predominates in Pears's extension of, or amendment to, Davidson's theory. Pears sees a subsystem (his word for a partition) as being 'built around the nucleus of the wish for the irrational belief', and as being 'organized like a person . . . [I]t is a separate centre of agency within the whole person' (1984: 87). Partitions, according to Pears, are homuncular in that they are considered rational, have (that is, contain) goals, develop strategies to achieve those goals, and so on. Homuncularity will require a certain well-roundedness and will also probably involve overlapping of partitions, since much common knowledge about the world will be required for any partition to be appropriately homuncular.

While my account is not committed to holism and does not require partitions to be homuncular, it ends up with a not dissimilar approach. In this sense, it contrasts dramatically with that which emerges from the theory of, say, Rescher and Brandom (1980). These authors allow that a partition might contain only a single belief (together with its logical consequences). Thus, although it will be true in some sense that any partition will exhibit more consistency and closure than the whole, nonetheless a partition might fail to be well rounded. It need not contain a host of beliefs, for example, that support and help define the content

---

[10] See Evnine (1991: *passim*, 1999) for explanation and critical discussion of Davidson's holism.

of a given belief in it. Non-well-rounded partitions are made use of in an intriguing way by Rescher and Brandom in their development of a model of degrees of integratedness that a belief can enjoy. A person who acquires the belief that p, but has not integrated it at all with any of her other beliefs, will in effect have a partition constituted by p (and its logical consequences) alone, in which the conjunction of p with any of the person's other beliefs is not believed. As a person integrates the belief more and more, other beliefs that were outside the partition with p will come to exist, as well, within that partition (hence, Rescher and Brandom are committed to the possibility of overlapping territories). A person whose beliefs are fully integrated will be one with no partitions. Here we see the use of a notion of partition quite divorced from the more substantive considerations I have introduced. Accordingly, I contend, the postulated partitions can hardly explain the gradual integration of a belief since they consist in nothing more than the failure of someone to believe certain conjunctions of things she believes. We have a formal model of integration but no explanation of it.

4.2 THE IRRATIONALITY OF PARTITIONS

CP, recall, is the principle that says that, if a person believes p and believes q, she believes p *and* q. The claim that CP is rational for persons was given two readings:

CPR1 if S believes p rationally and S believes q rationally, then, if S believes p *and* q, S believes it rationally,

and

CPR2 if S is rational, then, if S believes p and believes q, S believes p *and* q.

In the previous chapter I attempted to rebut a number of objections to both these theses. Given their initial plausibility, rebutting the well-known and obvious objections to them provides strong support for them. We are now in a position to expand on the plausibility of CPR2 by giving an argument for it. At the end of the previous chapter, I argued for the thesis that

BC under normal circumstances, what it is to believe a conjunction simply is to believe its conjuncts.

In this chapter, I have added to that claim a specification of what counts as normal circumstances in this connection: the absence of mental partitioning. This led to a variant of BC:

BC′ if a person is not engaged in mental partitioning, what it is for her to believe a conjunction just is for her to believe its conjuncts.

The argument, then, is this:

BC′ if a person is not engaged in mental partitioning, what it is for her to believe a conjunction just is for her to believe its conjuncts;

RNP if S is rational, then she does not engage in mental partitioning;

so,

CPR3 if S is rational, what it is for her to believe a conjunction just is for her to believe its conjuncts;

so,

CPR2 if S is rational, then, if S believes p and believes q, S believes p and q.

This argument is obviously valid and premise BC′ has been defended at length in this and the previous chapter. That leaves premise RNP (for 'Rationality of Non-Partitioning'). It is hard to give an argument for RNP (or against it, for that matter) that will not appear question-begging to its opponents. This is a sign that we are dealing here with a very fundamental issue, about which there are likely to be deeply felt, but opposing, intuitions. One of the most famous opponents of RNP is Walt Whitman, who sings of himself:

> Do I contradict myself?
> Very well then . . . . I contradict myself;
> I am large . . . . I contain multitudes.
> (1959, ll. 1314–16)

These justly famous lines articulate a sense of the self as multiplicitous, fragmented in a celebratory inclusiveness.[11] But they do not seem to offer (or invite) argument. Nonetheless, there are a few things that can be said.

---

[11] Of course, Whitman is not an academic philosopher and is not discussing the nature of rationality. He, or those who thrill to his incantation, might well put their

4.2.1 Objections to RNP deriving from objections to CPR1 and CPR2

In Chapter 3, we looked at a variety of objections to CPR1. These derived from three paradoxes: the Lottery Paradox, the Paradox of Compounding Doubt, and the Preface Paradox. No doubt many proponents of these paradoxes will not accept premise BC'. However, since the paradoxes concern what is rational, they are logically independent of BC'. So, do any of these paradoxes provide reasons for rejecting RNP? I think it is clear that they do not. This was already clear in our treatment of them in Chapter 3. If someone rationally believes, of each ticket in a lottery, that it will not win, and yet also believes that one ticket will win, she cannot avoid epistemic problems by appeal to partitioning. An invocation of partitioning in those circumstances would amount to nothing more than a foot-stamping refusal to believe a contradiction all of whose elements are consciously present to the mind. The idea of partitions as embodying different aspects of one's life simply has nothing to do with the case. This led me to say that whatever problems the Lottery Paradox exposes are as much problems for one who rejects CPR1 as for one who accepts it. We may emphasize the point once again: Lottery- and Preface-style paradoxes do not exploit the notion of partitioning and cannot be solved by its utilization.

The objections to CPR2 stemming from naturalized epistemology, however, may seem to play out more successfully as objections to RNP. I noted above that partitioning is approached from two different directions: irrationality and the architecture of mind. The account I have given above grew out of the connections between partitioning and irrationality. The objection to RNP we are about to consider, however, is an attempt to show that partitioning may be rational owing to features connected with the architecture of mind. So we should bear in mind that the kind of partitioning we are about to discuss may not be of exactly the same character as the one the irrationality of which is asserted by RNP. That noted, however, let us proceed.

---

point by saying that they are, precisely, rejecting rationality as an ideal, not articulating it. But such a response would rest on the mistaken idea that rationality in this context is tied, *by definition*, to unity and consistency. If that were so, one could not coherently argue over whether rationality demands unity or not. What a defender of RNP and a Whitmanesque opponent of it are genuinely at odds over is what the nature of our epistemic goal should be. I take it that this is a debate over what rationality requires and not a debate over whether rationality is a worthy ideal.

If there were computational and complexity-based reasons for not believing the conjunctions of one's beliefs, then these might equally serve as reasons for engaging in partitioning in a serious sense. An analogy may help here. Fodor (1983) argues in favor of a modular theory of mind. Modular cognitive system are ones that are 'domain specific, innately specified, hardwired, autonomous, and not assembled' (1983: 37). Most importantly, though, for both Fodor and us, is his view that the essence of modularity is informational encapsulation (1983: 71). If a system is informationally encapsulated, it has information that is not accessible to other systems. If that information were present in a person as a belief, then, if a mind were modular in Fodor's sense, it would be true that a person did not automatically believe the conjunction of her beliefs. Modules would constitute partitions (though, as I just noted, in a rather different sense from that we developed above, since the empirical facts that underlay modules would not be expected to track either real or anticipated inconsistencies). Now it might be thought—indeed Fodor does think—that there are very good reasons why a mind should be modular. Although a modular mind loses through informational encapsulation, it may gain in speed, efficiency, robustness, and so on. For a finite creature such as a human being to have a modular mind might well be among the best ways it could be organized, from an epistemic point of view. In that case, one might argue that rationality permits some kind of mental partitioning. Perhaps one could even go so far as to say that, for a finite creature such as a human being, it will always be an epistemic advantage for it to have a modular mind. Modularity might be an epistemic ideal, and hence not only permitted by rationality, but positively required by it. Such, I believe, is the underlying thrust of the position of authors like Cherniak (1986) and Kornblith (1989).

Fodor, however, was introduced as an analogy, not an example. That is because, on Fodor's views, the modular parts of the mind do not possess their information in the form of beliefs. The paradigm of a module, for Fodor, is a perceptual system. Belief fixation, even of perceptual beliefs, however, is the job of a central, non-modular system that takes into account not only the outputs of various modular systems but everything a person knows that might be relevant. Hence, for the central system, non-partitioning is clearly an ideal. Since our notion of partitioning was given in terms of belief, Fodor's case for modularity cannot simply be taken over as a rebuttal of RNP. Indeed, Fodor's views on the central system seem to support RNP, given that the partitions referred to in the premise are partitions of beliefs.

It is surely essential, if a number of perceptual systems are all to belong to a single person, that, modular though they may be, their outputs all debouch into a common area, a central system that forms and manages belief. All their outputs contribute to a single, integrated informational system provided by belief. Without this, it would be hard to see what their use was to a person. If one attempted to transfer the Fodorian arguments about modularity to belief itself, arguing that beliefs belonged to modular subsystems of belief, it seems that one would be pressed to look for some higher-order part of the mind that could survey collectively the beliefs of each module. Without some way of integrating them it would again be difficult to see how they could be, overall, useful to a person. Belief, after all, controls behavior. If beliefs are encapsulated in modules or partitions, then a person's behavior will have to be directed, at any given time, by one or another module without the benefit of the information available to it in other modules. In the case of perceptual modules, we might suppose that an organism evolved in an environment in which the outputs of the various modules never conflicted: sight never tells us to go one way when scent tells us to go the other. In such an environment, total modularity, with no central system, might be harmless. But, of course, the world is not in fact so cooperative, and it is precisely through the synthesizing phenomenon of belief that we can cope with discrepancies when they arise. If belief were to come in modules, however, there is no higher function in a person to resolve discrepancies. There is nothing that stands to belief as belief does to information encoded at a sub-doxastic level; there is nothing to perform the essential synthesizing that persons must perform in all but the most artificially helpful of environments. The very point of belief is to allow flexibility in behavior that is not afforded by informationally encapsulated modules.

Fodor's views aside, however, is there any argument along the lines suggested above for accepting the rational permissibility, perhaps even necessity, of mental partitioning in the sense of belief compartmentalization? If partitioning is to serve goals of cognitive economy, it must be because it will save us from various cognitive operations that would relate beliefs in different systems. What are these operations? I have already argued that believing a conjunction is, in the absence of partitioning, nothing more than believing the conjuncts. No cognitive work, therefore, is required to believe the conjunctions of all our beliefs. I have not said anything about other cognitive activities such as reasoning or choosing, but let us suppose that partitioning would also save us the bother of having, say, to think about seventeenth-century history when choosing curtains. But why think that absence of partitioning should require one actively to go through all one's beliefs about the seventeenth century in those circumstances? I have no theory to offer as to how we reason or choose, but it would be a caricature of RNP, or anything remotely like it, to take these cognitive activities to require always running through all one's beliefs. That, clearly, is not how thinking works.

One can, of course, imagine particular circumstances in which partitioning is useful to some being. If keeping apart my long-held religious beliefs and my emerging acceptance of a scientific world view is essential for me to avoid a nervous breakdown, then clearly it is, in some sense, good for me to enforce a kind of partitioning of my belief system. But one cannot go from such examples to the view that it is not, in general, rational for a person to avoid mental partitioning. The need to avoid it is fundamental and pervasive; reasons for enforcing it are temporary, circumstantial, and haphazard. And, even when such reasons obtain, there is still a strong necessity for as much integration and synthesis as possible. (This theme will be taken up again below.)

4.2.2 The unity of the world

At bottom, I do not think that the objections to RNP at which we have so far looked are of the kind of which Whitman is thinking. Whitman is much closer to Nelson Goodman's views (1978) and to a torrent of work in the humanities in general that tout the death of the Cartesian subject and the birth of a fragmented, postmodern self. To understand this, let us go back to the work on partitioning of Rescher and Brandom (1980). These authors use the machinery of worlds to model belief states. A person's beliefs at a given time can be identified with a world at which all those beliefs are true. In the course of pursuing this strategy, Rescher and Brandom have recourse not only to ordinary possible worlds but to what they call non-standard worlds. Non-standard worlds come in two varieties, schematic and inconsistent. Schematic worlds are incomplete worlds, and they model the beliefs of those who do not have beliefs about everything (that is, all finite believers). Inconsistent worlds are worlds that model the beliefs of those whose beliefs are inconsistent. (These are not, in the ordinary sense, possible worlds, since possibility is constrained by consistency. They are, as many authors say, impossible worlds.) A problem arises, however, over the fact that, according to classical logic, in an inconsistent world, everything ought to be true (since anything follows from an inconsistency). Since people can have inconsistent beliefs and yet not believe everything, inconsistent worlds, if they are to model inconsistent believers, must satisfy a further odd condition (besides being inconsistent). Such worlds must be fragmented. They must be such that two propositions can be true at them and yet their conjunction not. Hence, at such a world, it can be true that p and true that *not-p*, but not true that *p and not-p*.

Now all this clearly recalls the discussion of Section 4.1.2 about the fragmentation of beliefs into partitions. But what is distinctive about Rescher and Brandom's position is that they bravely insist their ontology precedes their epistemology. Inconsistent worlds are not simply technical devices to model the beliefs of those whose beliefs are inconsistent; they are real ontological possibilities, on the same ontological level as standard possible worlds. To put it bluntly, on their view it is possible that the actual world is inconsistent. To the extent that we think that *p and q* follows from p and q, no matter what (that is, with no need to make a distinction between, as they say, taking p and q collectively and taking them distributively), we accept a theory about the actual world to the effect that it is not inconsistent. This theory could, in principle, be wrong.

If one thought that the actual world were inconsistent, one would have a powerful reason for mental partitioning. If the world were itself partitioned, mental partitioning would be the most adequate epistemic response to this fact. Without mental partitioning, we could not accurately represent the world. To insist on unity of the mind might then be held to betray a naive fixation on the unity of the world that the mind acquires knowledge of. Give up the unity of that world, and the requirement of mental unity, as articulated by RNP, becomes a hindrance. In Rescher and Brandom, the appeal to the notion of a fragmented world is resolutely realist; there may really be a non-unified world out there, and, if there is, then mental partitioning is an essential part of an adequate grasp of this situation. More often, in Whitman (one suspects), Goodman, and the various postmodern versions, appeal to a fragmented world acquires an idealist tinge. The world, as an independent object of knowledge, is relinquished, and all that remain are 'versions,' languages, and so on. Now the demand for mental unity is taken not as a hindrance to an adequate representation of a genuinely fragmented world, but as a killjoy repression of the creative stitching-together of a multifaceted self/world. It is the small-mindedness of which narrow consistency was Emerson's hobgoblin. Partitioning is seen as the freedom to move from one world to another with no thought for their consistency.

The idea that mental partitioning might be rational because of the disunity of the world is, I think, unconvincing in both its realist and its idealist forms. The best, and, as far as I can see, the only, resistance to the idealist form is to press hard on a robust notion of truth. When idealism becomes a license to move around from 'world' to 'world' or version to version, it cannot preserve a significant role for truth as a regulative ideal for belief. But, without the regulative ideal of truth, the very notion of belief cannot survive. Since we here come up against vast and fundamental debates in philosophy, I shall say no more. Against the realist version of the disunity of the world thesis, of the kind found in Rescher and Brandom, there is, I believe, a more self-contained and simple argument. One should ask how we could ever have evidence that a world was inconsistent. Of course, if we had conclusive evidence that p was true and that *not-p* was true, then, since a contradiction can (they assert) never be true, we could conclude that the world must be inconsistent. But what about inconsistent worlds without contradiction? If a world can genuinely be such that two propositions are true in it and their conjunction not, what allows us to decide, given arbitrary consistent propositions p and q, whether their conjunction is true or not (that is, whether the world is consistent or not)? Rescher and Brandom might argue that there are no such worlds—that the only fragmented worlds are ones in which the fragments involve inconsistencies. But, if their insistence that such fragmented worlds are real ontological possibilities is to be taken seriously, it is hard to see on what basis they could rule out the real ontological possibility of worlds that are fragmented without being inconsistent. This line of thought seems to me to show that the notion of a genuinely inconsistent world, as a real ontological possibility, borders on incoherence.[12] Rescher and Brandom's inconsistent worlds can, all their assertions to the contrary notwithstanding, be understood only in terms of the partitioned belief systems they model. Their possibility, therefore, cannot provide an argument for the rationality of partitioning.

---

[12] It should be emphasized that this is different from a repudiation of the possibility of true contradictions. If there were true contradictions, as some have held, the world would be inconsistent, but not in Rescher and Brandom's technical sense. The idea of a world in which p *and not-p* is true is far less perplexing than the idea of one in which p is true, *not-p* is true, but p *and not-p* is not true. The mystery of how p and *not-p* could both be true in the same world is compounded, not ameliorated, by the denial of their conjunction.

4.3 THE NECESSITY OF SATISFYING CP

At the beginning of Chapter 3, I said that not only is satisfaction of CP rational, but that satisfying it to some sufficient degree is necessary for something to be a person. I now take up this claim.

Our ordinary concept of a person does allow for some degree of partitioning but nonetheless requires what Dennett aptly calls 'a center of narrative gravity' (1991: 410 ff.). Too much partitioning would certainly challenge the existence of any center of narrative gravity in a life.[13] As I have indicated above, agency, in particular, would be frustrated by too much partitioning. Consider first the case in which, of my different partitions, now one and now another gets to control what I do. In that case, it seems unlikely that my sequence of actions could constitute any long-term, coherent plans. The idea of me as an agent, the author of my life, the one who deliberates, plans, chooses, and so on, could find no place. (The claim here is not that this can never happen, but that it cannot happen too much.) On the other hand, suppose one partition remains in control of action throughout. It then becomes doubtful what it means to attribute to a person those beliefs that are only in the non-operative partitions. If they had no tendency to influence action, even where they are relevant to the determination of action in the situations in which the agent finds herself, what would it mean to say that the person really believes them? (It should be remembered that asserting is itself a kind of action. Insulation from all action would mean that such beliefs could not even be asserted.)

There are, in fact, two ways in which too much partitioning could threaten the kind of coherence that Agency and a center of narrative gravity require. The first way is in the dimension of breadth. This means the existence of too many partitions. Suppose, for example, that there were, associated with a person, a thousand overlapping partitions, in each of which one belief was not part of the overlap. There would be a thousand beliefs that would, by that very fact, be insulated from each other. If partitions competed for control of action, that means that there would be a thousand different directions between which a person might vacillate. Since each partition would differ from the others only in respect of one belief, this might not seem so serious (though the sheer number of them would disrupt narrative unity in a life). However, given that we have, albeit impressionistically, tied the notion of partitioning to

[13] The following line of thought is indebted to Christine Korsgaard (1989).

what I called fault lines in a person's life, partitioning will, *ipso facto*, be of some significance. So, although it would be absurd to try to quantify the matter with any precision, it seems that too many partitions would be inconsistent with the demands of Agency.

The second way in which partitioning could threaten the coherence required by Agency is in the dimension of depth. That is to say, even if there were only a few partitions, if they had too little overlap, there would be nothing to hold them together as partitions of a single mind other than their association with a single body. It is not clear how much the importance of overlap here should be cast in terms of belief, and how much in terms of sub-doxastic states, abilities, and so on.[14] But, to give some idea of the problem, if the partition of the Japanese astronomer's mind that treated the sun as an object of mathematical physics did not also include all the beliefs necessary to speak Japanese, to know what to do in Japanese religious rituals, to tie his shoelaces, and so on, then it would be difficult, if not impossible, to take those beliefs as beliefs of the same person who knew and could do all those things. Thus, to be consistent with personhood, partitioning must be relatively superficial, not in the sense of being insignificant to the person (we have argued just the opposite), but in terms of not cutting too far down into basic beliefs and abilities that are crucial to coherent functioning. This is not to deny that deep divisions within one organism can occur. Cases of Multiple Personality Disorder include not only alters that speak different languages but alters with different physiological characteristics.[15] My point is that, the deeper the divisions, the more difficult it is to see the divisions as divisions within a single person. If they fight for control over action, then the 'person' will in fact be like two very different people alternating in their use of the body.

Suppose a case of an organism subject to maximal partitioning; that is to say, every single belief in the organism is isolated from every single other belief. It is not obvious that this is even a possibility. Even if one does not subscribe to all-out Davidsonian holism, many beliefs are identified by their places in various theoretical networks. For example, it seems impossible that one could believe that roses are red without believing its logical consequence that roses are colored. So, either suppose

[14] The idea that abilities, rather than beliefs, provide the crucial unity behind multiplicity in cases of what used to be called Multiple Personality Disorder is argued for by Braude (1991: ch. 7).

[15] For example, in one case, described by Braude (1991: 49), all the alters of one multiple were allergic to citrus juice except one.

the case *per impossibile*, or suppose that each of the beliefs involved is one that can be held in isolation from all other beliefs. It seems that, in such a case, there would be no person at all. We cannot take as a person the organism in which these many disconnected beliefs lie, since that organism would be incapable of acting like a person at all. No action could result from the joint effects of several of these beliefs. No belief could logically combine with any other to allow for means–end reasoning to achieve any goals. There would be no pressure towards any consistency among beliefs, and so nothing to regulate the acquisition of beliefs that could 'add up' to a coherent theory of any part of the world of that organism, and so on. But nor could we take each belief to be associated with a distinct person. For a single belief could not, by itself, sustain any form of activity appropriate to a person.[16]

What this shows, I think, is that everyone must recognize the importance of coherence, system, and connection to at least some degree. Any kind of activity that we value as persons depends on it to at least some extent. Thus, even those who boast of containing multitudes must see each of those multitudes as displaying some coherence and well-roundedness. And, if they wish it to be true that there is a self that contains the multitudes, these multitudes cannot be too numerous or too deeply fragmented but must overlap to a considerable degree. Those who love extreme sports may find a thrill in the idea in pushing fragmentation as far as possible without tumbling over the abyss of non-personhood. But it is quite clear that the abyss yawns.

---

[16] Fodor and Lepore (1992) are critical of arguments from holism against the possibility of what they call punctate languages and minds—i.e. languages that include only one sentence and minds with only one belief. Though I find the idea of a punctate mind or language absurd, my argument at this point is independent of considerations of content, and hence of holism. The point is not that it is impossible for something to have but a single belief but rather that something that had only one belief could not be a person. It is the nature of minds or persons that I claim here makes this impossible, not the nature of belief or content.

5

The Epistemic Shape of a Person's Life

> The passage of time does not destroy or diminish but rather
> multiplies and increases the quantity of valuable things.
>
> (Mikhail Bakhtin, 'Forms of Time and of the Chronotope in
> the Novel', 1937–8)

This chapter both continues and extends the approach developed in
the previous two chapters. In those chapters, we were concerned with a
synchronic, first-order principle, CP, governing persons' beliefs, to the
effect that they are closed under conjunction. I argued that this principle
was both rational for persons and such that nothing could be a person
unless it satisfied the principle to a sufficient extent. In this chapter,
I will look at another principle that I shall also argue is both rational
for persons and such that nothing can be a person unless it satisfies
it to a sufficient extent. The principle, however, will be unlike CP in
two respects. First, it is a second-order principle, dealing with belief
about one's own beliefs. Secondly, it is a diachronic principle, in that
it concerns beliefs about future beliefs. I call the principle Reflection,
since it is a version of (or at least extremely similar to) a principle of
that name introduced and defended by Bas van Fraassen. It says that
a person should treat her future selves as general experts.[1] By treating
someone as an expert about an area, I mean that, if one came to know
what the expert believed about something in that area and did not come
to know any reason why one should not, one would adopt that belief
oneself (if one did not already have it). A general expert is one whose
expertise is unconfined to a particular area. So Reflection holds that,

---

[1] Bas van Fraassen (1984, 1995). I use the expression 'future selves' without meaning
anything of ontological import by it. It is simply easier to speak that way than to talk of
oneself at future times. For more on this point, and for the significance of 'future selves',
rather than 'future self', see Evnine (2005).

if one were to come to know one's future beliefs and not learn of any reason why one should not, one should make those beliefs one's current beliefs.[2] Satisfying Reflection means giving a vote of confidence to your future selves, *qua* epistemic agents.

5.1 REFLECTION

As I just mentioned, Reflection is a version—an informal and generalized version—of a principle that goes by the same name, introduced into the philosophical literature and defended by Bas van Fraassen. That principle has been considered primarily in the context of formal epistemology and is expressed as a principle of second-order conditional probability:

$$P_{a, t}(Q | P_{a, t'}(Q) = r) = r.$$

This says that a person a, at a time t, should accord a probability r to Q conditionally on the hypothesis that a will accord r to Q at some later time, t'.[3] The principle thus stated becomes relevant to epistemology through an explication of degrees of belief in terms of (subjective) probability, a conception that lies at the basis of much formal epistemology. (See Sections 1.2.1 and 3.2.2 for some discussion of degrees of belief.) The statement of Reflection with which I opened this chapter is free of this formal apparatus.[4] I prefer to discuss Reflection in an informal manner for several reasons. (1) The formal apparatus gives a principle that pertains to partial belief. The formal principle will extend to full belief if and only if one takes full belief to be degree of belief at or above a certain threshold (perhaps one). This is known as the Lockean Thesis. In Section 3.2.2, I gave reasons for

---

[2] Treating Reflection in terms of expertise in this way derives from Haim Gaifman (1985).

[3] For treatments of Reflection in the context of more general theories of second-order probability, see Brian Skyrms (1980) and Gaifman (1985).

[4] Is the principle I defend a version of Reflection or a distinct, albeit similar, principle? There is probably no non-arbitrary way to answer this question. If Reflection is, by definition, a formal, probabilistic principle, then clearly my principle is not a version of it. If, however, the formal statement of Reflection is supposed to capture a more general thesis, then my principle seems to be getting at the same thing. In favor of the latter, van Fraassen, in the lead-up to his statement of the formal principle, says his principle will enjoin us 'to form as a matter of principle an exceptionally high opinion of [our future judgments]' (1984: 243).

rejecting the Lockean Thesis. Without it, two distinct principles would be needed to comprehend both partial and full belief. In my informal statement, in the gloss on what it is to take someone as an expert, 'belief' can refer ambiguously either to full or to partial belief. (2) The formal statement commits one to thinking of partial belief in terms of probability. This is a commitment I do not wish to make. (3) It will turn out that some of the most interesting issues concerning Reflection cannot be dealt with within the limits imposed by a probabilistic formal theory. The formalism simply does not represent all the factors that are pertinent to a discussion of Reflection. I conjecture that it is because Reflection has been discussed almost exclusively in this formal, probabilistic context that some of the issues I discuss here have not been considered explicitly.[5]

Reflection, especially in its formal guise, is treated as a principle of belief updating, a principle that says how your current beliefs should be affected by coming to know about your future beliefs. However, in reality, the only circumstances under which we might get to know something specific about our future beliefs will be extraordinary ones (in most of which Reflection clearly should not be applied to update current beliefs).[6] Its interest as a principle of belief updating is in fact marginal. Rather, the principle is of interest in so far as a general attitude of confidence towards our future selves as epistemic agents, on the one hand, flows from interesting features of our epistemic situation and our knowledge of it, and, on the other, is presupposed by our practice of making plans. (Once again, these kinds of issues do not typically feature prominently in formal epistemology, which is, by contrast, much preoccupied with problems of belief updating.)

A variety of arguments as to why one should satisfy Reflection have been offered, but these arguments have been vigorously contested.[7] The most prominent argument advanced for Reflection is the Dutch Strategy

[5] Needless to say, none of the above is meant to suggest that there is anything wrong with formal epistemology. It is simply not the best framework within which to approach the issues I am interested in.

[6] Richard Foley (1994) has usefully emphasized this point.

[7] The following is a sampling of the literature. For the principle are van Fraassen (1984), Jordan Howard Sobel (1987), and Mitchell Green and Christopher Hitchcock (1994). Against the principle are David Christensen (1991), William Talbott (1991), and Richard Foley (1994). More equivocal positions are taken by Patrick Maher (1993: ch. 5) and John Vickers (2000).

argument (also known as the diachronic Dutch Book argument).[8] It shows that someone who violates Reflection is open to a series of bets, offered over time, each of which she will find fair by her odds at the time the bet is offered, but which together guarantee a net loss. This argument, like the better-known (synchronic) Dutch Book argument for probabilistic constraints on degrees of belief, is a coherence-based argument. The guarantee of a net loss is supposed to indicate a certain internal incoherence in the beliefs of someone who fails to satisfy Reflection. What distinguishes it from the synchronic version of the argument is that the coherence it enjoins is of a diachronic variety. This has made the argument seem suspect to some who nonetheless have sympathy with the synchronic version of the argument.[9] By contrast, the arguments I will give here are of quite different characters. The first is a truth-based argument, an argument that shows that satisfaction of Reflection is rational because it will promote true beliefs. The second argument will show that satisfaction of Reflection is a necessary condition of making plans, which is itself an essential part of being a person. Satisfaction of Reflection is therefore a necessary condition of being a person.

5.2 THE RATIONALITY OF REFLECTION

My argument for the rationality of satisfying Reflection depends on two substantive premises about fundamental features of our epistemic situation and our knowledge of those features. The first premise is that, in general, people's beliefs get better over time. Call this principle Ameliorism. The second is that it is an essential feature of being a person that one have some knowledge of Ameliorism. Call this Self-Knowledge. Given Self-Knowledge and Ameliorism, the rationality of satisfying Reflection is obvious. If the beliefs of one's later selves are, by and large, superior to those of one's current self, and if one has knowledge of this fact, then it is rational, in general, to treat those later

---

[8] The argument is given in van Fraassen (1984) and is adapted from one given by David Lewis in favor of conditionalization (which, as van Fraassen (1995) shows, implies Reflection). Lewis's presentation of the argument was not published until (1999) but it had entered the literature through a presentation of it in Paul Teller (1973).

[9] See especially Christensen (1991, 2004: ch. 5).

selves as experts in the sense defined above. So, what is to be said in favor of Ameliorism and Self-Knowledge?

5.2.1 Ameliorism

Time, I maintain, is generally the friend of belief. This manifests itself in several ways. First of all, since persons are subject to the condition of Finitude, we are located, limited creatures whose conceptions of the world have to be put together bit by bit, largely on the basis of experience. The more time we have, the more experience we have, the more complete our picture of the world becomes. Not only does increased experience enlarge the scope of our beliefs, it provides materials for their refinement and correction. The more experience we have, the less likely it is that a false belief will endure unchallenged. Time has other salutary, if somewhat vaguer, effects on our beliefs. We gain in wisdom and understanding. Whatever exactly these are, they are likely to improve our beliefs. There are also problems that take time to think through, or opinions on which we can benefit from a second thought. The picture I am painting is hardly unfamiliar. Societies have typically treasured their elders as experts. They have seen more of the world, experienced its vicissitudes, and had time to see the effects of their own and others' actions, and to ponder the meaning of it all.

It is, admittedly, hard to make Ameliorism precise. I have talked vaguely about improving one's beliefs. This includes both gaining true beliefs and shedding false ones. But the question of whether and how beliefs can be quantified, thus enabling precise measurement in both these respects, is itself controversial. Nor are all beliefs equal in their value. Some account ought to be given of relevance, or importance, of beliefs acquired, lest age be seen, ultimately, as an opportunity to stockpile trivialities that are bound, one way or another, to get in the way of more important things. Nevertheless, experience, wisdom, and understanding, universally admitted as the prerogatives of age over youth, must themselves bring discernment as to what is important. And the sheer accumulation of experience is an ungainsayable and impressive (though perhaps easily overlooked) fact of life.

The Ameliorist idyll, of course, is only part of the story, at least as the story pertains to persons who are human beings. Time has other, less salutary effects on human belief that must also be taken account of. But for the present, let us pretend that an unqualified Ameliorism characterizes the shape of the epistemic lives of persons.

As it happens, literature provides us with a case with which further to explore Ameliorism. The wizard Merlin, in T. H. White's *The Once and Future King*, lives his life backwards, getting younger with each passing day.[10] How does Ameliorism stand with respect to his situation? In getting younger, one supposes, he loses, along with his wrinkles, wisdom and understanding and, at a certain point, even cognitive skills that, for human persons, come with growing up. To the extent that the overall quality of one's opinion depends on cognitive skills, wisdom, and understanding, his later (younger) opinion is not superior to his earlier (older) opinion. In this sense, Ameliorism is false for Merlin. However, the case is not as simple as that. For we have to deal with the issue of those beliefs about the world that come simply with the increased opportunity to experience it that time affords. At his origin, did Merlin come into the world with a stock of beliefs about all sorts of empirical things (the address of that witch who could supply liver of blaspheming Jew, and so on) and does he then gradually lose these beliefs throughout the course of his life? If so, the story borders on incoherence. For all his wizardly qualities, Merlin has the form of a human person. He has eyes and ears with which he goes through time, seeing and hearing more and more as he gets younger. Why, then, should he not be gaining empirical beliefs? Does the world make no impact on his senses as he goes through it? If, on the other hand, he begins his existence with little or no empirical information, and acquires it in due course as he progresses through the world, then, despite his getting younger all the time, he will still be acquiring more and more beliefs through ordinary empirical means. To this extent, Ameliorism would still apply. Only when he became too young to have the beliefs (that is, when his cognitive skills became too immature to support the beliefs) would his later beliefs on empirical matters cease to be superior to his earlier beliefs. He would fade into the imbecility of a first childhood.

What this fantasy reveals (if it is coherent at all) is that time actually plays two distinct roles in improving the beliefs of human persons, one necessary and the other contingent. The contingent role affects

[10] White's conceit is actually more complicated than this and clearly incoherent for reasons unrelated to those I discuss in the text. Merlin's living backwards is supposed to explain his knowledge of the future. For that to work, he must not be moving forwards in time but getting younger, as I pretend in the text, but getting older, like everyone else, while going backwards in time. But that, in turn, would be inconsistent with how he is represented by White: the order of the phonemes in the English sentences he speaks, for example, is the same as for everyone else.

those persons, like human persons, who have cognitive skills, neural hardware, and so on, that develop rather than senesce over time. There might be (non-human) persons who were born at their cognitive peak and thereafter suffer a steady cognitive decline, or who, over the course of their necessarily finite existences, suffered no change in the equipment underlying their cognitive skills. But that is not how human persons are. Rather, human persons grow into their cognitive peak just as they grow into their physical peak. Cognitive decline may occur later in life (I will return to this issue below), but it is worth remembering that what faces us (human persons) all with such high probability now is a recent feature of human life. Until only a short time ago, life expectancy would have most of us dying long before our cognitive equipment could go into decline. Let us call this aspect of the improvement of our beliefs over time Contingent Ameliorism. Contingent Ameliorism is contingent in (possibly) two senses. First, it is true of human persons but cannot be assumed to be true of any person whatsoever. Hence it is not a necessary truth about personhood. And, secondly, it might be argued that it is only contingently true of human persons. In both these respects, it is to be contrasted with Necessary Ameliorism, which is based on the fact that beliefs accumulate over time. The Ameliorism here is a consequence of the necessity with which persons live in time. No person can fail to satisfy Necessary Ameliorism.

How much, exactly, of the cognitive improvement of human persons is owing to Contingent Ameliorism? In the previous paragraph, I spoke of cognitive skills and neural hardware. A baby is born unable to see and requires some short time to develop sufficiently to process information in this way. (Though, presumably, this development of the hardware is complete long before the child starts to have beliefs at all.) Other forms of development of hardware are more subtle. A normal 6-year-old, while able to have beliefs, presumably cannot have them about quantum mechanics. Perhaps, before puberty, one cannot have beliefs involving concepts of sexual desire or romantic love. (In this case, it is not the *neural* hardware that needs developing.) In describing Merlin's case, however, I also suggested that he would lose wisdom and understanding. I have no analysis or empirical theory of these phenomena. While they may depend on developments in neural or other hardware, they may also (or only) depend on experience and other features associated with Necessary Ameliorism. If they depend only on features associated with Necessary Ameliorism, then even Merlin will gain in wisdom and understanding as he gets younger. If they depend on factors of both these kinds, then the story of Merlin may not be coherently describable in terms of these concepts.

5.2.2 Self-Knowledge

The second premise of the argument for the rationality of Reflection is Self-Knowledge. Since Self-Knowledge is itself a second-order claim, a claim about what persons must believe or know about themselves as believers, the basis for the claim that all persons must satisfy Self-Knowledge will lie in the condition on personhood that I called, in Chapter 1, Second-Ordinality. Second-Ordinality says that persons must be able to attribute beliefs to themselves and others. I shall argue here that Self-Knowledge is implied by Second-Ordinality. What is the importance of the existence of beliefs to persons? The answer surely lies in their connections to action. Even though not every belief a person has must be acted upon, the very existence of belief is bound up with action. Action is the means by which persons navigate through their environment and shape that environment to suit their ends. Action, therefore, must be accompanied by representation of the environment, and, for persons, belief is one of the primary forms that such representation takes. Belief, in its primary function, is a conduit through which the environment in which persons exist affects the actions of those persons. Of course, belief is a lot more than just a conduit for information. In belief, the informational link between environment and person exists in a manner that is susceptible to rational consideration. In Chapter 1, I suggested that Agency implies Belief—that is, that engaging in long-term agency requires having beliefs. But, even if one challenges that connection, given that persons (by stipulation) have beliefs, it remains the case that, at its core, belief must play the role of conduit between environment and action.

   This essential feature of belief has repercussions for the practice of attributing it. (I focus here on the attribution of belief to others. Self-attribution poses a host of well-known problems that I cannot go into here. I do say something relevant to the issue, though, in Chapter 6.) Attributing beliefs to persons helps us understand them; that is, it helps explain and anticipate their actions by connecting those actions to ways in which the world impinges on the agents. If the attribution of belief is to do this, then it must be done in the light of certain basic principles that govern the relations between persons, beliefs, and their environments at the most general level. I call these principles the framework conditions of belief attribution. These framework conditions will include, though not be limited to, Necessary Ameliorism, for the following reason. It must be part of the framework conditions that belief is positively impacted by experience. It is a consequence merely of being in time that creatures increase the amount of experience they have.

Although not all this experience need result in an accumulating and improving stock of beliefs, some of it must. To attempt a little more precision, the knowledge necessary for belief attribution to work must include at least the following: that there is a default condition that, absent special circumstances, if a belief is attributed at one time, it is available at a later time for use in explanation and interpretation; that new experience leads to new belief; and that experience is capable of leading to rational revision of belief. Without knowledge of such factors, it would be impossible to use information about the environment—here including the history—of an agent, including the history of its locations, activities, and circumstances, to infer the existence of beliefs that would, in turn, be able to play a role in rational explanations of that agent's actions. Thus, being a person entails having knowledge of Necessary Ameliorism. As we shall see below, it also entails having knowledge of a variety of qualifications to Necessary Ameliorism.

Although ordinary human experience provides us with knowledge of Contingent Ameliorism fairly easily, I do not think one can argue merely from framework conditions of belief attribution to knowledge of it, as one can with Necessary Ameliorism, even supposing we restrict ourselves to beings for whom Contingent Ameliorism is true. One could engage in belief attribution, with knowledge of the framework conditions that imply Necessary Ameliorism, without having knowledge of what effects differences in person's ages had on what kinds of beliefs they could have. No doubt one's practice of belief attribution would be less successful than if one knew more specific details about a creature's epistemic profile. But such ignorance would not eviscerate the whole point of attributing beliefs to predict and explain action. Below, we shall return to issues of belief attribution to show that such a practice requires knowledge of more than Necessary Ameliorism. Those considerations will show, I think, that it would be very strange (though not impossible) for creatures for whom Contingent Ameliorism was true not to have knowledge of it. But, for the moment, we may note that, as long as one had no good reason to believe in the falsity of Contingent Ameliorism (to believe in Contingent Senescence, for example), the argument for Reflection given above will still go through with knowledge of Necessary Ameliorism alone.

5.3 APPARENT COUNTER-EXAMPLES
TO REFLECTION

I noted above that Ameliorism will certainly be thought to paint too rosy a picture of our epistemic lives. There are all sorts of ways in which our beliefs do not get better over time. Consequently, there are a number of apparent counter-examples to Reflection. In this section, I shall consider three types of problem cases. There will be specific things to say about each, but, following my discussion of them separately, I shall attempt to bring them together under a single rubric.

5.3.1 The classic counter-examples

The mere observation that there will, even inevitably, be cases in which my future beliefs will be inferior to my present ones is not enough to challenge Reflection. Our lapses are unpredictable in type and in content. Recognition of such future deficiencies is compatible with a general satisfaction of Reflection. But what about cases where specific lapses can be predicted? A host of counter-examples of this sort have been proposed in the critical literature on Reflection. In order to provide such cases, resort is almost always made to such things as mind-altering drugs, hypnosis, or other 'external' disrupters of rational belief formation. To give one example, suppose you believe that you have just taken a drug that will make you believe that you can fly. You will, naturally, not want now to adopt the belief that you can fly (Christensen 1991). Do cases of this kind show that satisfaction of Reflection is not rational? I do not think so, for two reasons. First, I have argued that it is rational to satisfy the principle because of our *general* expectations of what our future beliefs will be like. Generality should not be confused with universality. An attitude of confidence towards our future beliefs may still be rational even if we have good reason to believe, as we do in the kind of counter-example just illustrated, that, in some particular case, a future belief will be wrong or otherwise inferior to one's current beliefs. The second reason is that the definition of treating someone as an expert requires us to adopt the expert's belief only if we do not, in learning of that belief, also learn some reason why we should not adopt it. In the cases under consideration, this proviso is clearly not met. To see this, consider another alleged counter-example, this one from Patrick Maher

(1993: 107). Suppose one envisages having ten drinks at a party, and considers it certain that, as a result of the alcohol, one will incorrectly judge, at the end of the evening, that one is sober enough to drive home. I should not now adopt the belief that I will be sober enough to drive home at the end of the evening. But the force of this example depends on knowing the circumstances under which the future judgment will be formed. Without those circumstances, or something like them, it *would* be rational for me now to believe that I will be able to drive home safely at the end of the evening, on the condition that I will then judge that I am able to drive home safely. Other things being equal, I will be in a much better position to know then than I do now whether it would be safe for me to drive. So, in a case where there is nothing in the belief itself to make one question Reflection, we get what looks like a counter-example only if the hypothesis about a future belief includes something in addition—namely, the circumstances under which that belief is acquired. In another case (Christensen 1991), I envisage that I will, at some point in the future, judge that I am the Messiah. Christensen argues, rightly, that it would be irrational for me now to believe that I am the Messiah on that condition. But in this case too, in learning that I am to have this belief in the future, I would also be learning something about the circumstances under which it was acquired. For the very content of the belief is such that (as I now judge) I could never have that belief unless I were insane. So here, too, the proviso in the statement of Reflection would not be met. Consequently, these kinds of cases are not, after all, counter-examples to Reflection as understood here.

Let us distinguish *following* Reflection from *satisfying* it. Following Reflection means being such that you would, if you learned of your future opinion, adopt it currently. Satisfying Reflection is being such that, if you were to learn of your future opinion, you would adopt it now, unless you learned of some reason why you should not. So, one can satisfy Reflection without following it in all cases. The counter-examples above show that it is not always rational to follow Reflection, precisely because in some circumstances, in learning of our future beliefs, we may also learn some reason why we should not adopt those beliefs now. The counter-examples do not challenge the claim that it is rational to satisfy Reflection.

Now one might feel that the defense of (satisfying) Reflection that I have given against the classic counter-examples, and the attendant distinction between satisfying and merely following the principle, will be subject to a serious objection. For one might fear that, if one tried to give a general account of the reasons for which one might, rationally, not follow Reflection, one would be able to do no better than specify them as 'being a case in which it is rational not to follow Reflection'. In other words, satisfying Reflection will amount to following it, unless it is not rational to do so. And this, in turn, sounds vacuous.[11] This objection seems to me, however, overly pessimistic. It is not the case that beliefs acquired as a result of madness, drugs, and alcohol are deficient *because* it is not rational to follow Reflection with respect to them. It is, rather, that it is not rational to follow Reflection with respect to them because they are deficient. Even if one were to despair of giving a precise account of their deficiency, the core of such an account is easily forthcoming. Such beliefs are deficient because they do not result from the proper functioning of our cognitive faculties. I shall not attempt a more precise characterization here but I see no reason to think that one could not be forthcoming. (Obviously, such an account may leave room for cases that are hard to classify.)

5.3.2 Methods of belief acquisition

The considerations of the previous section should make us see that whether it is rational to follow Reflection depends not only on the content of the belief in question but also on the way in which the given belief was acquired. And this, in turn, suggests other kinds of cases that put pressure on Reflection. Roughly put, different methods of belief acquisition are sensitive to temporal considerations in different ways. Out of these differences, apparent counter-examples to Reflection can be constructed. One kind of case is as follows. I now believe, on the basis of perception, that the walls of the room I am in are blue. Suppose I know, or hypothesize, that in a week's time someone will ask me about the color of the walls of the room I was in a week previously and I will form a belief as to their color based on memory. My predicted or hypothesized memory-based belief will not be superior, in reliability, to my current perception-based one, for two reasons. First, a memory is a doxastic presentation of a fact that occurs at a temporal distance from the point at which that fact was initially registered. The greater the temporal distance, the more opportunity for degradation of information preserved. But, secondly, the initial registration of the fact was the perception-based belief itself; hence, it cannot be less

---

[11] A version of this objection is endorsed by Maher (1993: 114–16).

reliable than the memory-based belief that derives from it.[12] And, given
the possibilities for degradation of information just mentioned, it will
typically be more reliable than the memory-based belief. Thus, even if
I now knew what my belief would be one week from now, it would
be irrelevant to what I should now believe about the color of the walls.
Another example: suppose I am now eating spaghetti for dinner.[13] I
believe this on the basis of perception and perhaps other sources (such
as knowledge of my own actions and intentions). If asked whether I ate
spaghetti for dinner today two years from now, having no memory at
all, I might estimate its probability on the basis of, say, my memory that,
at that time in my life, I was not eating a lot of pasta. Once again, this
future belief, even if I knew now what it would be, would be irrelevant
when set against my current belief. One could put the message of these
examples crudely by saying that, other things being equal, perception
trumps memory or retrospective statistical estimates. Since perception
is always of things present, whereas memory and retrospective estimates
are always of things past, here is a way in which present selves are bound
to be more expert than future selves.

Perception is one kind of present authority. Another is derived from
the privileged access we have to our current mental states. It has often
been alleged that such access yields infallible belief. If so, beliefs based
on privileged access are clearly more expert than any beliefs we can have
in the future about the same things, since beliefs about past mental
states are never plausibly thought to be infallible. But, even if privileged
access does not lead to infallible belief, it is hard to deny that it leads to
belief with greater authority than any other methods of forming beliefs
about past mental states.

5.3.3 Mental decline and personal identity

A final kind of worry people often express about Reflection is that we
have every reason to expect, or at least to treat as a vivid possibility,
a variety of types of mental decline as we age. Not all types of mental

---

[12] Not all memory-based beliefs come from perceptual beliefs. One can remember
something about an incident that one did not notice at the time and hence about which
one did not have a belief at the time. If such a phenomenon were extensive, my remarks
about memory in general would have to be relativized specifically to those memory beliefs
that were formed from original perception-based beliefs.

[13] Adapted from William Talbott (1991). Talbott was, as far as I know, the first to
point the way to these kinds of issues.

decline are threatening to Reflection. For example, the fact that we will, no doubt, forget many things we now know is not, in itself, a problem. For Reflection tells us to value our future opinion, whereas forgetfulness induces a lack of opinion. Still, forgetfulness may create problems less directly. If we forget having done something, we are more likely to believe (falsely) that it still needs to be done.[14] And, of course, other forms of mental decline may directly induce opinion that we would not now want to privilege over current opinion. In such cases, there may or may not be something wrong with the way a given individual belief is acquired. If it is acquired as a result of organic degeneration of the brain, then the case will be similar to those we examined in Section 5.3.1, cases in which we hypothesize a future belief arising as the result of drugs, brainwashing, and so on. If, however, the case is one in which, as a result of ordinary forgetfulness, I forget that I have walked the dog, and thus believe that the dog has not been walked, it is hard to dismiss it as one in which the proviso in Reflection ('as long as we don't learn anything else. . .') is not met. So satisfying Reflection would require following it in this case. However, the other answer to the classic counter-examples of Section 5.3.1 must also be taken into account. It will be compatible with my treating my future self as an expert that I hypothesize that that future self will, owing to forms of mental decline, have a variety of beliefs that I should not value over my current beliefs. For the sheer number of such suspect future beliefs may be fairly small relative to the number of my future beliefs in total. It is only when we hypothesize sufficient mental decline that most of my future beliefs are suspect that we have a new problem for Reflection.

Van Fraassen supplements the Dutch Strategy defense of Reflection with a line of argument that, when I fail to satisfy Reflection with respect to some future belief, either the subject of that belief is not me or the belief is not really mine.[15] Concerning this kind of claim, in the context of the sort of example examined in Section 5.3.1, in which one foresees getting drunk and believing, as a result, that one can drive safely, Patrick Maher, writes: 'this is a desperate move. Nobody I know gives any real credence to the claim that having ten drinks, and as a result thinking he or she can drive safely, would destroy his or her personal

---

[14] I owe this point to Dana Nelkin.

[15] This theme is sounded in van Fraassen (1995) and also in Richard Jeffrey (1988: 126–32).

identity.'[16] Maher is quite right about the kind of case he describes. However, in cases in which we consider the possibility of massive loss of future expertise, owing to such things as senility, the response is, it seems to me, not a desperate move at all. It is quite plausible to suppose that there are epistemic constraints on personal identity over time such that, at least in some cases, facts about beliefs and their formation can be sufficient for the non-identity of a person at one time and a person at another.[17] These epistemic constraints on identity should not be framed in terms of relations of content of earlier to later beliefs. For example, it would be absurd to suggest that identity over time required identity of beliefs over time. What lies behind the invocation of considerations of personal identity by van Fraassen in this context is that, if some future person is to be me, at a minimum, I must be able to consider his beliefs as my beliefs. I cannot say what experience will bring, so I cannot expect him to have the same beliefs as I do now. But at least, for his beliefs to be my beliefs, they must be formed in ways that I now consider appropriate ways of forming beliefs. I must, as it were, be able to vouch for them in advance, whatever they may be. Generalizing this, we obtain, as a necessary condition of a person Q's (at time t') being the same person as P at some earlier t that Q's beliefs at t' should be acquired from P's beliefs at t in ways that P at t finds reasonable. Of course, all this is a matter of degree. I can easily contemplate the prospect of my forming some unsavory habits of belief acquisition. In practice, the most prominent way in which this necessary condition will fail to hold is when I contemplate future madness or senility. (I will make explicit here what should be obvious anyway, that it is consistent with judging that a future person will not be me that I should still have an intimate and special concern for his fate.)

5.4 AMELIORISM AND SELF-KNOWLEDGE DEEPENED

I want now to draw together some of the results of the previous section. The kinds of potential challenges to Reflection that we have been

---

[16] Maher (1993: 107–8).

[17] Like Carol Rovane (1998: 59–64), I think that our ordinary conception of what a person is is probably too confused to avoid conflicts of intuition over analytical claims such as the one I go on to make in this paragraph. I discuss this at somewhat greater length in Section 1.1.

considering all stem from specific features of human belief acquisition. It is a fact about the psychology of humans, for example, that they can have their beliefs altered by hypnosis, drugs, and madness; that they are subject to increasing forgetfulness and dementia, and so on. Earlier I made a distinction between Necessary and Contingent Ameliorism. That distinction is, in fact, better drawn as follows. There are some features that characterize the temporal epistemic profile of any person, as such. I have argued that Ameliorism is such a feature. But any person will be a person of some given type: human, simian, Martian, android, or what have you. Such types also have their own, distinctive temporal epistemic profiles. *Qua* person, any particular person will have these characteristics contingently. All persons, therefore, will have epistemic lives that are subject to two distinct profiles. One of these profiles is ameliorist and is connected to the most basic facts of having a temporally extended epistemic life. The other profile stems from the specific ways in which a person of a given kind acquires and processes beliefs. While these profiles are not always entirely harmonious, they must, to some large enough extent, allow for co-realization. If members of a given kind are to be persons, the distinctive creaturely ways of handling belief that pertain to that kind cannot undermine those features that are necessary for personhood, though they can mitigate them, to a greater or lesser extent, 'around the edges'.

Naturally, the details of the second profile will vary from person to person (or type of person to type of person). Yet there are characteristics we can expect any such profile to have. Let me concentrate here only on issues deriving from the different (normal) methods of acquiring belief such as we examined in Section 5.3.2. Persons of whatever kind, being subject to Finitude and Agency, must have ways of gathering information about the environments within which they act. This means they must have faculties of perception. One cannot generalize too much about what kinds of perception. Persons must be able to acquire information about those aspects of the environment that affect them and that they can act on. Which those features are will depend on what those persons are like. If, for example, there could be ghostly individuals that passed through walls, information about the hardness or softness of things in their environment might be unimportant. Creatures that, say, consumed their own bodies for nutrition, until those bodies were exhausted, might need nothing like faculties of smell or taste. But the demands of Agency do require locating particular things. Hence, all persons must have some perceptual means of learning about the positions of things in their environment.

Because action takes time, information, once acquired through perception, must be preserved. Hence, persons must have memory. And, since Agency was taken to comprehend not just single actions, but courses of action, plans, and projects (more on this soon), their memory must be relatively long term. And not only will it be necessary for persons to have some kind(s) of perception and memory. It is in the nature of such faculties that perception will be more reliable than memory. This is because, as we noted above, memory-based beliefs (at least in a large class of cases) will be derived from initial perception-based beliefs. In addition, there will always be opportunities for degradation of stored information.

We saw in Chapter 2 that persons must be able to engage in certain inferences. Therefore it is immediately necessary that they have inference as a method of belief acquisition. Making an inference, of course, takes time. One might, therefore, come to a mistaken conclusion because one has forgotten, during the course of making the inference, what one of its premises was. This is a way in which problems with memory may ramify through other epistemic areas. And inference about things that can be observed will always, like memory, cede authority to the immediacy of perception of such matters. The other traditional source of belief is introspection, the nature of which is very much in dispute. For some it is merely the application of perception and inference to oneself; for others, it is a special kind of inner vision. Which of these models one accepts will radically affect the kind of temporal profile one assigns to introspection. I shall not engage with this debate here, however. Nor will I consider whether there are further *sui generis* types of belief-acquisition processes (such as moral intuition). Suffice it to say that one can determine a fair amount about a person's methods of belief acquisition, and their relative temporal merits, with necessity.

How does Self-Knowledge stand in the light of our more complex picture of the temporal epistemic profiles of persons? I think one can argue that persons must have knowledge not simply of the general truth of Ameliorism. They must also have knowledge of just those ways in which we have seen Ameliorism should be complicated owing to such things as the relative merits of perception and memory, and so on. In other words, Self-Knowledge must extend to at least some of the second, specific temporal profile that characterizes the epistemic life of persons. The argument for this is an extension of the argument for

Self-Knowledge given above based on the practice of attributing beliefs. Beliefs arise, and must be seen to arise by creatures who attribute them to themselves and others, as part of our interactions with the world. They cannot, therefore, be attributed where we have no conception of the modes by which beliefs are affected and acquired. Knowledge of these modes, needless to say, will not take the form of a scientific psychology; it is knowledge that must be available to all creatures, however undeveloped, that have and attribute beliefs. This knowledge will include (*a*) a basic classification of the avenues by which beliefs can be acquired into categories such as perception, memory, and inference; and (*b*) some conception of the conditions of operation of these different methods. Such knowledge amounts to knowledge of precisely the ways in which Ameliorism must be qualified. In the absence of such knowledge, it is hard to see how the attribution of beliefs would be constrained in such a way as to make beliefs plausible elements of rational explanations of behavior. Take perception, as an example. The folk psychological notion of perception as a means of acquiring beliefs will recognize the existence of appropriate sensory organs and contain the knowledge of the obvious and basic ways that such organs can be impeded in their operations (a person in the dark or with eyes closed cannot form beliefs on the basis of visual perception). It must also recognize the ways in which memory-based beliefs can derive from perception-based ones.

It thus turns out that not only must persons be subject to Necessary Ameliorism; not only must this Ameliorism be qualified in ways owing to the natures of their belief-forming abilities; but persons must have knowledge of both Ameliorism and its qualifications. It does not follow that the recognition of the ways in which methods of belief formation are sensitive to time must be codifiable in some set of principles. This kind of knowledge is not meant to be able to settle all difficult questions about the comparative worth of the epistemic warrants of different beliefs. Rather, such knowledge is required as a background against which the attribution of beliefs acquired by the different methods is anchored to the circumstances in which these beliefs are attributed and used to explain the actions of their owners. To serve this purpose, the conception of our epistemic situation, the existence of which is claimed by Self-Knowledge, can be somewhat vague.

Let us now recap some of the proceeding discussion. Satisfaction of Reflection means treating our future selves as experts. To treat someone as an expert is to adopt her opinion—if we don't already share it—on learning what that opinion is, *unless* we learn of some reason why we should not. We have now seen a variety of factors learning about which might lead us not to follow Reflection. But one can satisfy Reflection without always having to follow it. Opinions with respect to which we would not follow Reflection might be the result of some disruptive, external influence on our belief-forming processes, such as a drug or hypnosis; they might be formed on the basis of a (normal) method of belief acquisition that is, in its nature, inferior to the methods we have currently for arriving at an opinion on a given subject; or they might be formed in the context of (severe) mental decline. These, of course, are not the only things learning about which would incline us not to follow Reflection with respect to some future opinion. Simply learning that that opinion is false should be sufficient. But what all these cases have in common is that they concern issues of the nature of our cognitive apparatus in acquiring beliefs.[18]

Discussions of Reflection in the context of formal epistemology do not address these issues for the simple reason that they find no representation in the probabilistic framework employed.[19] That framework gives us no way of representing information about the way in which either the current conditional opinion, or the hypothesized, future unconditional opinion is reached. But, once one begins to think of Reflection in terms of expertise, this limitation becomes a serious liability. The reason is that expertise itself cannot be conceptualized in terms only of opinions and persons. An expert is a person whose opinions (on the subject of her expertise) we trust—but only if they are formed in the right way. Thus, all the various types of things learning of which would cause

---

[18] It is, in fact, highly plausible to suppose that the rationality of a belief that p will be affected by beliefs we have about how the belief that p was acquired. As Laurence BonJour (1985: 38–45) argues with his clairvoyance examples, epistemic externalism, which seeks to analyze rationality and justification in terms of methods of belief acquisition, comes up short if it leaves out of the equation the beliefs subjects have about those methods.

[19] The only way to represent facts about how a hypothesized future belief is acquired in the probabilistic formalism is to specify them explicitly as part of the hypothesis conditionalized upon. Reflection would thus look like this: $P_{a,t}(Q|P_{a,t'}(Q) = r$ and $S) = r$, where S specifies something about the method on the basis of which, either by hypothesis or prediction, a assigns a probability of r to Q at t'. As John Vickers (2000) points out, a demand that one satisfy Reflection cannot be confused with a demand that one satisfy the above expansion in full generality. If S states simply that Q is false, then it would obviously be irrational to satisfy the expanded schema even in cases in which it would not be irrational to satisfy the original one. Thus, to allow information to enter about method of belief acquisition, one would have to express Reflection by the expanded schema, restricted to cases in which S says something only about method of belief acquisition. This, I believe, is pretty much equivalent to where I have ended up in the text.

us not to trust our future selves have their counterparts for experts in general, and the distinction between satisfying Reflection and following it is reproduced analogously for Reflection-like principles in which the expert is not one's future self but someone else. (This should silence the objection that, by distinguishing satisfying Reflection from following it, and noting the variety of reasons for which we might not follow it, we are left with a principle too *ad hoc* to be of any interest.) If I consider someone an expert, were I to learn only that she believed that *p*, I would make that opinion my own. But, if I learned also that she believed that *p* because she had been brainwashed to believe it, I would not treat her opinion as a guide to my own. Similarly, an expert astronomer who tells me, without leaving her darkened study, on the basis of complex calculations, that there is currently an eclipse of the sun will not be heeded in the face of my being able to look up at the daylight sky. Her calculation is superseded by my perception precisely because, with respect to such things as whether the sun is shining, perception is a more reliable method of belief formation than is calculation. The doctor who tells me that, since my test is negative, there is nothing wrong with me, and so I cannot be in pain, should be disregarded. My knowledge of my own pain, afforded by a method that has privileged access to its objects, is superior to any other method.[20] Experts are experts about their fields of expertise in virtue of being able to form beliefs about them on the basis of appropriate methods. They may form beliefs about a field on the basis of other, less reliable methods (the astronomer falls to tea-leaf reading to predict an eclipse), and, in that case, their beliefs will not carry any special authority. Or, there may be different ways of forming beliefs about the same subject matter that are available to others, which beliefs will then supersede the experts' (I judge about my headache by a method with privileged access, which the pain specialist cannot do). Thus, no principles about the way in which expert opinion should influence us can afford to ignore issues of the methods of belief acquisition. And no such principles can be qualified with complete precision. It follows that Reflection, itself such a principle, must also take account of these issues and will also itself be somewhat vague. Thus, although Reflection turns out to be a

---

[20] In all these cases, it is nonetheless possible that the expert is right and I am wrong. (At least, in the last case, it is possible if one does not consider privileged access a source of infallible beliefs.) What is at issue is simply the rationality of adopting, or not adopting, a belief on the basis of someone else's having it.

messier principle than it first appeared, it would be unrealistic to expect anything else.

5.5 THE NECESSITY OF SATISFYING REFLECTION

So far, I have offered a defense of Reflection in which issues of personal identity have surfaced to ward off a potential objection. The objection was that, in cases of anticipated or hypothesized madness or senility, we might have good reason to believe that our future opinion will be, from our present point of view, highly inferior to our current opinion. The defense was to note that there are epistemic constraints on personal identity over time such that it is a necessary condition for a future person to be me that his beliefs bear certain relations to my current beliefs. In the alleged counter-example to Reflection, those conditions are violated. Hence, I cannot consistently suppose that some future person will both (*a*) have beliefs seriously inferior to my current ones and (*b*) still be me. A deeper link between Reflection and personhood, however, was manifested in the argument to show that satisfaction of Reflection is rational. The premises for this argument were concerned with necessary features of the shape of the epistemic life of a person and, more importantly, with the way in which being a person requires knowledge of such features. Thus, the notion of personhood was important in understanding why one should accept the premises of the argument. I turn now to an argument that satisfying Reflection is itself a necessary condition on personhood.

In Chapter 1, I laid down as a necessary condition on personhood the satisfaction of the condition Agency. This, in turn, was explicated in terms not just of being able to perform intentional actions but also of being able to engage in temporally structured, goal-directed behavior; to have, in other words, plans and projects.[21] Minimally, plans are likely to have the following structure. A goal is set at one time for which action at one or more subsequent times is necessary. This is what distinguishes plans from intentions that immediately manifest themselves in action. Where, for a goal adopted at one time, action is needed at some later time, one effectively delegates responsibility for bringing about the goal, by performing the relevant action, to one's later self. Given that action

---

[21] I use Michael Bratman's (1987) terminology here. Roughly, according to his usage, plans are intentions writ large, and projects are plans writ large.

is guided by the beliefs of the agent, it is very important for agents to ensure that those, including their future selves, to whom they delegate actions that are necessary for their current goals have belief systems that they judge are up to the job of doing what is important by their current standards. *In extremis*, one may delegate responsibilities to people about whom one is very doubtful. (I will return to this point later.) But one cannot routinely engage in meaningful planning without reasonable confidence in the abilities (including the cognitive abilities) of those to whom actions necessary to the plan are delegated. Thus we can say in general, that insofar as persons are, in Bratman's phrase, planning beings, they must have some confidence in the beliefs of their future selves. We can, however, be a little more specific about the circumstances of this confidence.

There are many reasons why a person may delegate actions necessary to accomplish present goals to future selves. She may not currently have time to perform them; circumstances may not be appropriate; she may simply be lazy. But one reason for such delegating that is endemic to persons is that they currently lack pertinent information. The reason I do not book my train ticket now is because I have not yet consulted the timetable. I do not yet have the relevant beliefs to guide my action. I delegate the purchase of the ticket to a future self who will have such beliefs. That is to say, I intend to look at the timetable and then book the ticket. Thus, plans often come into being precisely because we judge that our future selves will be superior, with respect to the relevant beliefs, to our current selves.

I say that this reason for planning is endemic to persons because, by definition, persons are epistemically limited creatures. (This is a consequence of Finitude.) They always operate under conditions of partial knowledge. Under favorable circumstances, this partial knowledge may be sufficient not to require them to defer action to accomplish present goals because they do not yet have a pertinent piece of information. But, even where deferred action is called for for some other reason (perhaps the circumstances are not yet in place for the necessary action), I know now that I will later need beliefs that I do not yet have, beliefs about, for example, the exact location of an object to be affected by me, and about a whole host of other concrete details of the situation in which I will be acting. I must also have confidence that I will still have many beliefs that I now have that are relevant. When I do come to book my train ticket, I must not have forgotten what I now know about when I must arrive by, who may be available to meet me, etc. Nor must I have forgotten what a train is, or that taxis exist, or that people cannot be in two places at once. There are no doubt many present beliefs that it will not matter whether I still have when I come to book my ticket. My belief about which pair of socks I am now wearing, for instance, will be very unlikely to be relevant to my future booking of a train ticket. But, along with my necessary confidence that I will have acquired the pertinent new information (what times the trains are), and that I will be able to take account of the circumstances in which I will have to act (I will know where a telephone is, what the right phone number is), I must also have confidence in the general integrity of my future beliefs about a large but indefinite range of things.

These considerations amount to a limited defense of the necessity for persons to satisfy Reflection. It is limited for two reasons. First, as I noted above and will explore further below, one can sometimes plan with little confidence in those (including future selves) to whom one delegates actions. Secondly, the argument as given does not yet show that, at any given time, one must satisfy Reflection with respect to one's future selves in general, but only that one must satisfy it with respect to those of one's future selves to whom one's current plans delegate some responsibility.

The second limitation is not, I think, very serious. A person's life cannot very well consist of a number of plans formed and executed serially, with no overlapping. Such an unstructured arrangement of plans would not be adequate to most of the characteristic features of personal life. And in fact, as Bratman emphasizes, plans are typically arranged in complex patterns of hierarchy and interlocking. Some have thought that a person's life must involve a single plan or goal by which all others are hierarchically subsumed.[22] If this were true, then the second limitation on the argument for the necessity of satisfying Reflection would be decisively removed. But, even if it is not true, leading the life of a normal person means that one must always be involved, as it were, in a continual warp and woof of plans at different levels of generality. This means (supposing an answer provided to our first limitation) that one must have a general confidence in one's future selves as epistemic agents. One must suppose that they will, generally, preserve a vast background of beliefs that one already has, that they will have the means of adequately determining, at future times of action, the situations in which they will be acting, and that they will acquire those particular

---

[22] Aristotle, *Nicomachean Ethics* I. i, and Sartre (1958: 433–556) may be of this view.

bits of information that are now lacking but that are necessary for the execution of many actions if those actions are to serve one's current goals.

I now come to the first, more interesting limitation. We do sometimes plan even in circumstances in which the people to whom we delegate important parts of the plan are not thought to be reliable. Consider first the case in which I must act through others. To some extent, others are always unreliable in this sense: my intention that they do something is not, in general, sufficient to bring it about that they do it. With others, one must always take certain measures to get them to do what one intends them to do. At a minimum, one must inform them of one's intention. I can intend for A to make the salad for tonight's dinner, but, unless I take the step of informing her of my intention, there is no reason to think she will. Even when informed, others can be more or less reliable, and further engineering may be required to get them to act as one intends. If I know A is forgetful, I may phone her in the afternoon to remind her about making the salad. Or I may tell not only A but also B, with whom she lives, that I intend for A to make the salad. People may be unreliable not only for epistemic reasons (they do not know of our intentions or they forget them) but also for non-epistemic reasons: they are disinclined to be helpful, they do not care, they are easily distracted, they overcommit themselves, and so on. In all these cases, we may take appropriate measures to forestall predicted failures. The general point here is that, where our plans require the actions of others, we must always, to a greater or lesser extent, take measures to ensure fulfillment of our intentions. This is to be contrasted with the case of our own actions. Under favorable, but not unusual, circumstances, no measures need to be taken to bring about action in line with our intentions. Merely to intend to do something is sufficient for us to do it (or, at least, to try to do it). This distinction should feature in an account of personal identity. It is an important fact about someone's being me that I can control his behavior through my intentions in this direct way. Conversely, it is an important fact about someone's being distinct from me that my attempts to control his behavior through my intentions must always rely on what I have called taking measures. My intentions cannot control the behavior of others in the same way that, under normal circumstances, they control my own behavior.[23]

---

[23] Exactly how they control one's own behavior is a further fascinating and difficult question that it is not necessary for me to take up here. I do not mean to imply that a current intention in any way locks a future action into place.

Now it often happens, in a host of small ways, that I predict that my current intention to do something at a later time will not, by itself, bring about my doing that thing. Every time I write an appointment in a diary, we are dealing with just such a case. I predict that I will very likely forget, when the relevant time comes, that the meeting is scheduled for just that time. I therefore act now to lay down a clue that will remind me, at a relevant point in the future, that the meeting is at hand. In a small way, the relation between my current intention and the future action of mine towards which it is directed becomes more like the relation between my intention and the action of someone else towards which it is directed. I must, as it were, inform myself (that is, remind myself) of my intention just as I must inform A of my intention that she make the salad for dinner. I must, in short, take measures to see to the fulfillment of my intention.

When the extent to which I cannot control my future actions merely by intending them becomes too great, we have a breakdown in personal identity. In Derek Parfit's example of the Nineteenth Century Russian, a young, idealistic nobleman intends to give land he will inherit in middle age to the peasants.[24] But he predicts that as a middle-aged man he will no longer share his youthful ideals and so will not act then in accordance with his current intention. He thus seeks to bind himself by taking such measures as we have been looking at. He makes a contract now that will give away the land then and that can be revoked only with his wife's permission. He then makes his wife promise that she will never give that permission. Parfit, rightly, argues that it is quite acceptable to characterize the case in terms of different selves. The young man feels the older one will be a different person; the wife will argue that the older man cannot release her from the promise made to the younger one precisely because the promise was made to a different person.

This is a case concerning values. Reflection is an epistemic principle.[25] But we can doubt the future fulfillment of my current intentions for epistemic reasons, and not just for the already-noted reason that we may forget we had the intention. Suppose I intend now to sell my house when I retire in order to move to smaller accommodations. I predict, however, that I will be suffering from dementia at that point. The problem that I may forget that I had the intention can be remedied by, say, writing it down in a way that I will find at the relevant time.

---

[24] Parfit (1984: 327–8).

[25] I briefly discuss a value-based analogue of Reflection in Evnine (2003: 381–4).

But my dementia is likely to affect much more than that. There may be cognitive deficiencies concerning how to sell a house, where the title is, what my name is, and so on. The only way now to ensure against such large-scale future epistemic deficiency is analogous to the Nineteenth Century Nobleman's recourse. I must take serious measures, say by now handing over power of attorney to someone who will be cognitively able to execute my current intention. As in Parfit's case, I reveal the otherness of the future self for whom I act precisely by having to act through another person who stands in an appropriate relation both to me and to that future self. The argument here thus confirms, though by a different route, the point made in the previous argument that serious breakdowns in Reflection are associated with disruptions of personal identity over time. Not only does personal identity over time require that I see the beliefs of my future self as being acquired in ways I now consider reasonable; it also requires that I be able to exert a certain kind of control over my future actions, a kind of control that does not involve having to externalize my current intentions and knowledge in someone who will carry them forward for action relative to a future person who may not have either the intentions or the knowledge to carry them out. Indeed, these are two sides of the same coin. If beliefs of a future person are formed in ways I now think are unreliable, then I will judge this future person to be deficient in executing my current plans, and hence will take whatever measures I can to remedy this deficiency.

One can bring out further the relation between the argument for the rationality of Reflection and the argument for its necessity by saying that planning itself has implicitly, and often explicitly, an epistemic dimension. It has an epistemic dimension implicitly in that agents must work on the assumption that their future selves will be epistemically capable of performing the actions that are delegated to them. Without this assumption, one part of the contrast between the way in which one's intentions control one's own actions and the way in which they can control the actions of others would be lost. For that distinction relies on (among other things) the way in which, for my intentions to be effective in controlling the actions of others, I must take measures to remedy their expected epistemic deficiencies (something I can do in my own case as well, but not too much without threatening personal identity). The need for epistemic planning becomes explicit when the reason for delegating actions to future selves is precisely to acquire necessary information that one does not now have. In that case, an agent must have knowledge of her epistemic situation in order to plan how to acquire that information. Plans must take into account what avenues an agent has for acquiring knowledge and under what circumstances they can operate effectively. If I plan to shoot an arrow at the castle door with a proclamation tied to it, I had better make sure I do it at a time at which I can see where the castle door is. If I plan on asking for directions when I get closer to my destination, I had better be sure I can speak the language they will be given in. Thus, in a variety of ways, the kind of epistemic self-knowledge the existence of which is asserted by Self-Knowledge, the self-knowledge that makes Reflection rational, also plays an integral role in planning, an activity for which Reflection is a necessary condition.

5.6 PAST, FUTURE, AND OTHERS

One of Reflection's critics is Richard Foley (2001). Foley argues for a symmetry in our attitudes to the beliefs of others, to our own past beliefs, and to our own future beliefs. In all these cases, there are three elements that he says should inform our attitudes: a credibility thesis, a priority thesis, and a special-reasons thesis. According to the credibility thesis, beliefs in all these three categories should carry some *prima facie* weight with respect to what we believe now. In other words, the information that someone (my future or former self, or another) believes *p* gives me a *prima facie* reason to believe *p* now. Foley's argument for this is as follows. We should recognize that our current methods and faculties of belief formation are similar in nature to those of others and our past and future selves. Not only that, but our current beliefs are largely the outcome of the beliefs of others and our former selves, and our future beliefs will be the outcome of our present beliefs and those of others. If one is not skeptical about one's current beliefs, one will be involved in a kind of inconsistency if one is skeptical about the beliefs in any of these other categories. And not being skeptical about them means according them some *prima facie* credibility. Hence, one should either be skeptical about one's own current beliefs (which is not an attractive option) or accept the credibility thesis.

The beliefs in these categories (past, future, and others), however, have only a *prima facie* credibility. We may often have good reason to discount them if we have further information about how they were formed or about their subject matter. An important additional reason for discounting them is if they conflict with one's current opinion. If

I believe *p* and you or my former or future self believes *not-p*, I am, according to Foley, justified in privileging my current opinion simply because it is my current opinion. Similarly, if I have just changed my mind from *not-p* to *p*, my current belief that *p* will outweigh the *prima facie* credibility attached to my former belief that *not-p*.[26] My current beliefs, in other words, have a kind of systematic priority over beliefs in the other categories. This is the priority thesis. Their priority, however, is not absolute. If I have some special reason for thinking that your opinion (or my former or future opinion) is more reliable, I should, even where my current opinion conflicts with it, relinquish my current belief and adopt yours. This is the special-reasons thesis.

How do the views argued for in this chapter relate to Foley's assessment of the issues? Let us grant, for the sake of argument (though I believe nothing I say in this chapter commits me either way), that some form of the credibility thesis holds in all those cases in which Foley thinks it does. Where my position differs most clearly from Foley's is over what one's attitude should be to one's future opinion. The point of Reflection might be put by saying that the priority thesis does not hold with respect to future opinion. If all I know is that I now believe *p* but will believe *not-p*, the priority thesis counsels me to maintain my belief that *p*. Reflection, by contrast, counsels me to abandon my current belief and adopt the belief that *not-p*. As I have argued above, this is because of the generally ameliorative nature of our epistemic lives and our necessary knowledge of this. Foley makes the point, which I quite agree with, that generally speaking we are likely to have knowledge of a future belief that differs from a current belief only under circumstances that provide a 'special reason' for not following the policy of Reflection. So, in some sense, the question of how future opinion should affect current (categorical) opinion is largely moot. But the general policy of Reflection, and the attitude it enjoins to the beliefs of our future selves, is warranted, and hence, I argue, Foley's priority thesis, as applied to future beliefs, is not. However, just as Foley takes the priority thesis to be mitigated by the special-reasons thesis, so too, as we have seen, Reflection is subject to something like the converse of the special-reasons thesis. The special-reasons thesis tells me, in the current context, that there may

---

[26] One might wonder whether the *prima facie* credibility of past beliefs can ever lead to their adoption. But it clearly can. Foley has in mind cases in which I discover that I believed *p* some time ago and now do not believe either *p* or *not-p*. Hence, there is no present belief to take priority over the past one.

be special reasons that should lead me to privilege my future beliefs over my present ones. I have allowed that there may be special reasons why my future beliefs should not be privileged over my present ones. Such special reasons include, for example, learning that the future beliefs in question will be acquired as a result of hypnosis or drunkenness.

As a consequence of this disagreement over the applicability of the priority thesis to one's own future beliefs, a second, and more general, point of disagreement emerges between Foley's position and the views I espouse here. To understand this crucial difference, we should turn to the question of what our attitude should be to our own past beliefs. In this case, like Foley, I do accept the priority thesis. Where current opinion conflicts with past opinion, we should give priority to our current opinion (although, as always, there may be special reasons for why one should not in particular cases). In supporting this position, however, Foley faces a dilemma. He seeks to support it by an argument that is not dissimilar in spirit to the argument I have been urging for Reflection. Here is what he says, of a case in which I now believe the opposite of something I believed five years ago:

> according to the credibility thesis, I have a prima facie reason to trust not just what I believed five years ago but also what I have believed in the interim . . . Indeed, what I am most pressured to trust, on threat of inconsistency, is not my opinions at any given moment in the past but rather *the overall drift of these opinions, the drift that eventually led to my current opinions.* (Foley 2001: 144; emphasis added)

Appeal to this argument, though, threatens to undermine the priority thesis with respect to my future beliefs, since, if I am most of all to trust the drift of my opinions, it is that drift that brings me to my future opinions. Unless there is some special reason to think the course of this drift is seriously impeded, I ought, as I have argued, to defer to my future opinions rather than my present ones. So, if Foley wants to justify the priority thesis with respect to our past beliefs on the basis of the arguments just given, he ought to give it up with respect to future beliefs. Conversely, if we are to continue to hold the priority thesis with respect to future beliefs, we need a different reason (one that is not forthcoming) to hold it with respect to past beliefs.

What this shows is that the kinds of arguments presented in this chapter, and hinted at by Foley's remarks about trusting the overall drift of our opinions, support an asymmetry in the attitudes we should have to our past and future beliefs. Foley is attempting to articulate a view in which there is no such asymmetry. But this comes to grief over the recognition of the generally salutary effects of time on our beliefs. The fact that believers, and hence persons, exist in time is of crucial importance. Any view that seeks to treat future and past beliefs symmetrically will miss a key aspect of the epistemic shape of a person's life.

The difference between what our attitudes should be to our past beliefs and to our future beliefs mirrors a difference in our attitudes to the beliefs of others between others who are experts and others who are not. We should treat our past selves as if they were generic others and our future selves as if they were experts. Foley's application of the credibility thesis to the beliefs of others generally obscures this distinction. Of course, he can always appeal to the special-reasons thesis to justify treating some others as experts. If I know you are an expert about something, that is a special reason for me not to give priority to my own opinions about that topic where they differ from yours, but rather to cede to your expert opinion. So, unlike the case of what our attitude should be to our future beliefs, there need be no substantive disagreement between Foley and me in this case. But it is, I think, illuminating to see that the asymmetry in our attitudes to our past and future beliefs is itself mirrored in a distinction we make among other people between those whose beliefs will not take priority over my own (even if they have, as the credibility thesis holds, some *prima facie* authority) and those whose beliefs are treated by us as authoritative. The temporal structure of a person's epistemic life casts a synchronic shadow, as it were, over the social field.[27]

---

[27] See Evnine (2003, 2005) for further exploration of this theme.

6

Oneself as Another

It's as though a man flies over his own head on the wings of reason, or some such thing. You join the universe and forget your worries.

(Bernard Malamud, *The Fixer*, 1966)

In the previous chapter, we examined something of the attitudes a person should have to her future beliefs and her past beliefs. But how do these attitudes compare to the attitude one should have to one's current beliefs? This turns out to be a complex issue. In this chapter, I shall argue that a person's current beliefs can be viewed by her in two different ways. They can be a transparent lens through which she sees the world, or they can appear to her like any other worldly phenomenon. When a person's own beliefs appear to her as worldly phenomena, they are of a piece with her own past and future beliefs and the beliefs of others. They are, as it were, the beliefs of no one in particular. The possibility of these two ways of seeing one's own beliefs sets the stage for certain kinds of conflict or tension. On the one hand, when one thinks of one's beliefs as the beliefs of no one in particular, one can apply to them certain canons of rationality that may lead to a variety of what are broadly speaking skeptical attitudes to those beliefs. On the other hand, essential features of being a person are tied to the ways in which one's beliefs can be transparent to their owners. Roughly, transparent beliefs constitute an epistemic perspective that is determinative of who, or what kind of a person, one is. When we think of our beliefs in this way, the kinds of attitudes that we might be rationally led to when we think of our beliefs as worldly phenomena are threatening to our identities and our very status as believing subjects. This chapter, therefore, deals with what one might think of as the epistemic dark side of personhood. Being a person means that there are ways in which one's beliefs cannot be completely susceptible to principles of rationality that apply to them when they are seen, not as *our* beliefs, but simply as the beliefs of some person or other. I shall end the chapter by locating its conclusions in a tradition of philosophical theorizing that goes back at least to Kant, a tradition to which I give the name aspectual dualism.

Before we embark on the business of this chapter, it will be well to recall a few of the features that I argued in Chapter 1 are necessary conditions of personhood. First, persons are necessarily located in space and time. Hence, they all have pasts, presents, and futures. Since it is also a necessary condition that persons have beliefs, it follows that they necessarily have past, present, and future beliefs. Anything that is necessarily true of any creature that has beliefs will, *ipso facto*, be necessarily true of persons. Finally, because of Second-Ordinality, it follows that persons necessarily are able to have attitudes to their beliefs. Hence, the discussion of what those attitudes should be is highly relevant to the discussion of the epistemic dimensions of personhood.

6.1 EPISTEMIC IMPARTIALITY

Careful readers may have noticed that my gloss of Bas van Fraassen's principle of Reflection in the previous chapter deviated in a small, but significant, way from van Fraassen's own. There, I said that the t' in the formula

$$P_{a,t}(Q|P_{a,t'}(Q) = r) = r$$

refers to a time *later* than t. The principle encapsulated a certain attitude I argued we should have to our future beliefs. According to van Fraassen, however, the principle holds when t' is *later than or equal to t*. In other words, it includes, as a limit case, a recommended attitude to one's current beliefs. Let us call this case, following van Fraassen, Synchronic Reflection:

Synchronic Reflection $P_{a,t}(Q|P_{a,t}(Q) = r) = r$

and continue to treat t' as later than t, yielding the principle of Chapter 5, to which we now give van Fraassen's official name Diachronic Reflection:

Diachronic Reflection $P_{a,t}(Q|P_{a,t'}(Q) = r) = r$.

Synchronic Reflection is a strange principle. It is not clear what, exactly, would be involved in a violation of it—what state of mind that would represent. Hence, it is equally unclear what is involved in putting it forward as a rational requirement on belief. If the interpretation of the conditional probability in Reflection is given in terms of learning and other temporal processes, it is not even obvious that Synchronic Reflection makes sense. If, that is, conditional probability is taken so as to yield the following as an interpretation of the principle—one believes Q to degree r at t *on coming to learn that* one believes Q to degree r at t'—the synchronicity of the two temporal indices seems to require that the learning take no time at all. But then it is obscure what is meant by learning. I am not sure whether this is a genuine problem or not. In any case, I have taken Reflection to be a principle about expertise. In line with that, one way to interpret Synchronic Reflection is as a requirement to take one's current self as an expert. Taking someone as an expert in general means adopting her beliefs if one learns what they are (and learns nothing else that leads one to question the expert's expertise). Although one might, in this sense, take someone as an expert without actually thinking of her as an expert (one might, for example, simply adopt her beliefs unthinkingly upon learning of them), typically one will take someone as an expert because one believes she is an expert. In that case, one will see the fact that she believes p as itself a reason or justification for believing p. So, if Synchronic Reflection is interpreted in terms of taking one's current self as an expert, in the case in which that is because one thinks one is an expert, it would imply that one takes the fact that one believes something as a justification for believing it or (to be more precise) for continuing to believe it. Whether or not this is a valid interpretation of Synchronic Reflection, this is certainly an important issue in epistemology. The view that the fact that one believes something is part of a justification for continuing to believe it is known as epistemological conservatism.[1]

My defense of the rationality of Diachronic Reflection in Chapter 5 was that one's future beliefs, in general (and with suitable qualifications), will be better than one's current beliefs. Given that our current beliefs are already what we *believe*, the fact that future beliefs will be better should lead us to prefer them to our current ones. But no such epistemic virtue can be found in our current beliefs themselves. Ameliorism may

---

[1] Discussions of conservatism include Sklar (1975), Foley (1982), Adler (1990), and Christensen (1994). Nothing actually hangs on whether conservatism is seen as an interpretation of Synchronic Reflection other than a certain neatness in bringing together the issues discussed in this chapter and those discussed in the previous chapter.

imply that our current beliefs are, necessarily, better in general (and with suitable qualifications) than our earlier beliefs. But, although this fact gives us reason to prefer them to our past beliefs, it does not give us any reason in itself to accept them. There is, therefore, no epistemic reason for satisfying Synchronic Reflection, as there is for Diachronic Reflection. Does that mean, then, that we ought not, at least without special reasons, take our current selves as experts? This is the view of David Christensen.

Christensen advances what he calls the Principle of Epistemic Impartiality (PEI):

> The considerations determining which beliefs it would be epistemically rational for an agent to adopt do not give special status to any of the agent's present opinions on the basis of their belonging to the agent. (2000: 363–4)

According to Christensen, our beliefs ought always to be governed by the best evidence we have, and the fact that we currently have, or that some particular person has, a certain belief is, *in itself,* no evidence for its truth, and hence does not affect what it is epistemically rational for us to believe. Although he does not say so explicitly, Christensen surely advocates a broader position of which PEI is a special case. Indeed, I assume that the plausibility of PEI is supposed to stem from its being an instance of this broader view. The broader position can be stated as follows:

> The considerations determining which beliefs it would be epistemically rational for an agent to adopt do not give special status to anyone's opinions merely on the basis of their belonging to that particular person.

Thus, PEI ultimately stems from an assimilation of one's own beliefs to the beliefs of persons in general.

It is important to see that epistemic impartiality does not commit one to denying that the fact that *someone* has a given belief may be evidence in favor of its truth. If only one person believes something, that is likely to be, at best, pretty weak evidence for it. But the old saying '60 million Frenchmen can't be wrong' could, with some plausibility, be amended to '60 million people are unlikely to be wrong—at least about certain kinds of things'. Hence, that people hold a given belief could, arguably, be seen as evidence in its favor. What epistemic impartiality does commit one to denying is that, without any special further reason, the fact that the belief is held by this or that particular person or persons (including oneself) is evidence in its favor. (An expert, of course, is someone for whom there are special reasons to take the mere fact that she believes something as evidence in its favor.) A comparison with Utilitarianism may help to clarify this distinction. According to that theory, that an action leads to an increase in happiness in someone is relevant to the morality of that action. But that the happiness accrue to some particular individual, without further considerations being in play, is morally irrelevant to the action.

Christensen's Principle of Epistemic Impartiality underlies his attack on a variety of interlinked positions in epistemology. He uses it to criticize coherence-based defenses of Diachronic Reflection, since these suggest that it is epistemically rational to treat one's future beliefs as expert merely because they *are* one's future beliefs, without regard to whether or not they are more likely to be true than one's current beliefs. (As we have seen, though, Diachronic Reflection can be defended on grounds other than coherence. These grounds do not involve giving any special weight to my future beliefs just because they are mine. Rather, they are given weight because they are, with all the qualifications we have noted, more likely to be true than my current beliefs.[2]) Another target that is aimed at by PEI is epistemological conservatism, which I associated above with Synchronic Reflection. Conservatism comes in a variety of guises, but the basic point is that the practice of conserving one's beliefs—that is, of continuing to believe what one believes—is epistemically recommended. The element of the conservative position that Christensen finds most objectionable, and that is clearly inconsistent with PEI, is that one's believing something already provides an epistemic justification for continuing to believe it. Christensen agrees that we might sometimes have reason to take ourselves as expert, in the sense that the fact we have a certain belief might be seen as evidence for the truth of the belief (and hence as justification for continuing to believe it), just in the way that the fact that a certain belief about physics is held by a prominent physicist may be evidence for its truth. Indeed, Christensen thinks that, at least in a weak sense, this is typically the case:

Typically, I have reasons to think that a given belief of mine is an accurate indicator of reality. The strength of the indication varies markedly, of course,

---

[2] In fact, Christensen himself seems to endorse something like the defense of Reflection given in the previous chapter. He writes: 'part of my confidence in my own cognitive abilities involves a belief in my own *general* tendency toward cognitive improvement . . . I suspect that my general trust in my own belief-acquisition processes would give me reason not only to take my future belief into account, but actually to *favor* my future belief over my present one' (2000: 367; emphasis in the original).

from belief to belief, depending at least in part on my background beliefs about the likely genesis of the belief in question . . . But in every case, any epistemic weight I attach to the fact that I have certain beliefs derives entirely from independent reasons for thinking that belief to be accurate. (1994: 75)

Typical or not, Christensen clearly thinks that it is an empirical and contingent matter to what extent one takes one's current self to be an expert. Assessments of one's current expertise are, he says, in principle no different from such assessments as 'in general, believe what you read in the *Times*' (1994: 76). It is, of course, empirical and contingent to what extent *The Times* is reliable and hence the extent to which the fact that something is asserted in *The Times* is a justification for believing it.

We can consider a few illustrations of PEI at work. The first two of these are explicitly discussed by Christensen, the third is strongly suggested by things he writes. A case he himself uses in connection with his argument for PEI is the following. (I shall refer to this case as the Belief Downloader case.) Suppose I encounter someone whom I take to be no better and no worse informed than I am on some subject matter. I have no special reason to take either her or myself to be more expert than the other on this subject matter. If I had a 'Belief Downloader' that could search our respective minds and, where we differed, could change my beliefs to conform to the other person's, Christensen (2000: 359–60) maintains that it should be a matter of epistemic indifference to me whether I activated this machine or not. This indifference is recommended by PEI. It manifests my not according any special epistemic status to my actual current beliefs in determining what I should believe. Note the example is not one in which I know what the beliefs are over which we differ. In at least one example of the latter kind of case, in which neither of us can actually cite any evidence for our conflicting beliefs, Christensen (1994: 76) thinks the rational thing to do is to suspend belief.[3]

Another case illustrating PEI is provided by the Preface Paradox. It is a presupposition of Christensen's, and of many others', treatment of

---

[3] It is interesting to note that, in one sense, the recommendation to suspend belief is equivalent to the recommendation of indifference in the actual Downloader case. If one adopts the language of partial belief and probability (and if one identifies belief with probability one), suspending belief over p means according a probability of 0.5 to p and 0.5 to *not-p*. Being indifferent over activating the Belief Downloader is according a 0.5 chance to giving p a probability of one and a 0.5 chance to giving it a probability of zero. The expected epistemic utility in both cases is the same. But, of course, the two cases, for all that, involve quite different epistemic outcomes.

the paradox that what he calls the Modest Preface Proposition, 'some of the beliefs expressed in the body of this book are false', is rational. Why is it rational? The reason generally accepted, though advanced in a number of different forms, is that it is rational, on the basis of experience, to accept that one's past books (or one's past beliefs) have contained errors and so have those of other people. Not to accept the equivalent proposition about one's current book (or one's current beliefs) would amount to giving the beliefs expressed in it some special epistemic status merely because they are one's current beliefs. It would involve treating like cases differently. This justification for the Modest Preface Proposition can be found, for example, in David Makinson's original formulation of the Preface Paradox:

If [an author] has already written other books, and received corrections from readers and reviewers, he may also believe that not everything he has written in his latest book is true. His approach is eminently rational; he has learnt from experience. The discovery of errors among statements which previously he believed to be true gives him good ground for believing that there are undetected errors in his latest book. (1965: 205)

Christensen himself takes belief in the Modest Preface Proposition to be justified along similar lines:

Given the comparisons our author willingly makes between his work and that of Professors Y and Z, it is simply not rational for him to believe their books to contain errors, but not to believe the same about his own book. (2004: 41)[4]

As a third and final example of PEI at work, consider Christensen's view, quoted above, that

typically, I have reasons to think that a given belief of mine is an accurate indicator of reality. The strength of the indication varies markedly, of course, from belief to belief, depending at least in part on my background beliefs about the likely genesis of the belief in question. (1994: 75)

Given this, it ought also to be possible for there to be cases in which the strength of the indication that a belief of mine is an accurate indicator of reality is negative. This is certainly possible with other people, and with my past and future selves. All these can be taken as 'counter-indicators',

---

[4] The comparisons 'our author' willingly makes, in Christensen's example, amount to an admission that Y and Z are more careful than he is, and therefore less likely to make errors in their books. But it is clear from the context that Christensen would hold our author to be equally irrational if the willingly made comparison were simply that Y and Z were not less careful than he was.

in the sense that their beliefs on a given subject matter might be indications that reality is what would be accurately represented by the negations of those beliefs. There are artificial cases of this. If someone is fitted with glasses that invert her visual field, and she does not know this but we do, then, if she believes that a given object is to her left, that will be evidence to us that the object is to her right (and hence not to her left). But there are also much less artificial cases. Some people, for example, are pretty reliably wrong about directions. If they say 'go this way', that is a good reason not to go that way. Some people are reliably wrong about whether a person will make a good romantic partner for them. It can be inferred of anyone they choose that she/he will make a bad partner. A final, real-life example of this phenomenon is when people are known to be optimists or pessimists. Description of this last kind of case are easier in a context of partial belief. If someone who is generally reliable but known to be an optimist tells you confidently that the weather will be fine, that may be a reason to believe the weather will be fine, but with less confidence than the optimist.

Since this attitude is quite possible towards other people, and since Christensen emphasizes that the degree to which we take our current beliefs to be reliable is an empirical matter, and since the point of PEI is to have us assimilate our treatment of our own beliefs to the treatment of the beliefs of others, it ought to be the case that one could, in theory, see oneself as a counter-indicator in the same way as I have just described we may see others. And, indeed, something like this does go on to some extent. People do (or can) know of themselves that they are optimists or pessimists. They can know that they always tend to misjudge romantic partners or get directions wrong. Such a person will therefore take her own belief that *p* as a reason for believing *not-p*; or her own very confident belief that *p* as a reason for a somewhat less confident belief that *p*.[5]

Here, then, we have a number of cases in which adherence to PEI seems at least somewhat plausible. And yet, I think, all three cases are

[5] There are a host of more bizarre examples, as well, often discussed under the rubric of belief instability. Arthur Collins (1979), for example, discusses a case in which the belief 'believing that I am in brain state B' is known to be correlated with being in brain state C ($\neq$ B). My belief that I am in brain state B would thus be evidence that would justify my believing that I am not in brain state B. (Collins deduces from the paradoxical nature of this example that beliefs cannot be identified with brain states.) See, for some other discussions, Tyler Burge (1984), Frederick Kroon (1993), and Byeong D. Lee (1998). A good treatment of the parallels between belief instability and an analogous problem of decision instability is provided by Roy Sorensen (1988: ch. 11).

actually rather strange. While it is easy to see the appeal of the impartial standards of rationality that would have us respond in these cases as PEI dictates, and while following these dictates does not seem impossible, there is, I suggest, something in all these cases that should make us wonder about just how far we can really take adherence to PEI. In order to see why, we need to take a step back and look at some deep features of belief itself.

6.2 BELIEFS, TRANSPARENT AND VISIBLE

Beliefs are states of mind, but they are states that naturally tend to efface their own presence and in which facts generally concerning the world beyond the believer's mind are made apparent. In this sense, I would argue, they are like optical instruments through which we look in order to apprehend the world. Like such optical instruments, we look *through* them, and not *at* them. Other people's beliefs, of course, and one's own past and future beliefs, are not transparent, in this sense. They are merely worldly phenomena that themselves become accessible to us through our current beliefs about them. One might say that a person's current beliefs do not generally appear to her as part of the world she lives in. Rather, they are like a mental eye with which she looks at the world.

At the same time, however, our current beliefs are the same kind of thing as our own future and past beliefs and the beliefs of other people. They are thus also worldly phenomena that can be looked *at* and not just *through*. All that is required for that is for us to have beliefs about our current beliefs. By having a belief about my belief that *p*, my belief that *p* becomes visible to me in exactly this sense: it now appears as the object of one of my beliefs (namely, my belief that I believe that *p*).[6] Since my beliefs are what make the world visible to me in the first place, the case in which I have a belief about a belief of mine is one in which that belief becomes visible. Our attitudes to them may resemble our attitudes to other worldly phenomena, and, in particular, to worldly phenomena of the same kind—that is, beliefs of others, or of our past or future selves.

It is sometimes suggested that our own beliefs are incapable of becoming visible to us. In particular, this line of thought is often

---

[6] The term 'visible', in its literal contexts, is used to mean both 'capable of being seen' and 'seen'. I preserve this ambiguity in the metaphorical use I make of the term here.

credited to Wittgenstein, who indeed made remarks that are strongly suggestive of this view. In the *Tractatus Logico-Philosophicus* he writes, in a very famous passage:

> If I wrote a book called *The World as I found it*, I should have to include a report on my body, and should have to say which parts were subordinate to my will, and which were not, etc., this being a method of isolating the subject, or rather of showing that in an important sense there is no subject; for it alone could *not* be mentioned in that book.
>
> You will say that this is exactly like the case of the eye and the visual field. But really you do *not* see the eye. (2001: 5.631, 5.633)

Wittgenstein is here discussing the subject, the self, and not simply the subject's beliefs. But a passage in the *Philosophical Investigations* that makes a similar point shows just how closely Wittgenstein was prepared to treat the subject and her beliefs: 'I say of someone else "He seems to believe...." and other people say it of me. Now, why do I never say it of myself, not even when others *rightly* say it of me?—Do I myself not see and hear myself, then?—That can be said' (1958: 191). Whether or not this is Wittgenstein's considered view on the matter, it is, I believe, not correct to say that our current beliefs *cannot* become visible to us.[7] They can—as I indicated above, all that is required is that we have second-order beliefs about them. But Wittgenstein is right to see something problematic here.

The phenomenon of the transparency of belief has been an object of philosophical theorizing for some time.[8] What exactly is it for a belief to be transparent to its bearer? One preliminary point that needs to be emphasized is this. As I am using the terms, 'transparency' and 'visibility' are not opposites. I have not yet said very much about transparency, but all that is required for a belief to be visible is that I have a second-order belief that I have that belief. Nothing in what I say about transparency will conflict with the existence of such a second-order belief. Indeed, it is likely that most of our beliefs are both transparent and visible to us. I shall reserve the terms 'non-transparent' and 'invisible' for the contradictories of 'transparent' and 'visible'. As will emerge, beliefs can be transparent and invisible or visible and non-transparent. A second preliminary point is that transparency (or visibility) is not a simple

---

[7] See Moran (2001: 69–77) for an interpretation of Wittgenstein that avoids attributing this view to him.

[8] A good, recent discussion, with references to other literature, is Moran (2001). Another important contributor to the debate is Sydney Shoemaker. See, e.g., his (1988).

property of beliefs, but rather a relation between beliefs and a person. Your beliefs, typically, will be transparent to you but not to me. Many of your beliefs, if I am acquainted with you, will be visible to me, and very likely visible to you too. It is, however, probably a conceptual truth that no belief can be transparent to anyone but its bearer.

What, then, is the difference between a belief's being transparent to its bearer and its lacking that relation (its being non-transparent) to the same person? It is tempting, and I think on the right lines, to identify this distinction with the distinction between a person's conscious and unconscious beliefs. (I use these terms in a not distinctively Freudian sense.) For a belief to be conscious is for it to be transparent to its bearer; for it to be unconscious is for it to be non-transparent to her. But, of course, the distinction between consciousness and unconsciousness is itself contested and difficult to make out. One feature that has figured prominently in discussion of transparency is self-knowledge. When beliefs are transparent to us, we can know what our beliefs are, not by looking in at the mind (in whatever metaphorical sense that might be meant), but by looking out at the world. This, indeed, was how the terminology of transparency was originally introduced in this context by Roy Edgley:

My own present thinking, in contrast to the thinking of others, is transparent in the sense that I cannot distinguish the question 'Do I think that P?' from a question in which there is no essential reference to myself or my belief, namely 'Is it the case that P?' This does not of course mean that the correct answers to these two questions must be the same; only I cannot distinguish them, for in giving my answer to the question 'Do I think that P?' I also give my answer, more or less tentative, to the question 'Is it the case that P?' (1969: 90)

In the case of beliefs that are non-transparent to me, other people's and possibly sometimes my own, I must distinguish these two questions. The questions of whether so-and-so believes that *p*, and whether *p* is true, are readily separable. Knowledge of a belief that is not transparent to me will be by inference from behavioral evidence. In the case of others, the inference may be based on their assertions expressing the propositions believed.[9] But, in most cases (certainly in almost all cases

---

[9] Burge (1993) argues that we have *a priori*, non-inferential knowledge of the meanings of others' assertions on the basis of our seeming understanding of their speech. His approach to the transparency of a person's beliefs to herself emphasizes their sensitivity to practical reasoning in a way that is not that dissimilar from Richard Moran's views, discussed below. Taking account of Burge's position would complicate my presentation of the issues I am interested in but not, I think, seriously undermine it.

concerning oneself), the evidence is likely to be more indirect. Typically we infer the existence of beliefs from behavior that would be rational only if such beliefs were present. Distinguishing the two questions 'does S believe that *p*?' and 'is *p* true?' means at least the possibility of actually giving them different answers. In my own case, that means that I might judge that I do believe that *p* on the basis of behavioral evidence ('I must believe *p* or I would not have done such-and-such') and yet judge that *not-p* (that is, have a transparent belief that *not-p*). Someone who is in a position to assert both of these is in a position to assert a Moore-paradoxical proposition of the form 'I believe that *p* but *not-p*'. It is non-paradoxical in these circumstances precisely because the belief reported on is non-transparent to the believer. Sydney Shoemaker (1988: 34–5) discusses the complementary case in which a person asserts *p* because she believes *p* but, owing to the condition of what Shoemaker calls self-blindness, an inability to know what one's beliefs are, may also assert that she does not believe *p*. (In my language, her belief that *p* is transparent but invisible to her.) This person would be able to assert the other kind of Moore-paradoxical sentence '*p* but I don't believe that *p*'.[10]

The idea that beliefs are transparent to someone owing to the way that person can have knowledge of them is given a distinctive spin by Richard Moran (2001). Transparency is explained in terms of a belief's connection to practical reason. When a belief is transparent to me, it may guide me in determining what I should do. (This, in turn, might prove a good way of getting at what it is for a belief to be conscious.)

[10] The views I express here, if they are correct, tell against two approaches to Moore's Paradox. First, they tell against the idea that Moore's Paradox depends on the proposition expressed (*that* not-p *and I believe that* p). Jonathan Adler (2002: 193 ff.), for example, holds that a Moore-paradoxical proposition is incoherent. On the basis of the cases I discuss, Adler is, implausibly, committed to denying the possibility that a person's beliefs can be either invisible or non-transparent to her. All beliefs would have to be both transparent and visible to their bearers to make what is expressed by a Moore-paradoxical utterance anything like incoherent. In fact, Shoemaker himself gives his example as part of an argument that self-blindness (i.e. invisibility of belief) *is* impossible. I agree that it is as a general condition (and my requirement that persons satisfy Second-Ordinality may rule out its generally being true for persons by definition), but I do not see why it should be impossible in isolated cases. And I certainly think non-transparency is possible, though, again, not as a general condition for persons.

The second approach to Moore's Paradox that my remarks would suggest is misguided is one that sees it as depending on the nature of assertion (see, e.g., Max Black 1952). For a claim such as '*not-p* but I believe that *p*,' under the circumstances suggested in the text, can certainly be asserted. Assertion is, one might say, indifferent to the epistemic status of the beliefs expressed or reported on.

Furthermore, in these cases I arrive at knowledge of what I believe, not by inspecting my mind, but by turning it outwards and determining what I should believe. The theoretical question 'what *do* I believe?' gives way to the practical question 'what *should* I believe?' If, by contrast, a belief of mine is not transparent to me, it must play no role in my practical reasoning (if it did, it would be transparent). That does not mean, though, that it plays no role in affecting my behavior. If I can have knowledge of it, that knowledge will come through inference from my behavior. (If I cannot have knowledge of it because it does not affect my behavior, one might wonder whether it qualifies as a belief at all.) Hence the non-transparent belief must affect my actions without playing a role in my deliberations over what to do. (And this seems just what we would expect of an unconscious belief.)

The connection with practical reasoning that Moran brings out is useful in understanding another feature of transparency. Those of one's beliefs that are transparent form a kind of epistemic perspective occupied by the person whose beliefs they are. Since they are the things one takes into account in deliberation, they shape the actions, plans, and projects that constitute one's life. They also constitute an epistemic perspective in the sense that the totality of one's transparent beliefs are that through which the world is accessible to a person. Thus, in a sense that is at once literal, since these beliefs will include many about one's position and surroundings, and metaphorical, these transparent beliefs locate one in the world. They make that world accessible to one and shape the ways in which one intervenes in it. Ultimately, then, they determine what kind of a person one is; or, to use a phrase that has many meanings in one of its prominent roles, they determine one's identity, who one is.[11]

I have discussed the notion of a belief's transparency and looked at what it is for a belief to lack that transparency. Above, however, I suggested that what is required for a belief to be visible to one is merely that one have a second-order belief about it. This means, as I explained, that visibility is not the contradictory of transparency; non-transparency is not synonymous with visibility. Beliefs may be both transparent and visible to the same person at the same time. A belief will be transparent insofar as it is conscious or I can have knowledge of it by considering what I ought to believe or it has an immediate significance to my practical reasoning. It will be visible just in case I believe that I have

---

[11] For a discussion of this notion of identity, see Oliver Black (2002).

that belief.[12] Although, where a visible belief is also transparent to me, it will not be true that I am confined to inferential knowledge of it, it will nonetheless be true that a beginning of an assimilation of my belief to the beliefs of persons in general has begun. In having a second-order belief about it, I will have a belief that relates to it in many of the same ways that my second-order beliefs about my past or future beliefs, or the beliefs of others, relate to their objects. This assimilation becomes even closer when one considers that my beliefs can be visible to me not only in particular but also in general. That is, I can have second-order beliefs that generalize over my first-order beliefs, as when I believe that some of my beliefs are irrational, or some are based on sensory perception. In most cases, there is no problem here, and no conflict between the belief as transparent, and hence as essentially mine, and the belief as visible and thus like the belief of no one in particular. The stage, however, is set for the possibility of such conflicts. The essential elements of the conflict arise from the combination of the notion of transparency of belief and the requirement on persons of Second-Ordinality. In what follows, I shall attempt to argue that, in the cases we examined above of the applicability of PEI, such a conflict is lurking.

One example of the kind of conflict I have in mind, already alluded to, is provided by Moore's Paradox. One of the ways in which we can unproblematically assess the beliefs of others, or our own past or future beliefs, is by judging them to be false. When a current belief of mine is visible to me, this attitude becomes a theoretical possibility. If I express my belief that I believe that p by saying 'I believe that p', but want also to express my judgment that that belief is false, I will end up with the Moore-paradoxical proposition 'I believe that p but p is false' (or 'I believe that p but *not-p*'). There need be nothing paradoxical or odd about this in the case in which my belief that p is not transparent to me. If I simply infer that I must believe that p from various actions of mine, but it is not transparent to me in exerting a force on my practical reasoning, then the assertion 'I believe that p but p is false' may be quite an ordinary thing to say. The problem arises in cases in which my belief that p *is* transparent to me but nonetheless visible in a way that allows the theoretical possibility that I should also judge the belief to be false.

---

[12] Indeed, it may well be the case that all transparent beliefs are visible to their owners, though I do not agree with Shoemaker's opinion (1988), already noted, that they must all be.

The conflict between the belief's transparency and its visibility (and the possible epistemic consequences thereof) is particularly dramatic in the case of Moore's Paradox. But the case does not necessarily show anything about PEI because it can be argued that, if a belief that p is transparent to a rational person, evidence that p is false will undermine the existence of her belief that p. Although one can recognize that a Moore-paradoxical proposition could be true of one, one could never be in a position rationally to accept or assert it if the belief that p were transparent to one. Thus, acceptance of PEI does not threaten any kind of conflict with the transparency of belief via Moore's Paradox. In the illustrations given above of PEI, there is less sense of oddness than one would get if it turned out that PEI led one to accept a Moore-paradoxical proposition. Nonetheless, there is, I shall argue, some oddness there.

6.3 THE LIMITS OF PEI

The way to see that there is something odd going on in the three illustrations of PEI considered above is to reflect on the fact that, in all three cases, the plausibility of the stance recommended by PEI is essentially linked to the small scale of the examples. If, however, one recasts the examples on a bigger scale, it becomes apparent that adherence to PEI would effect a serious undermining of personhood. Before I look at the cases, however, I would like to be clear about what I am trying to show here. First, I am not attempting to show, *contra* Christensen, that the deliverances of PEI in these cases are not, after all, epistemically rational. I am happy to grant that the verdicts of PEI do represent what is epistemically rational. Thus, I am not suggesting that our conception of what is (epistemically) rational should be enlarged to allow for some, broadly speaking, pragmatic component.[13] Nor do I want to argue that there is a broader conception of rationality than epistemic rationality and that, in these cases, we should follow this broader conception. There is, of course, a legitimate notion of pragmatic rationality, and, in many cases, for all I know, it is advisable to believe what is useful to us even when it is not (epistemically) rational to believe it. But that is not what is going on in the cases to be discussed. Rather, they represent ways in which epistemic rationality presents to us an ideal

---

[13] Whether this is a good idea for *other* reasons is something on which I take no stance here.

that is at odds with what it is to be a believer, and hence, since belief is a necessary condition of personhood, with what it is to be a person. That epistemic rationality is at odds with what it is to be a person does not mean that it is impossible, in these cases, for a person to believe what is epistemically rational. It is to say that personhood is in danger of being compromised by unattenuated adherence to what is epistemically rational. Looking at the examples writ large is a way of bringing out the nature of the potential compromise. On the small scale of the original examples, there need be no compromising of personhood, or at least none that is detectable. Although I have not dealt at all with moral aspects of personhood, the technique pursued here might seem more familiar in that context. One might, for example, attempt to show what was wrong with deceiving others by imagining cases in which deceit was practiced on such a large scale that it genuinely compromised the kinds of interpersonal relations that we think of as, in some loose sense, definitive of personhood. This does not mean that anyone who practices any small deceit is a monster in danger of losing her personhood. With these general remarks, let us now proceed to look at the individual cases we have described.

6.3.1 The Belief Downloader case

In the Belief Downloader case as originally presented by Christensen, we are to imagine a case in which I am with someone whose beliefs on, say, ichthyology are of the same level of expertise as my own. In that case, Christensen says, it should be a matter of epistemic indifference to me as to whether I activate the Belief Downloader that will search our respective minds and, where we differ in our ichthyological beliefs, will replace my beliefs with the beliefs of this other person. And this indifference is supposed to stem from PEI, since failure to recognize the indifference would indicate a partiality to my beliefs merely because they were mine.[14] (Remember that the case is not one in which I know which the beliefs are that will be affected.) Even on this original small scale, I have to say that I find the example somewhat strange. In one sense, of course, I can see that, given that we stipulate that this other

---

[14] In fact, his point would be the same if I preferred to activate the Downloader in this case as it would if I preferred not to activate it. In the former case I would be exhibiting partiality to the other person's beliefs merely because they were hers (or, perhaps, merely because they were not mine).

person is of the same reliability as I am, in cases in which we differ she is as likely to be right as I am. So I can see the point of saying that it should be a matter of epistemic indifference to me whether I choose to activate the Downloader or not. Yet, at the same time, such indifference seems almost pathological in the degree of alienation from one's own beliefs it recommends. It is not that I think my beliefs are more likely to be right, where they differ from the other person's, simply because they are mine. But still, they are mine—they represent how I think the world actually is. I identify with them, not epistemically, by weighing them more heavily, but simply by having them. To use the language introduced above, they form part of my epistemic perspective and thus, to some extent, are implicated in who I am. Of course, this does not preclude their being subject to change, to rational evaluation, and so on. It is, after all, even more part of who I am that I will revise my beliefs on being presented with certain kinds of evidence than that I hold some particular ichthyological belief. These kinds of changes of belief manifest my autonomy and come about precisely as a response to other beliefs of mine that also form part of my epistemic perspective. These beliefs are both about matters of fact and about the correct ways of weighing evidence, changing beliefs, and so on. But, in the Downloader case, we are contemplating allowing changes to our beliefs that do not stem from my existing epistemic perspective. To that extent, there is an element of arbitrariness to them. They do not manifest my autonomy but challenge it. At the end of the process, I will find myself with different beliefs without having arrived at them in a way that is responsive to my other factual and methodological beliefs. Even if, at second order, I recognize the new beliefs are as likely to be true as the beliefs they have replaced, they still represent something of an alien intrusion.

If this is not evident in the case as described, then imagine some variants of it. First, consider it on a much larger scale. Suppose I meet someone whom I take to be averagely reliable, as I take myself to be. And now I consider whether to activate the Downloader to replace *all* my beliefs where they differ from hers, and not just my ichthyological beliefs. I may recognize that there are some areas where this other person will be less expert than me. But, at the same time, there will be other areas where she will be more expert than me. On balance, let us suppose, she will be more expert than me in about as many cases as she will be less expert. Here too, then, it ought to be a matter of epistemic indifference to me whether I activate the Downloader. Yet the consequences of activating it could be huge. It is surely not fanciful to suppose that, in activating the Belief Downloader in a case like this, I put my very identity under threat. I may end up, on balance, with about as many true beliefs as if I do not activate it; but I will simply have wrenched myself from one epistemic point of view to another, without having traced a path through epistemic space to get there. I may, in a sense, become a different person. In a further variant, consider my confrontation with someone who is generally more expert than I am in a whole variety of areas. It is even possible that this person is more expert about my life and my friends and family than I am. In this case, PEI would not merely hold that I should be indifferent about whether to activate the Downloader, it would require that I do.[15]

Christensen will doubtless say that any reluctance I feel about activating the Downloader under these circumstances stem from non-epistemic considerations. The fact that activation of the Downloader may disrupt my epistemic perspective may, in some way, affect who I am has nothing to do with what it is epistemically rational for me to think or do in the circumstances. As I indicated above, I do not wish to challenge Christensen's verdict here. Perhaps it should be a matter of epistemic indifference to me whether I activate the Downloader, or, in the case of someone more expert, I rationally ought to activate it. My point is that, if that is true, then we have a case here where believers (and therefore persons), for whom beliefs can play this perspectival role in determining who one is, cannot look with equanimity on the demands of epistemic rationality. There is a tension here between epistemically rational indifference and the way in which our beliefs place us in the world in a way that is deeply determinative of who we are.

The advocate of PEI who aims to resist a tension with the demands of personhood will have to argue that, in a case where I confront someone more generally expert than I am, it is not epistemically rational to activate the Downloader. And likewise, when I consider someone equally expert as myself, it is not epistemically rational to be indifferent to activating the Downloader. To that end, one might argue that the problem here is not too much epistemic rationality but rather too little. If faced with someone who is more expert (or equally expert), I should not generalize about our respective beliefs but get down to brass tacks and look at particular beliefs. If I know that someone is more expert and may disagree with me about some things, the truly epistemically

---

[15] I am grateful to Christensen for suggesting to me this last twist to my problematization of PEI.

rational thing to do is to look at all my beliefs and re-evaluate their credentials. If their justification is good, I can keep them; if it is not good, I should suspend belief. The final outcome will be that I raise my assessment of my own level of expertise to the point at which I can say that, if the other person differs from me about something, so much the worse for her. (Of course, nothing prevents me from allowing that she may have many true beliefs on subjects on which I have no beliefs. In that case, if I were to help myself to her beliefs via the Downloader, there would presumably be none of the threats to identity that I worried about in the case in which her beliefs replace those of mine with which they disagree.[16])

The problem with this line of argument is that it seems simply to be denying that epistemic rationality can accommodate second-order generalizations about one's beliefs at all. It demands that rational assessment of one's own beliefs take the form of second-order beliefs about particular first-order beliefs. In fact, it is even more restrictive than that. Even if we reason about particular beliefs of ours, analogues of the Downloader case will arise if those particular beliefs are identified in any way that does not make their content explicit. If I think, for example, of the first belief I acquired on waking up this morning, I might, under certain circumstances, wonder whether I should activate the Downloader and swap that belief, whatever it may be, with the first belief acquired this morning by somebody cleverer than I am. It seems overly restrictive, however, to exclude reasoning about one's own beliefs in ways that do not identify their contents, or that generalize over them. (Indeed, as we shall see in the following section, Christensen, for one, thinks that rationality demands that I formulate certain generalizations about my beliefs.) As long as second-order generalizations about our beliefs are allowed as vehicles for rational self-assessment, we can begin to construct cases that will show how PEI, one element of epistemic rationality, can come into conflict with the demands of personhood. To sum up, one can avoid the potential for conflicts between reason and personhood in this manner only if one takes an overly restrictive view about the ways in which we can rationally assess our own beliefs.

---

[16] In fact, even in this kind of case, I am not so sure there are no threats to identity involved in, say, suddenly finding myself expert on quantum mechanics where before I knew nothing of it. But it is true that the threats would be considerably less than in the replacement case. I shall not argue the point, since I think this attempt to show that epistemic rationality cannot come into conflict with considerations of identity founders on other grounds.

6.3.2 The Preface Paradox

Our second example concerned the Preface Paradox. We saw that PEI recommends that the author believe that some of the beliefs expressed in the body of her book are false. More generally, it recommends fallibilism, interpreted as the view that we ought rationally to believe that some of our beliefs are actually false. PEI recommends these positions, since we take the books and the beliefs of others to contain falsities and resisting the same conclusions for our own books and beliefs would manifest a partiality to them just because they were ours, precisely the situation PEI forbids.

'Some', as in 'some of the beliefs expressed in the book' or 'some of one's beliefs', covers a multitude of sins. When an author expresses what Christensen calls the Modest Preface Proposition, we naturally take her to mean that *a few* of the beliefs expressed in the book are false. And, on this small scale, the author who embraces a Modest Preface Proposition seems nothing but eminently sane and reasonable. But how many errors can an author acknowledge in her book without, in some way, undermining her authority? Suppose she has written five previous books all of which have turned out to contain many serious errors? In each case, she worked hard to prevent errors, just as she has with her newest book, and yet they were there anyway. Perhaps the rational thing to believe now is that her current book also contains many serious errors. And yet, of course, an author who expressed that belief in her preface would probably have few readers. Such an admission, however rational, would be at odds with her role as author, as one who is genuinely asserting the propositions expressed in the book and thereby offering them to her readers as something they can rely on.[17]

As for the author and her book, so for a person and her current beliefs in general. If we are to accept fallibilism on the basis of assimilating our own current beliefs to our past beliefs and to the beliefs of others, all of which, it is alleged, are reasonably thought by a person to contain some errors, perhaps we should go further and draw the conclusion that our current beliefs are seriously and massively mistaken. One proponent of fallibilism does seem to suggest going this far, though without acknowledging the serious implications of it. Arguing for the fallibilist view, Jonathan Roorda writes: 'virtually everyone I know has some false

---

[17] I am, of course, presupposing something here about the nature of assertion, something of the kind argued for by Robert Brandom (1994).

beliefs, and I regard it as almost certain that the belief systems of most of the people alive in previous eras were wildly false with respect to nearly every question of intellectual significance. Why should I exempt myself from the obvious inductive conclusion?' (1997: 135).

Is not the obvious inductive conclusion from the evidence presented here that my current belief system is wildly false with respect to nearly every question of intellectual significance?[18] Yet, however rational such a conclusion might be, thinking that most of my beliefs are false, or that my belief system is wildly and massively in error, seems to undermine its very existence. While there appears to be nothing at odds with belief as such in holding that a few of my beliefs are false, an inconsistency of sorts does emerge when one ups the number of beliefs one takes to be false. Consider the limit case in which one believes that everything one believes is false (we can exclude this belief itself from the scope of 'everything' to avoid immediate Liar-like paradoxes). First of all, there is a danger of believing a contradiction constituted by the belief that everything one believed was false and any other of one's beliefs. (I say a danger of believing a contradiction because there is the issue of first- and second-order bridging beliefs, discussed in Section 3.2.3.) More seriously, it would be doubtful whether one actually believed anything at all. Since belief has truth as an intrinsic aim, there is a conceptual problem in supposing that a belief that is transparent to one is false. The person who, allegedly, believes that everything she believes is false reduplicates this conceptual problem at the global level. It would follow for her that every belief she had would be one she believed was false. This seems downright incoherent. As we move away from the limit case, the bizarre consequences of the inductive conclusion based on a grim assessment of others' beliefs diminish. But it seems that our general view of the beliefs of others *could* be bad enough to make the obvious inductive conclusion in our own case one that seriously threatens to undermine the very beliefs it is supposed to be about.[19]

---

[18] Even if we take the evidential situation to be better than Roorda presents it as being, still, strict adherence to PEI means that, *if* the evidence were to be that bad, then, insofar as our beliefs were going to be epistemically rational, we would be obliged to admit that our own beliefs were in as parlous a state.

[19] Christensen, and in general one seeking to show that there is no conflict between epistemic rationality and the demands of personhood, might fall back at this point on the Davidsonian claim that, although it may be rational to believe that some (few) of our beliefs are false, on the basis of evidence about the existence of false beliefs in other people, it could never be rational for us to believe that most, or all, of our beliefs were false, because we could never (*contra* Roorda's claim quoted above) have evidence

6.3.3 Taking oneself as a counter-indicator

Our final case concerned the taking of oneself as a counter-indicator of the truth. The considerations here are similar to those arising from the Preface Paradox except that here we deal with cases in which epistemic rationality affects our attitude to specific beliefs of ours, rather than to our belief corpus in general. Christensen says that it is an empirical matter how much to trust the reliability of one's beliefs. I suggested that, in that case, it ought to be possible for the reliability to be negative, and therefore that one ought, rationally, to be able to take one's belief that *p* as evidence that *not-p*. And, in fact, something like this does seem to happen when people know of themselves that they are optimists or pessimists, or reliably wrong about directions, and so on, But again, as in the Preface case, there seem to be limits as to how extensive such a situation might be. There is nothing in principle that should prevent us from taking another person to be a counter-indicator on a very wide scale.[20] Yet, although we might be able to take ourselves as counter-indicators about directions or about the likelihood of good weather, one's status as a genuine believer would be undermined if one thought one were a counter-indicator on a wide scale. Indeed, the very evidence that we would have to use to reach the conclusion that we were counter-indicators on a wide scale would itself become suspect. If one took one's believing that *p* as *prima facie* sufficient evidence that *not-p* over a wide range of propositions, the difference between what it is to believe *p* and what it is to believe *not-p* would be blurred. But, if the difference between believing a proposition and believing its negation were blurred, what sense could be made of believing anything? One cannot, therefore, take oneself to be a counter-indicator on a wide scale without undermining the existence of one's beliefs altogether. The nature of belief requires that we take ourselves generally as indicators rather than counter-indicators. It cannot, therefore, be an entirely empirical matter how much to trust the reliability of one's own current beliefs, as it is an empirical matter how much to trust the reliability of other people's beliefs or one's past beliefs.

that most, or all, of other people's beliefs were false. See Evnine (1991: 138–43) for discussion of this Davidsonian argument. If this is what it takes to obviate the problem of the conflict between PEI and the demands of personhood, let it be so noted here.

[20] Unless one invokes the Davidsonian considerations just mentioned in connection with the Preface Paradox.

6.4 ASPECTUAL DUALISM

What all these three cases show, I conclude, is that belief itself—and, with belief, being something, such as a person, that essentially has beliefs—places a limit on how far a person can follow the dictates of epistemic rationality, at least insofar as they are exemplified in PEI. This should not be taken to mean that PEI should itself be rejected as part of epistemic rationality. Rather, what it shows is PEI, and the demands of epistemic rationality in general, are in principle unfeasible and inappropriate as an epistemic ideal for persons, or for believers in general. PEI requires us not to make distinctions of persons in letting our beliefs be shaped by evidence. If there are limits to how far one can follow PEI without running up against the conceptual requirements of being a person, there are limits on how far a person can see her own beliefs as the beliefs of no one in particular. Though it may be epistemically rational not to take account of whose a belief is, and in particular whether it is one's own, this is an epistemic ideal that, as a matter of conceptual necessity, cannot be fully followed by persons. Thoroughgoing rational self-assessment would have us step outside ourselves in a way that a person necessarily cannot do. Being a person is essentially something perspectival: it involves having an epistemic perspective, a set of beliefs that are transparent to their bearer and in an important sense determine the identity of that person. The requirement on persons of Second-Ordinality demands that persons be able to make their own beliefs visible to themselves. As a result, persons can assess their beliefs in abstraction from the fact that they are *their* beliefs. But epistemic perspective, transparency, and identity, on the one hand, and visibility, Second-Ordinality, and rational self-assessment, on the other, are always in potential conflict. Since both terms of this conflict are necessary to being a person, persons are necessarily subject to this conflict. The conflict itself is an inescapable part of personal life.

What we are seeing here is a manifestation of what I call aspectual dualism, a philosophical tradition championed by, among others, Kant, Sartre, Strawson, Thomas Nagel, and, most recently, Richard Moran. What is characteristic of these various forms of aspectual dualism is that persons are seen both as the origin or source of something, and as something that occupies a place within that of which they are at the same time the origin. The sense in which persons are originators may vary across different forms of this dualism. In Kant, for example, they are originators in two senses. First, the empirical world is (at least in part) a product of the rational mind. Secondly, the rational mind is the uncaused cause of a person's actions. Yet, for Kant, the mind that originates the world is itself a part of that world and can itself be affected by the very actions of which it is the uncaused cause. Thomas Nagel, of course, has explored this kind of dualism in a vast number of forms.[21] One of the best known (1974) is that in which the brain, through consciousness, is the origin of appearance and at the same time an object that appears. In the kinds of cases I have been discussing in this chapter, the sense of origination is something different again. It is by having beliefs that the mind stands as an origin of the world. This origination is a feature of beliefs insofar as they are transparent to their bearers. In this mode, beliefs have the function of presenting a world to the person whose beliefs they are. They also constitute an epistemic perspective for their bearers that partially determines who they are. Other things that we encounter come to us largely, perhaps even exclusively, through our beliefs.[22] We encounter these other things by having beliefs about them, and our beliefs shape the way in which we access, weigh, and consider evidence about the world in general. As we have seen, those very beliefs can themselves be presented to us through our beliefs, our second-order beliefs about our first-order beliefs.

In all forms of aspectual dualism there is a sense of conflict that arises from the fact that persons are at once the origin of something and an element within that of which they are the origin. I have said that this potential for conflict is a necessary feature of personhood. Indeed, one might say that aspectual dualism is the conceptualization of a tension or sense of paradox that necessarily pervades the lived experience of persons. Yet the degree to which such tension or sense of paradox is felt can vary. Although Second-Ordinality is a requirement of being a person, some persons are more self-reflective, more aware that the very means by which they access the world are themselves shaped by that world, than others. Aspectual dualism, in one or another form, is more likely to be propounded by those who

---

[21] See Nagel (1970, 1974, 1979*a*, 1986).

[22] I say 'perhaps even exclusively' because even things that impinge on us directly through sensation may appear to us as 'other' only if conceptualized through belief. But this is a huge topic, which goes far beyond the point I am making here.

feel this tension or sense of paradox strongly; and it is likely to be looked at askance by those whose experience does not involve this kind of tension as much. I conjecture that one's sensitivity to this kind of tension is less a product of philosophical argument than of temperament. But philosophical argument is the tool that philosophers have, and I have attempted to provide arguments here to show that, alongside the more well-known cases of morality and consciousness, in epistemology too, there is a tension between a person's originating a world through her beliefs and her, and her beliefs', occupying a place within that world.

Conclusion

Persons, I have claimed, are finite beings that have beliefs, including second-order beliefs about their own and others' beliefs, and engage in intentional actions, not only immediately but in the form of long-term plans. I have treated these characteristics as (partially) definitive of personhood and I claim that this conception of persons is one that, almost certainly, all persons have. Whether or not all persons have it, all *human* persons do, and it functions within the context of a whole network of ethical, cultural, political, and legal institutions and practices that constitute the social sphere. If, however, one thinks that I am wrong that these characteristics (partially) define a concept that makes no essential reference to a real kind such as *human being*, and one thinks instead that persons just are, say, human beings, one should at least agree that the characteristics I have listed are key elements of the natural history of normally developed humans.

On the basis of this conception, I have argued for a number of conclusions about the epistemic nature of persons. First, persons necessarily possess certain core logical concepts (conjunction, conditionality, disjunction, negation, and quantification) and must grasp certain valid principles of inference and exclusion involving these concepts. The idea that there could be persons who have second-order beliefs and engage in intentional action yet cannot grasp these simple logical concepts or who, having grasped them, cannot infer and exclude with them in the ways I have detailed is an incoherent fantasy. Its incoherence, unfortunately, has not stood in the way of its popularity. One finds versions of the fantasy in a wide variety of contexts: philosophical, anthropological, psychiatric, and no doubt many others.[1] And, while the empirical claims of some of these fantasists have been refuted, it is important to argue, as I have done here, that such a mistake is not merely empirical but conceptual.[2]

---

[1] Philosophical proponents include Cherniak (1986) and Stich (1993); psychiatric proponents include Arieti (1955). Evnine (1989) provides critique of Arieti. Anthropological examples are harder to pin down. Lévy-Bruhl is the best-known name, but his doctrine of the prelogical mentality of primitive peoples is not a good example of the fantasy for a variety of reasons. A good discussion of the anthropological case generally can be found in Cooper (1975).

[2] Black and Overton (1990) give the empirical data on Arieti's views.

Persons, I have also argued, should and must generally believe the conjunctions of their beliefs. That they should believe them goes against a variety of philosophical positions. Many epistemologists have taken paradoxes like the Preface and the Lottery as refuting the view that it is always rational to believe the conjunctions of one's beliefs. Naturalized epistemologists oppose it on the grounds that they think it is an unrealistic demand. I have tried to address both these sources of worry. But the real issues, I think, run deeper. Conjunction gives us one way (though, of course, not the only way) of understanding what it is to have a unified mind. A mind is unified to the extent that its beliefs are closed under conjunction. Failure to believe the conjunction of some beliefs is an instance of mental partitioning, or compartmentalization, a defensive stance persons fall into when they sense the possibility of conflict in their beliefs. Thus, the requirement to believe the conjunction of one's beliefs is really a requirement to have, in the sense given, a unified mind.

Opposition to the ideal of a unified mind is apt to portray the ideal as a serious, plodding thing, oppressive and inimical to creativity, pluralism, and other desirable things. And so it might be, if it is taken to preclude such things as mixed feelings, change over time, mental states of which we are unaware, or a plurality of uncoordinated ends. But all these go way beyond the minimal understanding of unity that I have defended as an ideal for persons. When unity is seen in this minimal light, it is hard not to feel that a high degree of unity is a necessary condition for the very existence of persons.

I have also argued that there is a distinct temporal profile to the epistemic lives of persons. Roughly put, a person's beliefs get better over time. More accurately, the accumulation of experience gives an ameliorist thrust to a person's beliefs that is overlain by a variety of cross currents stemming from the details of the particular methods of belief acquisition a person has, and from the types of built-in obsolescence, as it were, of a person's cognitive hardware. Challenges to this Whiggish conception of a person's epistemic history may, as in the case of Foley (2001), come as support for a symmetry in a person's relations to her past and her future beliefs or they may, as in most epistemology, come as simple neglect of this issue altogether.

Not only do the epistemic lives of persons have characteristic temporal profiles, but persons must have knowledge of these profiles. Such knowledge is presupposed by the ability to attribute beliefs to others. The presence of this knowledge means that, were persons able to know what their future beliefs will be, it would be rational for them to adopt them straight away. Since such knowledge is usually denied to persons, in fact, they must grow into their later opinions at their own rate. Nonetheless, trusting our future selves is not only rational, but a condition of temporally extended agency. When we cannot, by and large, depend on the expertise of our future selves, those selves become as others—persons who must be coaxed, managed, cajoled, or made allowance for if they are to serve our current goals.

Finally, I have suggested that, through their beliefs, persons both constitute epistemic points of view (in the perspectival sense) and, simultaneously, may find themselves and their beliefs represented within the worlds of which they are the origins. This dual-aspect mode of existence brings in its wake the inevitable risk of certain epistemic distortions. On the one hand, insofar as reason requires us to be objective and impartial, that requirement should extend to the consideration of our current beliefs. These are, after all, just more beliefs, of the same kind as the beliefs of other persons and of ourselves in the past and future. On the other hand, things that we can obviously think about beliefs in these other categories cannot be thought, without great strangeness, about one's current beliefs. The starkest example of this is that we can judge that someone believes p but that p is false, where that someone is another or a past or future self. But we cannot think this about our current selves. There are a variety of other phenomena in which there are similar, if less dramatic, problems in thinking of our beliefs as the beliefs of no one in particular, phenomena we saw illustrated in the Belief Downloader case, the Preface Paradox, and taking oneself as a counter-indicator.

Uncomfortable as this aspectual dualism may be, it is the necessary fate of all persons. Persons are, in some sense, both inside and outside the worlds they represent to themselves. The sense of strangeness that comes with this is one of the most distinctive features of what it is to be a person, and it has been given prominence by Kant and, more recently, by Strawson, Nagel, and Moran. Its consequence is that being a person is inherently problematic. A variety of philosophical topics, ranging from skepticism to self-deception to alienation, doubtless derive their fascination from the way in which they reflect this problematic aspect of personal existence. Perhaps, then, the ultimate epistemic dimension of personhood is that persons are, necessarily, philosophers.

References

Adler, Jonathan (1990), 'Conservatism and Tacit Confirmation', *Mind*, 99: 559–70.

_____ (2002), *Beliefs' Own Ethics* (Cambridge, Mass.: MIT Press).

Arieti, Silvano (1955), *The Interpretation of Schizophrenia* (New York: Brunner).

Armstrong, David (1973), *Belief, Truth and Knowledge* (Cambridge: Cambridge University Press).

Barnes, Jonathan (1969), 'The Law of Contradiction', *Philosophical Quarterly*, 19: 302–9.

Belnap, Nuel (1962), 'Tonk, Plonk and Plink', *Analysis*, 22: 130–4.

Biro, John, and Kirk Ludwig (1994), 'Are there More than Minimal *a Priori* Limits on Irrationality?', *Australasian Journal of Philosophy*, 72: 89–102.

Black, Jeffrey, and Willis Overton (1990), 'Reasoning, Logic, and Thought Disorders: Deductive Reasoning and Developmental Psychopathology', in Willis Overton (ed.), *Reasoning, Necessity, and Logic: Developmental Perspectives* (Hillsdale, NJ: Erlbaum).

Black, Max (1952), 'Saying and Disbelieving', *Analysis*, 13: 28–31.

Black, Oliver (2002), 'What Makes Me the Person I Am', *Dialegesthai*, http://mondodomani.org/dialegesthai/ob01.htm.

BonJour, Laurence (1985), *The Structure of Empirical Knowledge* (Cambridge, Mass.: Harvard University Press).

Braine, M. D. S, B. J. Reiser, and B. Rumain (1984), 'Some Empirical Evidence for a Theory of Natural Propositional Logic', *The Psychology of Learning and Motivation: Advances in Research and Thinking*, 18: 317–71.

Brandom, Robert (1994), *Making It Explicit: Reasoning, Representing, and Discursive Commitment* (Cambridge, Mass.: Harvard University Press).

_____ (2000), *Articulating Reasons: An Introduction to Inferentialism* (Cambridge, Mass.: Harvard University Press).

Bratman, Michael (1987), *Intention, Plans and Practical Reason* (Cambridge, Mass.: Harvard University Press).

Braude, Stephen (1991), *First Person Plural: Multiple Personality and the Philosophy of Mind* (London: Routledge).

Burge, Tyler (1984), 'Epistemic Paradox', *Journal of Philosophy*, 81: 5–29.

_____ (1993), 'Content Preservation', *Philosophical Review*, 102: 457–88.

_____ (1998), 'Reason and the First Person', in Crispin Wright, Barry Smith, and Cynthia Macdonald (eds.), *Knowing our own Minds* (Oxford: Clarendon Press).

Carrol, Lewis (1895), 'What the Tortoise Said to Achilles', *Mind*, 4: 278–80.

Cherniak, Christopher (1986), *Minimal Rationality* (Cambridge, Mass.: MIT Press).

Christensen, David (1991), 'Clever Bookies and Coherent Beliefs', *Philosophical Review*, 100: 229–47.

—— (1994), 'Conservatism in Epistemology', *Nous*, 28: 69–89.

—— (2000), 'Diachronic Coherence versus Epistemic Impartiality', *Philosophical Review*, 109: 349–71.

—— (2004), *Putting Logic in its Place* (Oxford: Clarendon Press).

Churchland, Patricia (1989), *Neurophilosophy: Toward a Unified Science of the Mind-Brain* (Cambridge, Mass.: MIT Press).

Collins, Arthur (1979), 'Could our Beliefs be Representations in our Brains?' *Journal of Philosophy*, 74/5: 225–43.

Cooper, David (1975), 'Alternative Logic in "Primitive Thought" ', *Man*, 10: 238–56.

Davidson, Donald (1975) 'Thought and Talk', repr. in Davidson (1984).

—— (1982), 'The Paradoxes of Irrationality', repr. in Davidson (2004).

—— (1984), *Inquiries into Truth and Interpretation* (Oxford: Clarendon Press).

—— (1985), 'Incoherence and Irrationality', repr. in Davidson (2004).

—— (2004), *Problems of Rationality* (Oxford: Clarendon Press).

Dennett, Daniel (1976), 'Conditions of Personhood', in Amelie Rorty (ed.), *The Identities of Persons* (Berkeley: University of California Press).

—— (1991), *Consciousness Explained* (Boston: Little, Brown and Company).

Douven, Igor, and Jos Uffink (2003), 'The Preface Paradox Revisited', *Erkenntnis*, 59: 389–420.

Dummett, Michael (1991), *The Logical Basis of Metaphysics* (Cambridge, Mass.: Harvard University Press).

Edgeworth, Maria (1987), *Helen* (London: Pandora). Originally published in 1834.

Edgley, Roy (1969), *Reason in Theory and Practice* (London: Hutchinson).

Evnine, Simon (1989), 'Understanding Madness?' *Ratio*, 2: 1–18.

—— (1991), *Donald Davidson* (Cambridge: Polity Press).

—— (1999), 'On the Way to Language', in Lewis Hahn (ed.), *The Philosophy of Donald Davidson*. Library of Living Philosophers, vol. 27 (LaSalle: Open Court).

—— (2003), 'Epistemic Unities', *Erkenntnis*, 59: 365–88.

—— (2005), 'Containing Multitudes: Reflection, Expertise and Persons as Groups', *Episteme*, 2: 57–64.

Fodor, Jerry (1983), *The Modularity of Mind* (Cambridge, Mass.: MIT Press).

—— and Ernest Lepore (1992), *Holism: A Shopper's Guide* (Oxford: Blackwell).

Foley, Richard (1979), 'Justified Inconsistent Beliefs', *American Philosophical Quarterly*, 16: 247–57.

―― (1982), 'Epistemic Conservatism', *Philosophical Studies*, 43: 165–82.

―― (1993), *Working without a Net: A Study of Egocentric Epistemology* (New York: Oxford University Press).

―― (1994), 'How Should Future Opinion Affect Current Opinion?' *Philosophy and Phenomenological Research*, 54: 747–66.

―― (2001), *Intellectual Trust in Oneself and Others* (Cambridge: Cambridge University Press).

Foucault, Michel (1970), *The Order of Things: An Archaeology of the Human Sciences* (London: Tavistock Publications).

Gaifman, Haim (1985), 'A Theory of Higher Order Probabilities', in Brian Skyrms and William Harper (eds.), *Causation, Chance, and Credence: Proceedings of the Irvine Conference on Probability and Causation*, vol. i (Dordrecht: Kluwer), 191–219.

Gärdenfors, Peter (1988), *Knowledge in Flux: Modeling the Dynamics of Epistemic States* (Cambridge, Mass.: MIT Press).

Geach, Peter (1976), *Reason and Argument* (Berkeley and Los Angeles: University of California Press).

Gentzen, Gerhard (1964), 'Investigations into Logical Deduction', *American Philosophical Quarterly*, 1: 288–306.

Goldman, Alvin (1986), *Epistemology and Cognition* (Cambridge, Mass.: Harvard University Press).

Goodman, Nelson (1978), *Ways of Worldmaking* (Sussex: Harvester Press).

Green, Mitchell, and Christopher Hitchcock (1994), 'Reflections on Reflection: Van Fraassen on Belief', *Synthese*, 98: 297–324.

Harman, Gilbert (1986), 'The Meanings of Logical Constants', in Ernest Lepore (ed.), *Truth and Interpretation: Perspectives on the Philosophy of Donald Davidson* (Oxford: Blackwell), 125–34.

Hart, W. D. (1988), *Engines of the Soul* (Cambridge: Cambridge University Press).

Hawthorne, James, and Luc Bovens (1999), 'The Preface, the Lottery, and the Logic of Belief', *Mind*, 108: 241–64.

Heil, John (1989), 'Minds Divided', *Mind*, 98: 571–83.

Hintikka, Jaakko (1973), *Logic, Language-Games and Information* (Oxford: Clarendon Press).

Hunter, Daniel (1996), 'On the Relation between Categorical and Probabilistic Belief', *Nous*, 30: 75–98.

Jaśkowski, Stanisław (1969), 'Propositional Calculus for Contradictory Deductive Systems', *Studia Logica*, 24: 143–57.

Jeffrey, Richard (1970), 'Dracula meets Wolfman: Acceptance vs. Partial Belief', in Swain (1970).

_____ (1988), 'Conditioning, Kinematics, and Exchangeability', repr. in Richard Jeffrey, *Probability and the Art of Judgment* (Cambridge: Cambridge University Press, 1992).

Kahneman, Daniel, and Amos Tversky (1982) (eds.), *Judgment under Uncertainty: Heuristics and Biases* (Cambridge: Cambridge University Press).

Kaplan, Mark (1996), *Decision Theory as Philosophy* (Cambridge: Cambridge University Press).

Kenny, Anthony (1973), 'Mental Health in Plato's *Republic*', in Anthony Kenny, *The Anatomy of the Soul* (Oxford: Blackwell).

Kneale, William (1956), 'The Province of Logic', in H. D. Lewis (ed.), *Contemporary British Philosophy* (London: Allen and Unwin).

Kornblith, Hilary (1989), 'The Unattainability of Coherence', in J. W. Bender (ed.), *The Current State of the Coherence Theory* (Dordrecht: Kluwer).

Korsgaard, Christine (1989), 'Personal Identity and the Unity of Agency: A Kantian Response to Parfit', *Philosophy and Public Affairs*, 18: 101–32.

Kroon, Frederick (1993), 'Rationality and Epistemic Paradox', *Synthese*, 94: 377–408.

Kyburg, Henry (1961), *Probability and the Logic of Rational Belief* (Middleton: Wesleyan University Press).

_____ (1970), 'Conjunctivitis', in Swain (1970).

Lee, Byeong D. (1998), 'The Paradox of Belief Instability and a Revision Theory of Belief', *Pacific Philosophical Quarterly*, 79: 314–28.

Lewis, David (1982), 'Logic for Equivocators', in David Lewis, *Papers in Philosophical Logic* (Cambridge: Cambridge University Press, 1998).

_____ (1999), 'Why Conditionalize?' in David Lewis, *Papers in Metaphysics and Epistemology* (Cambridge: Cambridge University Press).

Lewis, H., and C. Papadimitriou (1978), 'The Efficiency of Algorithms', *Scientific American*, 238/1: 96–109.

Lowe, E. Jonathan (1996), *Subjects of Experience* (Cambridge: Cambridge University Press).

Lycan, William (1995), 'Conditional Reasoning and Conditional Logic', *Philosophical Studies*, 76: 223–45.

Maher, Patrick (1993), *Betting on Theories* (Cambridge: Cambridge University Press).

Makinson, David (1965), 'The Paradox of the Preface', *Analysis*, 25: 205–7.

Marcus, Ruth Barcan (1981), 'A Proposed Solution to a Puzzle about Belief', in Peter French, Theodore Uehling, and Howard Wettstein (eds.), *Midwest Studies in Philosophy*, vol. iv (Minneapolis: University of Minnesota Press).

Mele, Alfred (1987), *Irrationality: An Essay on Akrasia, Self-Deception, and Self-Control* (New York: Oxford University Press).

Mellor, D. H. (1993), 'How to Believe a Conditional', *Journal of Philosophy*, 90: 233–48.

Moran, Richard (2001), *Authority and Estrangement. An Essay on Self-Knowledge* (Princeton: Princeton University Press).

Nagel, Thomas (1970), *The Possibility of Altruism* (Princeton: Princeton University Press).

—— (1974), 'What Is It Like to Be a Bat?' reprinted in Nagel (1979*b*).

—— (1979a), 'The Subjective and the Objective', in Nagel (1979*b*).

—— (1979b), *Mortal Questions* (Cambridge: Cambridge University Press, 1979).

—— (1986), *The View from Nowhere* (New York: Oxford University Press).

Nelkin, Dana (2000), 'The Lottery Paradox, Knowledge, and Rationality', *Philosophical Review*, 109: 373–409.

Ohlin, Jens David (2005), 'Is the Concept of the Person Necessary for Human Rights?' *Columbia Law Review*, 105: 209–49.

Olin, Doris (1989), 'The Fallibility Argument for Inconsistency', *Philosophical Studies*, 56: 95–102.

Osherson, Daniel (1975), *Reasoning in Adolescence: Deductive Inference.* Logical Abilities in Children, vol. iii (Hillsdale, NJ: Erlbaum).

Parfit, Derek (1984), *Reasons and Persons* (Oxford: Clarendon Press).

Peacocke, Christopher (1987), 'Understanding Logical Constants: A Realist's Account', *Proceedings of the British Academy*, 73: 153–200.

Pears, David (1984), *Motivated Irrationality* (Oxford: Clarendon Press).

Popper, Karl (1946/7), 'Logic without Assumptions', *Proceedings of the Aristotelian Society*, 47: 251–92.

—— (1947), 'New Foundations for Logic', *Mind*, 56: 193–235.

Potter, Sally (2005), *YES: Screenplay and Notes* (New York: Newmarket Press).

Priest, Graham (1985/6), 'Contradiction, Belief and Rationality', *Proceedings of the Aristotelian Society*, 86: 99–116.

—— (1999) 'What not? A Defence of a Dialetheic Account of Negation', in D. Gabbay and H. Wansing (eds.), *What is Negation?* (Dordrecht: Kluwer).

—— (2005), *Towards Non-Being: The Logic and Metaphysics of Intentionality* (New York: Oxford University Press).

Prior, Arthur (1960), 'The Runabout Inference Ticket', *Analysis*, 21: 38–9.

Rescher, Nicholas, and Robert Brandom (1980), *The Logic of Inconsistency.: A Study in Non-Standard Possible-World Semantics and Ontology* (Oxford: Blackwell).

Roorda, Jonathan (1997), 'Fallibilism, Ambivalence, and Belief', *Journal of Philosophy*, 94: 126–55.

Routley, Richard, and Val Routley (1975), 'The Role of Inconsistent and Incomplete Theories in the Logic of Belief', *Communication and Cognition* 8, 185–235.

Rovane, Carol (1998) *The Bounds of Agency: An Essay in Revisionary Metaphysics* (Princeton: Princeton University Press).

Sanford, David (1989), *If P, then Q: Conditionals and the Foundations of Reasoning* (London: Routledge).

Sartre, Jean-Paul (1958), *Being and Nothingness: An Essay on Phenomenological Ontology*, trans. Hazel Barnes (London: Methuen).

Schotch, P. K., and R. E. Jennings (1980), 'Inference and Necessity', *Journal of Philosophical Logic*, 9: 327–40.

Shoemaker, Sydney (1988), 'On Knowing One's Own Mind', in Sydney Shoemaker, *The First-Person Perspective and Other Essays* (Cambridge: Cambridge University Press, 1996).

Sklar, Lawrence (1975), 'Methodological Conservatism', *Philosophical Review*, 74: 186–91.

Skyrms, Brian (1980), 'Higher-Order Degrees of Belief', in D. H. Mellor (ed.), *Prospects for Pragmatism* (Cambridge: Cambridge University Press).

Sobel, Jordan Howard (1987), 'Self-Doubts and Dutch Strategies', *Australasian Journal of Philosophy*, 65:56–81.

Soper, Kate (1986), *Humanism and Anti-Humanism* (London: Hutchinson).

Sorensen, Roy (1988), *Blindspots* (Oxford: Clarendon Press).

Stalnaker, Robert (1984), *Inquiry* (Cambridge, Mass.: MIT Press).

Stich, Stephen (1983), *From Folk Psychology to Cognitive Science: The Case against Belief* (Cambridge, Mass.: MIT Press).

——— (1993) *The Fragmentation of Reason: Preface to a Pragmatic Theory of Cognitive Evaluation* (Cambridge, Mass.: MIT Press).

Strawson, Peter F. (1959), *Individuals: An Essay in Descriptive Metaphysics* (London: Methuen).

Stroud, Barry (1979), 'Inference, Belief and Understanding', *Mind*, 88: 179–96.

Swain, Marshall (1970) (ed.), *Induction, Acceptance, and Rational Belief* (Dordrecht: Reidel).

Sylvan, Richard (1999), 'What is that Item Designated Negation?', in D. Gabbay and H. Wansing (eds.), *What is Negation?* (Dordrecht: Kluwer).

Talbott, William (1991), 'Two Principles of Bayesian Epistemology', *Philosophical Studies*, 62: 135–50.

Teller, Paul (1973), 'Conditionalization and Observation', *Synthese*, 26: 218–58.

Thomson, Judith Jarvis (1997), 'People and their Bodies', in Jonathan Dancy (ed.), *Reading Parfit* (Oxford: Blackwell).

Van Fraassen, Bas (1984), 'Belief and the Will', *Journal of Philosophy*, 81: 235–56.

——— (1995), 'Belief and the Problem of Ulysses and the Sirens', *Philosophical Studies*, 77: 7–37.

Van Inwagen, Peter (1983), *An Essay on Free Will* (Oxford: Clarendon Press).

Vickers, John (2000), 'I Believe It, but Soon I'll Not Believe It Any More: Scepticism, Empiricism, and Reflection', *Synthese*, 124: 155–74.

Weatherson, Brian (2005), 'Can We Do without Pragmatic Encroachment?' *Philosophical Perspectives*, 19: 417–43.

Whitman, Walt (1959), *Leaves of Grass* (1st (1855) edn.; New York: Penguin).

Wiggins, David (1980), *Sameness and Substance* (Oxford: Blackwell).

Wilkes, Kathleen (1988), *Real People: Personal Identity without Thought Experiments* (Oxford: Clarendon Press).

Wittgenstein, Ludwig (1958), *Philosophical Investigations*, trans. E. Anscombe (2nd edn.; Oxford: Blackwell).

—— (2001), *Tractatus Logico-Philosophicus* (London: Routledge).

Index

action, *see* agency
Adler, Jonathan 140n, 149n
agency 14–15, 16–18, 33–4, 36, 51,
    105–7, 115–16, 123–4, 163–5
  and deliberation 42–4, 47–8,
    149–50
  and plans 128–34
Agency 12 n.16, 14–15, 16–18, 33,
    39, 42–3, 47, 51, 105–6, 115,
    123–4, 128
Ameliorism 111–17, 122–8, 140–1,
    164
Arieti, Silvano 163 n.1
Aristotle 1, 4, 130n
Armstrong, David 77–8
aspectual dualism 21–2, 139, 160–2,
    165
assertion 15n, 105, 149n, 157
  of a conjunction 74, 77–8

BC 54, 73–82, 83, 97–8
BC′ 83, 98
Bakhtin, Mikhail 108
Barnes, Jonathan 78, 80–1, 92
Bayesianism 13, 62n
belief 11–14, 55n, 115–16, 153, 159,
    160–2, 163–5
  asymmetry of past versus
    future 134–7, 164
  attribution of 15–16, 75–9,
    115–16, 124–5, 164
  conditional 19, 75
  in a contradiction versus having
    contradictory beliefs 60, 67–8,
    70–3, 80–2
  degrees of 13–14, 19 n.23, 61–5,
    109–10, 111, 143n, 145
  and fallibilism 65–70, 157–8
  methods of acquisition of 119–20,
    122–8, 164
  partial *see* degrees of
  and probability 58–9, 61–5, 143n
  rational constraints on 18–22
  second-order 14–18, 21–2, 146–7,
    150–1, 154, 156, 163–5
  and time *see* Ameliorism, Reflection

transparency of 138, 146–52, 158,
    160–1
  and truth 104, 158
Belief 10, 11–14, 16–18, 42, 49
Belief Downloader Case 143, 153–6,
    165
Belloc, Hilaire 82
Belnap, Nuel 29 n.7
Biro, John 18n
Bishop, Elizabeth 52
Black, Jeffrey 163 n.2
Black, Max 149n
Black, Oliver 150n
Bloom, Allan 91
BonJour, Lawrence 126n
Bovens, Luc 61 n.6
Braine, Martin 41 n.22
Brandom, Robert 2 n.5, 38 n.19, 41
    n.23, 86 n.4, 89 n.6, 96–7, 91
    n.7, 102–4, 157n
Bratman, Michael 128n, 129–30
Braude, Stephen 106
Burge, Tyler 16 n.20, 145n, 148n

CP 19–21, 52–6, 73, 84, 97, 108
  necessity of satisfying 54–6, 84,
    105–7
  rationality of satisfying; *see* CPR1;
    CPR2; CPR3
CPR1 53–4, 56–70, 97, 99–102
CPR2 53–4, 70–3, 84, 97–8, 99–102
CPR3 98
Carroll, Lewis 40
charity, *see* Principle of Charity
Cherniak, Christopher 18n, 23–4, 27,
    31–2, 36–7, 71, 72n, 100, 163n
Christensen, David 13 n.17, 65n, 66,
    68, 110 n.7, 111 n.9, 117–18,
    140n, 141–5, 152, 153, 155–9
Churchland, Patricia 2 n.4
Collins, Arthur 145n
Compounding Doubt, Paradox
    of 60–5, 99
concepts:
  evolution of 31n
  individuation of 25–32, 36–7

concepts: (*cont.*)
  possession of 11, 18, 23–32, 163
conditionality 37–40, 46 n.32, 48, 163
  canonical role for 37–8
  material 38, 39–40
  and *modus ponens* 37, 44
  relations to entailment and
      validity 39–40
  truth-functional or not 38
conjunction:
  -adicity of 35 n.15, 43 n.26
  belief in a 14, 52–82, 164
  canonical role for 32–3
  closure of belief under, *see* CP
  concept of 18, 25, 30, 32–7, 38
      n.17, 39, 40, 46 n.32, 48,
      78–9, 163
  and unity of the mind 19, 52–3, 164
consistency 70–3, 86–97
Cooper, David 163 n.1
counter-indication 144–5, 159, 165

Davidson, Donald 15n, 16, 77 n.21,
  80, 92–3, 95–7, 106, 158 n.19,
  159 n.20
deliberation, *see* agency
Dennett, Daniel 2 n.5, 6, 15, 105
disjunction 18, 30, 40–4, 47, 48, 163
  -adicity of 43 n.26
  canonical role for 40–2
  and exclusion 42
  exclusive versus inclusive 42, 43–4
  and *modus tollendo ponens* 41
Douven, Igor 61, 68n
Dummett, Michael 15n
Dutch Strategy 110–11, 121; *see also*
  Reflection

Edgley, Roy 148
Edgeworth, Maria 81 n.24
eliminative materialism 2, 11–12
Emerson, Ralph Waldo 103
epistemic impartiality 21–2, 138–9,
  141–6, 151–62, 165
epistemic perspective 138, 150, 154–5,
  160–1, 165
epistemological conservatism 140,
  142–3; *see also* Reflection
  Synchronic versus Diachronic

expertise 108–9, 111–12, 117–18,
  120, 121, 125–8, 137, 140–3,
  153–6, 165; *see also*
  counter-indication; Reflection
Evnine, Simon 76, 84 n.1, 96n, 108n,
  132 n.25, 137n, 159 n.19, 163 n.1

falsity 15, 46–7; *see also* negation
Finitude 10–11, 12 n.16, 16–18, 33,
  45, 51, 112, 123, 129
Fodor, Jerry 100–1, 107n
Foley, Richard 13 n.17, 61, 80, 110
  n.6 & 7, 134–7, 140n, 164
Foucault, Michel 2, 12 n.16
Frege, Gottlob 27
Freud, Sigmund 1, 84

Gaifman, Haim 109 n.2 & 3
Gärdenfors, Peter 35
Geach, Peter 94
Gentzen, Gerhard 28–9, 30, 38 n.18
God 11 n.12
Goldman, Alvin 18n
Goodman, Nelson 102–3
Graham, Jorie 23
Green, Mitchell 110 n.7

Harman, Gilbert 41, 45
Hart, W.D. 10
Hawthorne, James 61 n.6
Heil, John 92n
hermeneutics of suspicion 1–2
Hintikka, Jaakko 48–51
Hitchcock, Christopher 110 n.7
holism 96–7, 106–7
human beings 3, 4, 6–10, 11, 112–15,
  163; *see also* persons
Hunter, Daniel 61 n.6

inference 18, 23–32, 37–40, 41–2,
  124
  and canonical roles 25–32, 34
  feasibility orderings of types of 23–4
  materially valid 38
  primitively obvious 28
Inference 38–40
introspective knowledge 120, 124, 127,
  148–50; *see also* Self-Knowledge

James, Henry 1, 2
Jáskowski, Stanislaw 89 n.6
Jeffrey, Richard 13, 62 n.8, 121 n.15
Jennings, R.E. 89–90

Kahneman, Daniel 2 n.3
Kant, Immanuel 22, 55, 139, 160–1, 165
Kaplan, Mark 13 n.17, 61 n.6
Kenny, Anthony 84 n.2
Kneale, William 28
Kornblith, Hilary 72n, 100
Korsgaard, Christine 105n
Kroon, Frederick 145n
Kyburg, Henry 57–8, 59, 80–2

Lee, Byeong 145n
Lepore, Ernest 107n
Lévy-Bruhl, Lucien 163 n.1
Lewis, David 86 n.4, 88–90, 92n, 111 n.8
Lewis, H. 71n
Locke, John 3n
Lockean Thesis 61–5, 109–10
Lottery Paradox 14, 19, 57–60, 61–3, 65, 68, 70, 99, 164
Lowe, Jonathan 5n
Ludwig, Kirk 18n
Lycan, William 44 n.27

Maher, Patrick 110 n.7, 117, 119n, 121–2
Makinson, David 60, 68, 144
Malamud, Bernard 138
Marcus, Ruth 81–2
Marx, Karl 1
Mele, Alfred 92n
Mellor, D.H. 75 n.19
mental partitioning 19–20, 53, 54, 83–107, 164
  breadth versus depth of 105–7
  and conflict 84–97, 164
  and disunity of the world 102–4
  and homuncularity 96–7
  irrationality of 97–104
  and the logic of belief 87–91
  and modularity 85, 99–102
  and reasoning 87, 89–91
  and well-roundedness 95–7, 107

Merlin 113–15
Moore's Paradox 149, 151–2, 165
Moran, Richard 147 n.7 & 8, 148 n.9, 149–50, 160, 165
Multiple Personality Disorder 106

Nagel, Thomas 15, 22, 160–1, 165
naturalized epistemology 70–3, 100–2, 164
negation 18, 28, 38 n.17, 41, 44–8, 163
  canonical role for 44–5
  and deliberation 47–8
  and exclusion rules 41–2
  and falsity 46–7
Nelkin, Dana 58–9, 121 n.14
neurophilosophy 2
Nietzsche, Friedrich 2

Ohlin, Jens 7n
Olin, Doris 61 n.4
Osherson, Daniel 41 n.22
Overton, Willis 163 n.2

PEI, *see* epistemic impartiality
Papadimitriou, C. 71n
Parfit, Derek 132–3
Parmenides 44 n.28
Peacocke, Christopher 25 n.3, 28, 41
Pears, David 86 n.3, 92n, 95–7
personal identity, *see* persons
persons
  and conflict 160–2
  forensic view of 3–4, 12, 15, 17–18, 163
  historicality of the concept of 8–9
  identity (over time) 120–2, 128, 131–3
  identity (who one is) 138, 150, 154–6, 160–1
  necessary conditions on being 6, 7–8, 10–18, 54–5, 139, 163–5
  nominalism about 4, 5–10, 17–18, 163
  non-human 1, 5, 7–8, 14, 114
  versus people 2–3
  as philosophers 165

persons (*cont.*)
  realism about 3–10, 12 n.16, 18,
    163
Plato 84, 91–2
Popper, Karl 28
postmodernism 2, 102–3
Potter, Sally 44 n.28
Preface Paradox 14, 19, 58n, 60–1,
    65–70, 73n, 99, 143–4, 157–8,
    159, 164, 165
Priest, Graham 45 n.29, 46 n.31, 75
    n.18, 82n
Prior, Arthur 29, 30, 38 n.18
Principle of Charity 30, 32, 35 n.14

quantification 48–51, 163

RNP 98–104; *see also* mental
    partitioning
Reciprocity 15
Reflection 14, 19–21, 55–6, 59,
    108–37, 142
  counter-examples to 117–22
  following versus satisfying 118–19,
    121, 125–7
  and forgetting 121
  and mental decline 120–2
  and methods of belief
    acquisition 119–20
  necessity of satisfying 108, 111,
    128–34
  rationality of satisfying 108,
    111–28, 133–4
  relation to van Fraassen's principle of
    same name 109–11
  Synchronic versus
    Diachronic 139–42
Rescher, Nicholas 86 n.4, 89 n.6,
    96–7, 102–4
Ricoeur, Paul 2 n.2
Rohrbaugh, Guy 20 n.26
Roorda, Jonathan 157–8
Routley, Richard 79, 81; *see also*
    Sylvan, Richard
Routley, Val 79, 81
Rovane, Carol 2 n.5, 3n, 7n, 15, 122
    n.17

Sanford, David 39 n.21
Sartre, Jean-Paul 89 n.5, 130n, 160
Schotch, P.K. 89–90
Second-Ordinality 11n, 13 n.16,
    14–18, 46–7, 115, 139, 149n,
    151, 160–1
Self-Knowledge 111–12, 115–16,
    122–8, 134
Shoemaker, Sydney 147 n.8, 149,
    151n
Sklar, Lawrence 140n
Skyrms, Brian 109 n.3
Sobel, Jordan 110 n.7
Soper, Kate 2 n.2
Sorensen, Roy 145n
Sorites Paradox 64–5
Stalnaker, Robert 19 n.24, 83, 86 n.4
Stich, Stephen 2 n.3 & 4, 11n, 163 n.1
Strawson, Peter 7n, 9, 15, 160, 165
Stroud, Barry 18n
Sylvan, Richard 44–5; *see also* Routley,
    Richard

Talbott, William 110 n.7, 120 n.13
Teller, Paul 111 n.8
Thomson, Judith 3
tonk 29, 30 n.10
truth 15, 46–7
Tversky, Amos 2 n.3

Uffink, Jos 61, 68n
utilitarianism 142

van Fraassen, Bas 19 n.23, 20 n.25,
    108–9, 110 n.7, 111 n.8, 121–2,
    139
van Inwagen, Peter 47
Vickers, John 110 n.7, 126 n.19

Weatherson, Brian 13 n.17, 61 n.6,
    63n, 64n
White, T.H. 113
Whitman, Walt 98, 102–3
Wiggins, David 4, 6–7
Wilkes, Kathleen 2 n.5, 6 n.9
Wittgenstein, Ludwig 147